# BERLITZ®

# DISCOVER
# IRELAND

D0063681

Copyright © 1994 by Berlitz Publishing Co. Ltd, Berlitz House, Peterley Road, Oxford, OX4 2TX, England. All rights reserved. No part of this book may be reproduced or transmitted in any form or by any means, electronic or mechanical, including photocopying, recording or by any information storage and retrieval system without permission in writing from the publisher. Berlitz Trademark Reg. U.S. Patent Office and other countries—Marca Registrada.

Edited and designed by
D & N Publishing,
Ramsbury, Wiltshire.

Cartography by
Hardlines, Charlbury, Oxfordshire.

**Photographic Acknowledgements**
All photographs by Pete Bennett and © Berlitz Publishing Company Ltd. except for the following: Martin Gostelow 26, 131, 132, 134, 136, 138, 151, 166, 196/97, 201, 217, 226, 237, 274, 280, 283, 287, 294, 315; Northern Ireland Tourist Board 279, 289, 290, 291, 297, 300/301, 303.

**Front cover:** Kinvarra Castle (Pete Bennett/ Berlitz)

**Back cover:** Killarney Pub (Pete Bennett/ Berlitz)

**Photograph previous page:** Slievemore on Achill Island.

*Although we have made every effort to ensure the accuracy of all the information in this book, changes do occur. We cannot therefore take responsibility for facts, addresses and circumstances in general that are constantly subject to alteration.*

*If you have any new information, suggestions or corrections to contribute to this guide, we would like to hear from you. Please write to Berlitz Publishing at the above address.*

Phototypeset, originated and printed by C.S. Graphics, Singapore.

# BERLITZ®

# DISCOVER
# IRELAND

Martin Gostelow

IRELAND

SCOTLAND

*ATLANTIC*
*OCEAN*

N

Londonderry

**NORTHERN**
**IRELAND**

THE NORTH
WEST

BELFAST

Sligo

DUBLIN
AND
ENVIRONS

Galway    THE WEST

DUBLIN

**THE REPUBLIC**
**OF IRELAND**

Limerick    THE SOUTH EAST

Wexford

THE SOUTH WEST

Cork

| 0 | 25 | 50km |
| 0 | 10 | 20 | 30 miles |

# Contents

**MAPS:** Ireland 4, 8; Excursions from Dublin 128; The South East 150; The South West 174; The West 208; The North West 246; Northern Ireland 276.
**Town Plans**: Belfast 292; Cork City 176; Dublin 94; Dublin Environs 130; Galway City 232; Limerick City 209; Londonderry 277; Sligo Town 256; Wexford Town 156.

# Planning Your Trip to the Enchanted Island

Whether you are making the journey of a lifetime to the land of your ancestors, or paying a regular visit, advance preparations pay dividends. This section offers practical information and advice. You will need to decide when and where to go, and in what order. The cities are full of interest, especially Dublin which it would take a year to explore and get to know properly, but it would not make sense to concentrate on them alone. Rural Ireland has an equal or better claim to being the real Ireland. More of your memories are likely to be of green pastures, mountains, lakes, bays and islands, and the characters you'll meet there.

## When to Go

The peak months of the tourist season are July and August, so consider visiting in May, June or September if you can. The weather is likely to be at least as good and hotels are less busy. Spring flowers are at their best in April and May, and October offers many arts festivals. Winter days have their own sort of atmosphere but darkness falls early, and many sites and attractions are closed, as are a lot of the hotels in holiday areas.

*You can have magnificent beaches like Rosses Point near Sligo Town all to yourself, but it may be too cold to swim.*

## Climate

In the path of moist Atlantic air and the moderating effect of the Gulf Stream, Ireland is rarely hot or very cold. You might be lucky enough to encounter a warm dry spell in summer, but showers and bright intervals are far more likely. Take raincoats and umbrellas and be prepared for what the locals call 'soft' days, which are warm with fine misty rain that goes on for hours, keeping the emerald isle green. The west, where it rains on at least half the days of the year, tends to be wetter than the south east.

Don't be fooled by bright mornings – the sun may not last. On the other hand, don't despair if you wake up to pouring rain. The sky could quite possibly be cloudless by midday.

# Time Differences

From late March to the end of October, all of Ireland is on GMT + 1, the same as Britain. When it's 12 noon in Ireland in summer, it's 4am in Los Angeles, 7am in New York, 1pm in Paris and Johannesburg, 9pm in Sydney and 11pm in Auckland.

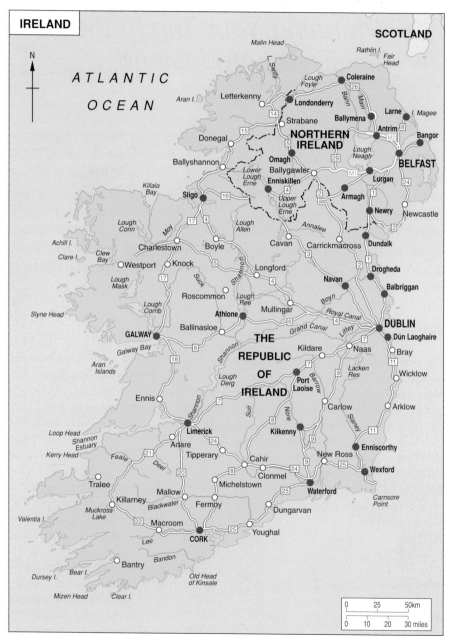

## REMEMBER TO TAKE

• A torch (flashlight) for looking inside ancient tombs at the intriguing patterns carved on the stones.
• A flash for your camera if it doesn't have a built-in one (for indoor sights and outdoors too when dark clouds hover).
• Binoculars, not only for bird-spotting but to look at inaccessible details in churches and ruins.
• Raingear and an umbrella.
• Sunscreen (yes, you *can* burn in Ireland).

*A new sort of farming: harnessing the energy of the wind on the Atlantic coast of Connemara.*

# Getting to Ireland

### By Air

Direct scheduled flights (more in summer) go from Atlanta, New York, Chicago and Boston to Shannon and Dublin. From elsewhere in the USA and Canada, you'll need to connect with one of those departure points. Charter flights operate in summer from several North American cities, offering flight-only or a range of package holidays and fly-drive and fly-bicycle combinations. Fares may be lower for short stays or if you fly mid-week. It may also be less expensive to go to Britain first and then to Ireland. Check with your travel agent.

*F*amous for centuries, the flower sellers in Dublin's Grafton Street have a colourful opinion on just about anything.

You can fly from a dozen cities in Britain to various points in Ireland. If you book in advance and accept that the dates can't be changed, remarkably low-cost fares arc available on these routes. If you are aged 26, 25 or under (the small print varies), always ask about youth and student fares, whatever the route. Some surprising savings are possible.

A few western European cities have direct flights to Dublin and Belfast; passengers from other European cities will probably have to change planes in London, Manchester or Glasgow.

If you buy your ticket for the journey home in Ireland, you'll have to pay a departure tax, currently £5. It will usually be added to the ticket price.

### Airports

Dublin, 8km (5 miles) north of the city, and Shannon, 26km (16 miles) west of Limerick, are the two principal gateways to the Irish Republic, with the usual facilities of major international airports. Shannon is well known for its shopping facilities.

Cork, Waterford, Galway, Knock (listed in some schedules as Connaught) and Sligo handle some direct international flights, mostly to the UK. Taxis serve the airports and bus services link the major airports and city centres. In Northern Ireland, Belfast International (Aldergrove) is 21km (13 miles) west of the city, with a frequent bus service. Belfast City Airport is only 3km (2 miles) east of the centre, linked by rail and bus. Eglinton Airport near Londonderry (Derry) has daily flights from Manchester and Glasgow.

## By Sea

Ferries carry passengers and cars between **Britain and Ireland** on the following routes:

Fishguard (Wales) to Rosslare or to Dublin

Pembroke (Wales) to Rosslare

Swansea (Wales) to Cork

Holyhead (Anglesey, Wales) to Dublin or to Dún Laoghaire (near Dublin)

Liverpool to Belfast

Stranraer and Cairnryan (in Scotland) to Larne, Northern Ireland

Stranraer to Belfast

Buses and in some cases trains connect with the ferries and inclusive bus-ferry-bus or train-ferry-train fares are available from, for example, London to Galway. Sailings are more frequent in summer but you are strongly advised to reserve early for holiday periods, especially if you plan to take a car.

Some of the schedules are inconvenient, either leaving or arriving at an unearthly hour when you would prefer to be in bed. You can avoid the problem by taking daytime crossings – between Fishguard and Rosslare, for example – or by taking an evening sailing on the Swansea-Cork route which can let you get a full night's sleep in a cabin.

Services also link **France and Ireland**: Both Le Havre and Cherbourg to Rosslare all year round

Roscoff, St Malo, Le Havre and Cherbourg to Cork (summer only)

# Customs and Entry Regulations

British travellers arriving in the Republic from Britain or Northern Ireland don't need a passport or identity document, but if you were not born in either the UK or Ireland, it may be useful to carry one. In fact there is no passport control between the UK and Ireland, although all other nationals should have their passports with them.

All travellers arriving from mainland Europe, North America or elsewhere need a passport (a national identity card will do for certain western European nationals). Visas are not required by citizens of a long list of countries including the USA, Canada, Australia, New Zealand and South Africa.

You can bring pets in from the United Kingdom if they have spent the previous six months or more there. Otherwise, any animal is liable to six months' incarceration in expensive quarantine.

If you are arriving with a car, bring the registration document, insurance certificate valid for Ireland (and Northern Ireland if you are going there) and your driving licence. The car should have a nationality plate or sticker.

## Duty-free Goods

The allowance of goods bought *duty-free* which you can carry into Ireland is: 200 cigarettes (or 50 cigars or 250g of tobacco); 1 litre of spirits (liquor) – OR 2 litres of liqueurs or fortified wines below 22 percent alcohol – OR 2 litres of sparkling wine; 2 litres of wine; 60ml of perfume and 250ml of toilet water. There's generally no evidence of customs officers at the entry points. The quantities are regulated by the duty-free shops themselves who are not permitted to sell you more – they will mark your boarding card.

The allowance does not apply between Northern Ireland and the Republic, or between Britain and Northern Ireland.

Travellers within the European Community may import any reasonable quantity of *duty-paid* goods, provided they are for their own use.

# Money Matters

## Currency

The Republic's monetary unit is the Irish pound or punt, abbreviated as £, or IR£ to distinguish it from sterling. Banknotes are issued in denominations of 5, 10, 20, 50 and 100 pounds. The pound is divided into 100 pence (p). There are coins for 1, 2, 5, 10, 20 and 50p and £1 (a large silvery coin).

Northern Ireland uses the pound sterling: Bank of England and Northern Ireland banknotes circulate side by side. Some British and Irish coins are similar in size and shape and may find their way across the border. Although there's not much difference in value between the two currencies, the rate does vary from day to day and they are not interchangeable. You should not take more than IR£150, or foreign currency worth more than IR£1200 (unless you brought it in and declared it) out of the Republic.

## Changing Money

Major banks and main post offices in the cities provide exchange facilities. So do large travel agents, the bigger tourist information offices and a number of other enterprises have a Bureau de Change. The rate at the banks and Irish Tourist Board *(Bord Fáilte)* offices is generally better than at the post offices and other places. Ask about commission rates and avoid changing small amounts where there's a fixed minimum commission.

## Credit Cards, Traveller's Cheques and Eurocheques

'Plastic' is widely accepted in the bigger shops, hotels and restaurants, as are traveller's cheques. To cash Eurocheques, you need the Eurocheque encashment card.

Banks throughout Ireland have cashpoint machines outside which issue cash when an acceptable card is inserted, and the correct PIN (personal identification number) is tapped in. Check with your credit card company or issuing bank to see which banks to use.

# Getting Around

## By Car

You will find the roads pleasantly uncrowded, especially away from the cities and off the major highways. In any case, it's much more fun on the minor roads: just watch out for wandering farm animals. You won't be able to keep up a high speed on the narrower sections, but then you won't want to. **Speed limits** in the Republic are 50km/h (31 miles per hour) in built-up areas and 96km/h (60 miles per hour) on the open road, unless marked otherwise. In Northern Ireland the limit in built up areas is 48km/h (30 miles per hour); other limits will be marked and on the stretches of motorway (freeway), the limit is 113km/h (70 miles per hour). Front seat belts must be worn (rear seats too, in Northern Ireland).

If you are not used to **driving on the left,** you will soon become accustomed to it. Do stay alert: it's too easy to set off on the wrong side after making a stop, especially first thing in the morning. Local standards of driving can be erratic, notably during city rush hours and in the most rural areas

*E*xpert opinion: all over the country, weekly markets bring farmers together to buy, sell and argue over a drink afterwards.

(where drivers tend not to use direction signals, probably assuming that everyone will *know* where they habitually turn).

Check the local regulations before parking. Some towns have meters, in some you buy a pay-and-display ticket, in others you must buy a disc (many shops sell them). Don't park on yellow lines in business hours, or on double yellow lines or zigzag lines at any time.

In Northern Ireland, signs saying 'no unattended vehicles' mean just that: a suspicious car is liable to be subjected to a controlled explosion.

The laws regarding alcohol levels and driving are strict. Only a couple of drinks could put you over the limit as assessed by breath or blood tests. Jail or heavy fines and the loss of your licence can result.

## Car Rental

Many local and international companies have offices at the airports and in the towns. Rates are comparable with the UK, and high by US standards. They're usually lower outside the peak summer months if you reserve a car in advance, especially as part of a fly-drive or sail-drive package. A local company may have lower rates but is more likely to make a 'drop-off' charge for leaving the car at a different location. Per kilometre or unlimited distance rates are available; many companies will make the calculation at the end of the hire period and apply the lower rate. Basic third-party insurance is included but there is generally a supplement for full collision cover.

You must have your national licence and be over 21 (25 for some companies; others require the licence to have been

13

held for two years). If you don't have a major credit card, a large deposit will be required.

**Tip:** From the point where you return cars at Dublin Airport to the terminal is a long uphill walk, and there aren't always trolleys available. If you have heavy baggage, drop off bags and a passenger at the departure hall before returning your vehicle.

## Fuel

Unleaded, super unleaded and premium leaded petrol (gasoline) and diesel fuel are widely available. If you hire a car, make sure you know which grade it uses. Few stations are open on Sunday in rural areas, especially out of season.

*When the humour isn't verbal, it's visual: 'neighbours gossiping' in Killarney.*

## Signs

International pictograms are in use, with local variants whose meaning is obvious. Place names are given in both English and Irish, and in a few areas in Irish only. Don't put too much trust in direction signs. Some are broken, some turn with the prevailing wind and plenty have been bent or twisted round by jokers. So if a sign conflicts with your expectations or your map, be at least suspicious of it.

The older black and white distance signs are generally in miles, the newer green ones in kilometres. Old signs to sites of interest to visitors are in green (and miles) and new ones in brown (and kilometres).

All but the most minor roads are numbered. In the Republic, N (National) signifies a main road, though it may have just two lanes. R (Regional) roads are less important. In Northern Ireland, the corresponding categories are A and B. The fairly short lengths of motorway (freeway) carry M numbers in both parts of Ireland.

## Rail Travel

The main cities are linked to Dublin by the quick and comfortable trains of Iarnród Éireann-Irish Rail. Since the lines mostly fan out like spokes from Dublin, rail travel is no use for travelling up or down the west coast, for example. If you have a Eurailpass, it's valid here (but not in Northern Ireland).

DART (Dublin Area Rapid Transit) serves 25 stations in the vicinity of the capital.

Northern Ireland Railways operate to Larne, Ballymena, Coleraine and Derry, and across the border to Dublin.

## Buses

Éireann-Irish Bus has a nationwide network, charging lower fares than the trains

*Y*esterday's hard life is today's precious solitude in Ireland's wilderness country. Shepherds used to spend the summer months with their flocks among the mountains and bogs.

and reaching more places. It also operates the services in and around Dublin, Cork, Galway, Limerick and Waterford. Northern Ireland's Ulsterbus network covers the province thoroughly, and some services extend to the border towns of the Republic and to Dublin.

Daily and weekly 'go anywhere' tickets are available. You can buy a pocket-size timetable at bus stations and tourist offices – it's useful for translating place names which are given in Irish only on some buses. *An Lár* on the front of some city buses isn't a place name; it means town centre.

*Rail/Bus Rambler Tickets*
You can buy 8- and 15-day tickets for unlimited travel on the trains, or the buses, or – for a supplement – both. Rambler tickets are valid on the Republic's services, but the more expensive Overlander ticket includes Northern Ireland as well.

**Taxis**
Dublin, Cork and Belfast taxis have meters. Most others apply standard fares – ask what the charge is likely to be before setting off. In cities, a few taxis cruise the streets looking for business, but most wait at taxi ranks, stations, airports and big hotels. Telephone directories list radio controlled taxi numbers under 'Taxicabs'.

**Domestic Flights**
You probably won't need to fly from city to city within Ireland, and you will miss the sights on the ground if you do. Poor sailors especially will appreciate the short flights to the Aran Islands from the Galway Coast.

*L*ike Dublin's commuters, you can cover the capital area conveniently by DART (Dublin Area Rapid Transit).

*E*ven a bus stop can be turned into street sculpture, and a reminder that the Vikings were the first to build a settlement at Dublin.

## Ferries

Dozens of offshore islands have more or less regular boat connections with the mainland, usually more frequent in summer. Some are run primarily for the island dwellers themselves. Some, especially to uninhabited islands such as Skellig Michael or Scattery, are mainly for visitors and operate only in summer. Depending on the route, you might find yourself on a converted World War II landing craft, fishing boat, luxury waterbus or modern hydrofoil. The most popular trips are to the Aran Islands from Galway or the Connemara coast or from Doolin, County Clare.

The Irish Tourist Board publishes details in the booklet *Island Boat Services*.

## Bicycle Hire

Dealers all over Ireland, especially in the popular touring areas, will rent out bicycles by the day or week. You can even have one ready to meet you on arrival at the airport. A big company will allow you drop the bike off at its other locations. A deposit is required, and you should check that insurance against theft and a strong lock are included (except on small islands where they aren't considered necessary). At the luxury end of the market, tour companies offer cycling safaris with pre-arranged accommodation and a vehicle to carry your baggage.

### Go Gypsy

If you fancy a really gentle pace and don't want to cover a lot of ground, you might like to hire a horse-drawn caravan. The Tourist Board's booklet *Equestrian Ireland* lists some operators. Full instructions on caring for the horse are provided!

### Take to the Water

The Shannon and the lakes and canals that connect to it make up a vast network of inland waterways. You can hire a two to eight-berth cabin cruiser, as simple or as luxurious as you wish. Novices are given

*If you pick a sunny day, you'll have a great view of Dublin's many attractions from the upper deck of an open-top tour bus.*

the necessary lessons in handling a boat before they set off on their adventures.

'Pick up here, drop off there' arrangements are possible, usually for an extra charge.

### Hitchhiking

You'll see a lot of people, including single women, standing by the road waiting for a ride, but most of them are locals. They'll know the drivers who are likely to come by, and the drivers will know them and where they want to get to. It isn't the same for a stranger, so apply the usual common sense rules. Ireland is safer than most places, but women alone are advised not to hitch. In rural areas, you may face a long wait, often in the rain.

## Guides and Tours

At some prehistoric sites, monuments and great houses, you have to go round with a guide but it's usually part of the pleasure: they are well informed and full of entertaining stories. Otherwise, the Tourist Boards can find guides for you but with all the available literature, they are hardly necessary.

Bus tours from half-a-day to a week or more cover all the well-known destinations. You'll be relieved of all the trouble of planning, navigating and finding accommodation, and you'll certainly see some great scenery through the windows, but you will not be able to get off the beaten path from one tourist attraction to another, and will travel from souvenir shop to 'singing pub' packed with other tour groups. There may be little chance to meet the people, the far from ordinary Irish. If you take a tour, try to arrange a schedule that gives you some free days as well.

# Tourist Information Offices

The **Irish Tourist Board – Bord Fáilte** (Fáilte sounds like 'Foiltya' and means 'Welcome') has international offices which can provide lots of literature and ideas to help you plan a trip.
Australia: 5th level, 36 Carrington Street, Sydney 2000; tel. (02) 299-6177
Canada: Suite 1150, 160 Bloor Street East, Toronto, Ontario M4W 1B9; tel. (416) 929-2777

---

**SEASON TICKETS**

A lot of the Republic's major historic sites – castles, great houses, parks, abbeys and monuments – are in the care of the Office of Public Works (OPW). If you intend to do even a limited amount of touring, it's well worth buying a yearly ticket covering them all. Do it when you make your first visit to an OPW site.

If you're a member of the National Trust in Britain, take your ticket with you to Northern Ireland. The Trust has some great properties there.

---

New Zealand: 87 Queen Street, Auckland; tel. (09) 793708
United Kingdom: 150 New Bond Street, London W1Y OAQ; tel. (071) 493-3201 (and the British Travel Centre at 12 Regent Street, London SW1Y 4PQ; tel. (071) 730-3400 has information on all of Ireland)
USA: 757 Third Avenue, New York, NY 10017; tel. (212) 418-0800
and in several western European cities.

The **Northern Ireland Tourist Board** has some offices abroad:
11 Berkeley Street, London W1X 6BU; tel. (071) 493-0601
276 Fifth Avenue, New York, NY 10001; tel. (212) 686-6250
and it is also represented worldwide by the British Tourist Authority.

All over Ireland, local offices are ready to provide you with information on accommodation and facilities, maps and leaflets and help of all kinds. (It's worth noting that Bord Fáilte gives very little away: it's quite commercially minded.) You'll find offices at all main arrival ports and airports.

Here are the addresses of some Irish Tourist Board city offices:
14 Upper O'Connell Street, Dublin 1; tel. (01) 8747733
Tourist House, Grand Parade, Cork; tel. (021) 273251
Aras Fáilte, Victoria Place, Eyre Square, Galway; tel. (091) 63081
Arthur's Quay, Limerick; tel. (061) 317522
Aras Reddan, Temple Street, Sligo; tel. (071) 61021
41 The Quay, Waterford; tel. (051) 75788
The Irish Tourist Board has offices in Northern Ireland, at:
53 Castle Street Belfast BT1 1GH; tel. (0232) 327888

Bishop Street, Derry; tel. (0504) 369501
The Northern Ireland Tourist Board head office is at:
River House, 48 High Street, Belfast BT1 2DS; tel. (0232) 246609
In the Republic, the NITB office is at 16 Nassau Street, Dublin 2; tel. (01) 679 1977

## Maps

Tourist offices may have free or low cost maps of their immediate areas and will usually have other maps for sale. Car-hire companies may provide a road map but you'll need one for advance planning. The Ordnance Survey, the Automobile Association and Euro-Map publish useful road maps to a scale of 1:300,000 (about 1 inch to 8km/5 miles). If you're walking or cycling, or driving on the back roads, you will need something more detailed or specialized. Hill walkers and climbers should note that the Irish Ordnance Survey's maps of mountainous areas are based on work done in the early 19th century so they may not be entirely accurate! In any case, unfortunately, not all the sheets are in print. There are local alternatives, so try a good book shop.

*T hatch has been the traditional roofing material in Ireland since the first Stone Age settlers arrived.*

## Travellers with Disabilities

Many hotels and restaurants are now catering for wheelchair travellers and others with special needs. The Irish Tourist Board's accommodation guide gives details, and the board also publishes a county-by-county fact sheet. Not all tourist sites are accessible to wheelchairs and the terrain means that some never will be. Special toilet facilities are still far from universal.

## Children

They will probably love Ireland, as long as you don't overdose them on ruined monasteries and castles. Working farms, wildlife parks, boat trips, a chance to try fishing and a couple – not all – of the folk parks (Bunratty, and the Ulster American and Ulster History Parks at Omagh are popular) should appeal to all ages. The beaches can be gorgeous: seize your chance when the weather is favourable.

*T*he Fota Island Wildlife Park has had great success in breeding cheetah. They're one of the few species that don't mingle with the visitors.

Otherwise, indoor entertainment includes some imaginative modern attractions (such as Celtworld at Tramore, see page 163 or Kerry the Kingdom at Tralee, see page 204).

Children can be taken into pubs, which is useful when you want to eat there. Some ask that you don't bring children in later in the evening.

## Health and Medical Care

Your travel insurance policy ought to include medical expenses although Residents of European Community countries are entitled to free medical treatment in Ireland. (There is a charge for medicines.) UK residents should carry identification such as a driving licence, and know their National Insurance number. Other European residents need to bring the E.111 social security form. Make it clear to the doctor that you wish to be treated under the EC regulations.

## Embassies and Consulates

You will find a list of all diplomatic representatives in Dublin in the telephone book, under 'Diplomatic and Consular Missions'.

Australia: Fitzwilliam House, Wilton Terrace, Dublin 2; tel. (01) 6761517
Canada: 65 St Stephen's Green, Dublin 2; tel. (01) 4781988
UK: 33 Merrion Road, Dublin 4; tel. (01) 6695211

USA: 42 Elgin Road, Dublin 4; tel. (01) 6688777
US Consulate in Northern Ireland: Queen's House, Queen Street, Belfast BT1 6EA; tel. (0232) 328239

# Accommodation

The Irish Tourist Board publishes an excellent *Accommodation Guide* each year, listing hotels and guest houses, working farms and other homes offering accommodation, as well as youth hostels. They can also help with details of self-catering accommodation at country cottages and even castles.

**Hotels** are graded A\*, A, B\*, B and C according to facilities. The gradings are also a rough guide to standards and prices. The approved places can display a green shamrock sign. General standards are good, and there has been a lot of recent upgrading with the aid of grants from the European Community. At the top end of the scale, **country house hotels** in former stately homes will cosset you in the lap of luxury at a price to match. More economically, if you want to stay in a great house or country mansion that hasn't been turned into a hotel but takes paying guests, look for the booklet *Hidden Ireland,* available from booksellers and Bord Fáilte offices. It lists private country houses all over Ireland offering bed, breakfast and dinner with the family. Most have only a few rooms, so you'll need to make reservations. **Guest Houses** are usually family-

*Many stately homes and castles have found a new rôle as luxury hotels and country clubs, like Mount Juliet in County Kilkenny.*

run and friendly and may offer full board or half board. Many **pubs** have rooms too, but it may be worth checking on the likely noise level, especially on Friday and Saturday nights. A list of hotels is given at the end of this guide (see page 320).

## Bed and Breakfast

The 'B & B' signs are everywhere in the holiday areas, more sparsely across the rest of the country, outside farmhouses, cottages, townhouses and mansions. The best are a wonderful way to meet local people in their homes, at less than the cost of a guest house. Rooms and standards of comfort vary enormously, so it's a good idea to take a look and ask the price before making a decision to stay.

Especially on the west coast, many houses have been radically adapted for the 'B & B' business, and new houses are frequently designed for it. 'En suite' bathrooms, or shower rooms, are the norm now. The rooms are usually spotless, often looking as if they have never been used. Some excellent places may not yet be on the Tourist Board's list.

## Camping and Caravanning

Sites range from a farmer's field to leisure parks with hot showers, shops and sports facilities. Lists of approved sites are published by:
Irish Caravan Council, 2 Offington Court, Sutton, Dublin 13; tel. (01) 323776 and the Northern Ireland Tourist Board (see page 18).

The Bord Fáilte *Accommodation Guide* also lists approved sites and a few companies which hire out motor homes.

## Youth Hostels

Concentrated in the most beautiful areas of Ireland, dozens of Youth Hostels are available to members of affiliated associations (you will need your membership card). For details, write to An Oige, The Irish Youth Hostel Association, 61 Mountjoy Street, Dublin 7; tel. (01) 304555. For Northern Ireland, the address is Youth Hostel Information, 56 Bradbury Place, Belfast BT7 1RV. In holiday areas you'll also find dozens of hostels which are unrelated to any organization. Standards are variable so it's worth taking a look before registration.

# Hairdressers

Every sizeable town has its unisex salon as well as traditional ladies' and old style gentlemen's hairdressers. Take advice, and take a look, if you want to get an idea of how up-to-date they are.

# Laundry and Dry Cleaning

The bigger hotels provide a same day or next day service. Thoughtfully, many provide a washing and drying room for guests to use, and heated towel rails in some bathrooms are a boon for drying small items overnight. Kindly landladies in bed-and-breakfast establishments may do some washing for you if you stay more than one night. Large camping and caravan sites have washing machines and the bigger towns have laundromats and fast dry cleaners.

# Photography and Video

International brands of film are available, and rapid processing of colour prints can be done in most towns. Transparencies (slides) will take longer – in most cases it's worth taking films home with you.

All sorts of videotape are on sale. Note that pre-recorded tapes bought in Ireland will not work on North American systems, or vice versa.

## Electric Current

The standard supply is 220-230V, 50Hz, with square three-pin plugs. Most hotels provide a 110V shaver outlet, but otherwise, US-made equipment will need an adaptor and transformer.

## Water

It's safe to drink the tap water anywhere in Ireland, unless there is some indication to the contrary.

*Imagine the controversy when Henry Moore's bronze tribute to WB Yeats was unveiled in St Stephen's Green, Dublin.*

## Weights and Measures

Ireland is gradually going metric (the Republic faster than Northern Ireland), but you'll still find foods sold in pounds as well as kilograms, and it's hard to imagine that the Irishman's favourite tipple will ever be measured in anything other than pints.

## Communications

### Post
Green is the colour of the post boxes in the Republic, red in Northern Ireland. Look out for antique ones marked *V R* for Victoria Regina and *E VII R* for Edward VII, even in the Republic. The service is modern enough and reasonably quick.

### Telephone
Direct dialling is now virtually universal throughout the island. Payphones (cream/green or blue/metallic in the Republic, brown/yellow or red in Northern Ireland) are widely distributed. Card-phones are at least as common as the coin-operated ones: you can buy the cards in post offices and many shops and petrol stations, in denominations of £2 to £15 (up to £20 in Northern Ireland).

Dial 10 for the operator (100 in Northern Ireland); 114 for international operator (153 in Northern Ireland); 1190 for directory enquiries (192 in Northern Ireland). Making international calls, dial the prefix 00-, then the country code. (In Northern Ireland, the prefix is 010-.)

Making calls to Ireland, dial the international access code used in your country, then 353 (44 for Northern Ireland) and then the area code (omitting initial zero) and local number.

*A coat of green paint put the stamp of independent Ireland on old red mail boxes dating from the days of Queen Victoria.*

Making calls between the Republic and Northern Ireland, first dial 08-, then the area code (omitting the initial zero) and number. Check with the operator if in doubt.

### Telemessages, Telex and Fax
Dial 196 for telemessages (190 in Northern Ireland) which have superseded telegrams. Telex is increasingly being replaced by fax: larger hotels and business service bureaux can send faxes for you.

### Newspapers and Magazines
The national dailies are the *Irish Independent, Irish Times* and *Irish Press,* all published in Dublin, the *Cork Examiner,* and in Belfast the *News Letter* and *Irish News.* In addition, the London papers (some in special Irish editions) reach most of Ireland on the morning of publication and the *International Herald Tribune* is sold at the bigger newsstands. Local, British and international magazines are widely available.

The local evening papers are a good source for entertainment listings. Look for the 'What's On' type of magazine – for Dublin, the free *Event Guide* publishes lists and reviews and *In Dublin* is good on pub music. The *Phoenix* is an irreverent satirical and critical magazine (like a cross between London's *Private Eye* and *Time Out* or New York's *Spy*). Other cities and towns, especially holiday centres, have their own guides.

### Radio and TV
Radio Telefis Eireann (RTE) has two TV and several radio channels including Gaelic stations. TV and radio from the UK can also be received over wide areas. Many of the larger or more expensive hotels have a selection of satellite or cable channels.

## Religious Services

Well over 90 percent of the population of the Republic and over 30 percent in Northern Ireland declare themselves to be Roman Catholic, and church attendance is high, although less diligent than it was. Mass is normally said on Saturday evening, Sunday and certain weekdays. The Church of Ireland, the Anglican

Protestant church, has a small minority of members. The Presbyterian church is stronger in Northern Ireland. The biggest cities have synagogues and Islamic centres. Concierges at main hotels have details, and addresses and service times are published in local Saturday papers.

# Etiquette

Friendly informality may be the norm, but people are punctual for appointments and social events. In the business world, it's usual to shake hands on meeting and taking leave, and to exchange business cards. People very quickly switch to first names, as part of a general friendliness. National pride has caused many people to restore the ancient versions of their names, such as Pádraig (among other variations) for Patrick, or Dálaigh for Daly: you may have to ask how to say them.

Business dress is quite formal, but if you're on holiday you can be as casual as you like. Men need a jacket and tie in more formal restaurants.

# Opening Hours

Most banks open from 10am to 12.30pm and 1.30pm to 3pm (3.30pm in Northern Ireland), Monday to Friday. Some stay open through the lunch hour. City and large town branches stay open until 5pm one day a week (Thursdays in Dublin).

Offices and businesses usually operate from 9am to 5.30pm, Monday to Friday. Shops open from 9 or 9.30am to 5.30pm, Monday to Saturday (later in big shopping centres) and some are even open on Sunday. In small towns, they may close for lunch and one afternoon a week.

# Public Holidays

Fixed calendar dates:

| | |
|---|---|
| 1 January | New Year's Day |
| 17 March | St Patrick's Day |
| 25 December | Christmas Day |
| 26 December | St Stephen's Day/ Boxing Day |

Movable holidays:
Good Friday (not an official public holiday, but widely taken);
Easter Monday
(Republic of Ireland only): First Monday in June, first Monday in August, last Monday in October.
(Northern Ireland only): First Monday in May, last Monday in May, 12 July (Orangemen's Day), last Monday in August.

# Language

In the Republic of Ireland the official language is actually Irish Gaelic. If you don't speak it you will only be in the same position as the vast majority of the locals. Virtually everybody speaks English. In spite of a noble campaign to save Irish from extinction, and although it is taught in schools and some knowledge of it is required of civil servants and the police, the old tongue is struggling to survive. Signs of all kinds are often in both languages, more as a gesture of support than to fill a need. Only in the *Gaeltacht*, a few pockets of land mostly in the west, is Irish Gaelic truly alive. In Northern Ireland, it's sometimes used on signs to signal republican sympathies.

You will probably notice that Irish spellings are far from standardized. In this book we have used the most widely accepted, though they might not all please the purists.

## Yes, You Know Some Irish Gaelic

Perhaps only a **smidgen**? That word almost certainly comes from the Irish Gaelic *smeachán*, a small amount. The nearly opposite term **galore** is a corruption of *go leár*, which just means sufficient. Was it the Irish or the English who gave it today's exaggerated meaning? The fancy perforated style of shoe now called a **brogue** has also come some way from its origin, the rough leather *brog*. Calling an Irish

*Road signs can mix up miles and kilometres, and in Gaeltacht areas some don't even give an English translation of the place names. An Daingean is Dingle, Traigh-Li is Tralee.*

accent a brogue may be connected in some way that isn't clear now.

There's no doubt about the **leprachaun** (from the old Irish *luchorpán*, a little sprite) or the less appealing **banshee** (*bean sídhe*), a wailing female spirit portending death. And no sentimental 19th-century song about the homeland far away was complete without a sweet **colleen** (from *cailín*, a country girl) or **mavourneen** (*mo mhuirnín*, my darling) and mention of the **shamrock** (*seamróg*, diminutive of *seamar*, clover). Not so obviously Irish in origin is **hubbub**, probably from *abú*, a war cry. Funnily enough, a Scottish Gaelic war cry, *sluagh-ghairm*, gave English the word **slogan**!

Geographers worldwide give Irish labels to three landscape features. **Drumlins** (from *druim*, a low hill) are oval mounds formed under glaciers

*You can pick up some words of Irish Gaelic from the many bi-lingual signs.*

during the last Ice Age: the northern border counties of Fermanagh and Down are strewn with them. An **esker** (from *eiscir*) is a ridge left when the glaciers retreated, making a useful dry route through otherwise boggy land. And of course **bog** is an Irish word too (*bog* means soft).

A **spalpeen** (from *spailpín*), originally a seasonal or itinerant worker, came to mean a rascal. No doubt he was thought to drink potcheen or **poteen** (*poitín*) a powerful and illegally distilled drink which he might have bought at a **shebeen** (*síbín*), an unlicensed liquor house. (All these 'eens' are just diminutives, by the way.) There's no need to translate *céilí*, a gathering for an evening of music, dance and stories, and mere English simply doesn't have a word for that indefinable spirit of fun and repartee, fuelled by the company, the drink, the tall stories and the music that the Irish call **crack** (*craic*).

It's possible that 'smashing' in the sense of wonderful comes from the Irish *maith sín* which means something similar and sounds like 'mashin'. When Australians talk about the **sheilas** as slang for women, they're using an Irish female name which also became a generic term (*sile*). Not too flattering a connection, the word **hooligan** derives from the Irish Houlihan family who were often in court in London in the 19th century. It's said that hoodlum came from Muldoon (mis-)spelled backwards: for some now obscure reason it was devised by a US newspaper to refer to a suspect without risking a lawsuit. There's an unproven theory that the American 'sure' implying agreement may have come from the equivalent Irish *is sa* (it is).

Lots of 'Irishisms', constructions used by Irish speakers of English, are adapted from Gaelic grammar, even though the user may not know a word of the language now. Formations such as 'I am after seeing her' = I have seen her; 'He asked would I do it' = He asked if I would do it; 'so it is' at the end of a statement; and 'It will be fine, says he' all evolved that way. To 'get your death' is a straight translation and 'the dear knows' (= God knows) comes not from the French *dieu* but from the Irish for deer, *fiadh*, which sounds like the Irish for God, *Fiadha*.

The most remarkable case of derivation and gradual change of meaning must be the word **Tory**, in the sense of Conservative politician or voter. *Tóraidhe* (or *tóraighe*) was the Irish Gaelic for a bandit! It was used to describe outlaws who supported the Jacobite cause in the 17th century, and in the form 'Tory' was eventually applied to Jacobites in the British House of Commons. Reconciled to the Hanoverian succession, they evolved into today's Conservatives.

A few Irish or Gaelic terms crop up in the text, and are worked into place-names. There is a short glossary on page 316.

## Smoking

Major international and local brands are available. In general, smoking is commoner than in the US or UK. Some hotels and restaurants are introducing non-smoking areas but the atmosphere in some busy pubs can be torture for sensitive eyes and noses.

## Tipping

Hotels and most restaurants include a service charge, so only some special extra service would warrant an additional gratuity. In informal eating places you may like to leave a coin or two on the table. The total on credit cards may be left open in restaurants: before adding a tip, find out whether service has already been included.

Hotel porters will expect something for carrying cases and other services. Taxi drivers should be tipped about 10 percent of the fare.

*E*specially at weekends, half the pubs in Ireland turn into informal concert halls. If the music in one doesn't suit you, move on to the next.

## Toilets

Most towns have 'public conveniences'; so do virtually all tourist sites and they are better kept than in most other countries. Alternatively, try the larger hotels, the cafés and pubs – it would be polite to buy a coffee or a drink there as well.

Don't mistake *Mna* for Men; it's Gaelic for Ladies. *Fir* means Men.

## Lost Property

After checking with the hotel housekeeper or front desk, public transport authorities

(telephone numbers are obtainable from directories) or other obvious leads, contact the local police station for information and advice.

## Complaints

By far the best policy is to sort out any difficulty on the spot, in a friendly way if possible, with the shop or hotel manager or other responsible person. Writing a letter afterwards won't solve the problem when it matters most. In cases where accommodation approved by Bord Fáilte or The Northern Ireland Tourist Board isn't up to standard, tell them as well.

# Crime and Theft

Ireland is still a law-abiding place but sadly, as in most of the world, thefts from (and of) cars are on the increase, especially in Dublin, as well as big city street crime. Don't leave anything attractive on view in your car, either in towns or rural areas. Avoid parking in dark and unfrequented areas and don't carry lots of cash or valuables on a back street pub crawl. Beware of pickpockets in crowded places, such as public transport, markets and sports events.

# Police

The *Garda Siochána* (usually shortened and in the plural *Gardai,* pronounced Gor*dee*) take care of all police matters and traffic control. They are friendly and helpful, although you don't see many of them about. In Northern Ireland the Royal Ulster Constabulary (RUC) have been the target of bombs and bullets for so long they are understandably defensive. Police stations there are surrounded by high wire fences and blast barriers.

# Emergencies

For Police, Fire or Ambulance services, the telephone number everywhere in Ireland is 999. Calls are free. The operator will ask where you are and what service you need.

# Eating and Drinking

An abundance of salmon, sea-trout and brown trout comes from the bountiful rivers and lakes, shellfish are farmed in the bays and the fishing fleet lands a varied catch from the sea. Emerald green pastures nourish prime cattle. Irish lamb from the hill farms or salt-blown coasts rates with the world's best. Intensive farming and organic farming co-exist to produce quantity and quality. Pork, ham and bacon are excellent and figure in some of the most basic Irish dishes. Rabbits multiply and game bursts from almost every copse or wood.

A bigger range of fruit and vegetables is available since EC membership augmented it with imports from the sunny south. Ireland does best with the fruits that cool summers favour, raspberries and strawberries, and all sorts of mushrooms flourish, both farmed and wild.

The best ingredients are available, though they haven't always been put to good use. There are still places, from hotel restaurants to pubs and snack bars where the food is frankly dull, coming from catering packs, cans and freezers. Vegetables are often an overcooked mess on a side plate, salads tired and faded and there's all too much reliance on the frying pan.

Good news at last! Some chefs, Irish and foreign, are revelling in a new atmosphere where creative cooking with fine ingredients is really appreciated. Their customers have travelled more, for one thing: vast numbers of Irish take holidays in France, Spain or Italy and many have worked abroad, a lot of them in the hotel business. So there *are* fine restaurants, including some in the country house hotels. You'll have to ask around and search them out, and be prepared to pay for quality. (See page 320 for our selection of places to eat.)

## Seafood

'Cockles and mussels, alive, alive O!' sang Molly Malone in the old song about Dublin, and indeed shellfish were a staple in Ireland's diet from the time the first settlers combed the beaches 9,000 years ago. Neglected for most of the 20th century, **mussels** are back on some menus. Not only mussels, but excellent **oysters** and **scallops**, **crabs** and **lobsters** too, from the cool, clean Atlantic waters of the west coast or the farms that have multiplied in sheltered coves. Even so, most of the production is exported to France, Spain and the UK. You may still experience the frustration of dining beside a sea lough lined with oyster and mussel beds, and find that neither delicacy is on the menu. Even when they are offered, ask how they are prepared: menu descriptions may not coincide with what you expect.

**Fish**, even the noble Atlantic salmon, hasn't always been esteemed in Ireland, except by those who come to fish the famous rivers every year. It was something to do with religion, of course. Since Catholics

*The old-fashioned look may be real or facsimile, but the custom of serving meals in pubs is relatively new, and growing.*

### TAIL TALES

Dublin Bay prawns aren't prawns and they don't come from Dublin Bay! They're a species of miniature lobster with long thin antennae (*langoustines* to the French, *Nephrops norvegicus* to the scientist), caught off northern Scotland and Ireland. They used to be unsaleable in Britain and most went to places where they were appreciated, France and Italy. Boats landing catches in Dublin found a demand there from street traders who could sell them – hence the name. Then someone decided to market the tails, free of shell, under the label of scampi. Demand became so great that all sorts of fakes were concocted. In Ireland you should be sure of the real thing.

were forbidden meat on Fridays, fish was seen as a substitute and looked down on. Some Protestants made a point of not eating fish at all. Now many people are making up for lost time. Farmed salmon is in surplus and appears on a lot of menus, grilled or poached. Look for the wild variety, sea trout and brown trout during the long season. Sea bass, monkfish, Dover sole, black sole and skate are superb.

**Soups** can be filling: thick vegetable broths, seafood bisques or chowders or occasionally a tasty carrot and orange.

The quality of Irish **meat** ought to guarantee you a good steak or roast, though the habit of over-cooking dies hard. Chicken is a reliable stand-by, but do try the traditional **stews**: bacon, cabbage and potato; an 'Irish stew' of mutton or lamb, carrots, potatoes, onions and herbs; or Dublin Coddle using bacon, sausages, potatoes, onions and parsley. Colcannon is a traditional meatless stew of potatoes, cabbage and onions.

## Potatoes

From the 17th century when it was found how well it suited the climate (unlike cereals, it didn't need a dry spell for harvesting), the potato rapidly became the staple, almost the sole diet of poorer people. When the crop failed so disastrously in the 1840s (see page 54), famine was inevitable.

Potatoes still figure largely in Irish cooking. In stews of course, and chips (french fries), roast and mashed, but also in some delicious local specialities. Potato breads or pancakes are treats which you'll most probably be offered in the north where they're sometimes called 'fadge'.

---

**POTATO BREAD**

As many recipes exist as there are cooks. Here's one:

Take half a pound each of mashed potatoes, grated raw potatoes and white flour with a pinch of salt, 30g (1 oz) butter and half a teaspoon of bicarbonate of soda. Mix thoroughly, adding enough buttermilk to make a stiff batter. Roll out into flat cakes and bake on a griddle or fry them like pancakes in a little butter. Eat with butter and jam for tea, or with bacon for breakfast.

---

**IRISH STEW**

In case you aren't offered any in Ireland, make some yourself when you get home. To serve 4/5 people, you'll need:

1.2kg/2lbs 8oz mutton or lamb chops
10 small or 4 large carrots (some Irish disagree with their inclusion)
10 small or 4 large onions
half a swede or turnip and/or a parsnip
550ml/1 pint meat stock (preferably lamb/mutton)
6-8 medium potatoes
sprig of thyme
salt and freshly milled pepper
chopped parsley

Chop the larger vegetables into chunks. Trim some fat off the chops. Heat the fat slowly in a heavy frying pan and then discard the pieces that are left. Fry the chops briefly in the fat until slightly browned. Add the vegetables and mix over the heat for a couple of minutes. Transfer the mixture to a large casserole, forming layers of meat and vegetables. Sprinkle salt and pepper on each layer. Add the stock. Peel the potatoes and place on top of the mixture. Sprinkle the potatoes with salt and pepper and add the thyme. Bring to the boil, cover and simmer in the oven at 190°C/375°F for an hour and a half. Pour off the liquid, take off the fat, and thicken the remaining liquid slightly by stirring in a little roux of white flour and butter. Check the degree of seasoning. Pour the liquid back over the stew. Return stew to the boil, sprinkle with chopped parsley, and serve.

---

Home made **soda bread**, especially the brown variety, is the highlight of the bakery counter. Filling and appetizing at the same time, it's one of the taste sensations of Ireland. **Barm brack** is a yeasty cake laced with spices, currants and lemon peel. Gingerbread is another traditional favourite.

## SODA BREAD

Most visitors become addicted to this tasty, grainy and moist Irish treat, almost more like a cake than a bread. Everyone has a slightly different method of making it. Here's one suggestion from an expert, if you want to try making your own when you get home:

    450g (1 lb) wholemeal flour
    225g (8 oz) strong white flour
    1 tsp salt
    1 tsp bicarbonate of soda
    600 ml (1 pint) sour milk
    (Optional 'secret' ingredients to make a richer loaf include 1 tsp treacle or molasses, 30g/1 oz of oatmeal, a beaten egg and 15g/half an ounce.of butter)

Mix the dry ingredients, add the milk (and treacle if used) and make a firm dough. Mould into a round loaf or two smaller loaves. Slash across the top with a sharp knife. Cover each loaf with a large metal tin. Bake at 230°C (450°F) for 40 minutes. When cooked, the bread will sound hollow when tapped.

## Cheeses

Plain and simple cheddar-type cheese (dyed orange in accordance with Irish preference) and blended butter used to be the limits of the output of a massive dairy industry. Now you'll have a chance of finding superb hard and soft farmhouse cheeses and fresh creamery butter. Goats have become quite fashionable again, and goatsmilk cheeses here can rival the French.

*You'll find a surprising range of eating options in Dublin, formerly notorious for its dull food.*

There's limited production of some very special farmhouse cheeses: you are more likely to find them in the top restaurants than in shops. In the south west, look for Knockalara, made from sheep's milk, Gabriel, like an Emmenthal; or semi-soft Gubbeen from west Cork. Cashel Blue from Fethard in County Tipperary is making a name for itself – make sure it's fully ripe and soft. Croghan is a semi-soft goat's cheese from County Wexford.

## Desserts

Desserts mostly stick to the routine: sweet pastries, trifles and fruit pies. An unusual exception is made from carrageen moss, a

kind of seaweed rich in iodine and trace elements and containing a natural jelling agent. Growing in shallow water all round the coast it's gathered and laid out to be washed by the rain and dried by the sun and wind. Some boiled with milk produces a jelly, delicious with fruit and cream.

## Breakfast

Breakfast is something of a bright spot. Unless, that is, you're vegetarian, or worried about your cholesterol intake. You'll probably be eating it where you're staying: with the illogical exception of the most expensive international hotels, it's included in the room rate. The 'Irish breakfast' offered at typical bed-and-breakfast places and guest houses comprises fruit juice, porridge or cereal, a big plateful of salty bacon, egg and sausage, perhaps with an extra helping of tomatoes or mushrooms, fried potato cakes or slices of savoury black pudding (blood sausage) or white pudding, toast and soda bread. The tea tends to be extra strong but it's more reliably good than the coffee.

## Restaurants

The picture is patchy. Dublin naturally offers a huge choice of eating venues, some excellent. Cork has a handful, and other cities surprisingly few. Small towns might

have only a hotel with a routine set menu that features quantity rather than quality. Best served are the holiday centres such as Kinsale, Dingle, Killarney and Clifden where you can stroll the streets, checking the menus posted invitingly outside competing restaurants. The best are expensive by international standards, but to a great extent, you get what you pay for. The same applies in the increasing number of country house hotels which welcome non-residents to dine.

Especially in the cities, the better restaurants offer economical 'business lunches' of three courses, and many other places have some sort of lower priced deal at lunchtime.

**Ethnic restaurants** are fewer than you may be used to in other countries. Only in the cities might you find anything more than a run-of-the-mill Chinese. A **fast food** outlet may be your only option in some places, especially if you leave it late before looking for somewhere to eat. Follow your nose to find **fish and chips**, whether in a sit-down café or takeaway: they can be superb.

**Pub food** ranges from excellent to execrable, or none at all. There are those who insist that pubs have no business serving food; it only distracts the bar staff from their proper job. Such traditionalists are fighting a losing battle, and many pubs have ambitious menus as well as snacks in the bar. These are a welcome alternative to a lot of old-style hotel restaurants which assume you want a five-course meal, and don't cater for anything less.

### Drinks

Some seek to portray all Irish pubs as a round-the-clock riot of good humour and great music. Many may indeed be the warm, welcoming, spontaneous theatres of fond memory, but others are grim, sepulchral and empty. Drink prices are high (and lists are displayed to warn you of this), so there's good reason to look for somewhere agreeable. Chances are it's just round the corner. Hotel lounges are a comfortable alternative, and prices are much the same.

### Black and Beautiful

You don't *have* to drink Guinness when you come to Ireland, but unless you don't touch alcohol, it would be a pity not to try one – you'd be missing an Irish experience. Nearly black, smooth and creamy, it has been called an acquired taste. If so, it's one that many visitors acquire remarkably quickly.

Ordering one involves a little ceremony and self-discipline. If you want a pint, just ask for 'A Guinness, please'; if you mean half a pint, say 'A glass of Guinness'. The barman or barmaid will then partly fill your glass with the foaming fluid – up to about four-fifths full – and leave it, perhaps for several minutes. You can enjoy the anticipation, and watch an extraordinary phenomenon. The bubbles appear to *fall* through the dark liquid, though you know they must be rising, unless the laws of physics don't apply here. Then the glass is topped up and set before you, with fully a thumb's thickness of creamy head that

*T*he fashion is growing for naming pubs after characters from literature or history. Gogarsty was the poet who invited James Joyce to the tower at Sandycove.

you practically have to bite through to get to your first mouthful.

Of course there are other brands of stout – the sweeter Murphy's and Beamish for example – each with their admirers. And the choice extends to domestic beers and lagers, imports and locally bottled versions of British, American, Canadian, Dutch and German brands. Low- and zero-alcohol beers and the usual international brands of **soft drinks** are available for the benefit of abstainers and drivers. Except in the better restaurants, **wine** lists tend to be short and simple. Ask what the house wines are before ordering: they can be good or dreadful.

*P*lenty of water and a gentle climate means flowers flourish.

*L*earn a little Irish Gaelic as you go along – the law requires signs and official documents to use the old language.

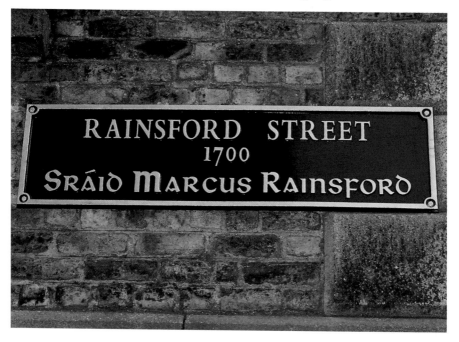

---

**FACTS AT YOUR FINGERTIPS**

**Geography**
The western outpost of Europe, between Britain and the Atlantic, Ireland is 475km (295 miles) from north to south and no more than 275km (171 miles) from east to west. The island is shaped like a shallow bowl, with a flat central lowland of pasture, lakes and bogs. Mountains and moors, rarely rising over 900m (about 3,000ft) but often picturesque, form a rough rim to the bowl. Much of the west coast is wild and beautiful, indented with bays and fringed by islands.

**Republic of Ireland (Poblacht na hÉireann or Éire)**
Population: 3.5 million
Area: 70,282 km² (27,136 square miles)
Capital: Dublin (Baile Atha Cliath) 478,000
(Greater Dublin 1 million)
Other main cities and towns:
Cork (Corcaigh) 127,000
Limerick (Luimneach) 60,000
Dún Laoghaire 55,000
Galway (An Ghaillimh) 47,000
Waterford (Port Láirge) 40,000
Government: An independent republic and parliamentary democracy, with an elected president whose role is largely ceremonial.

**Northern Ireland**
Population 1.6 million
Area: 14,129 km² (5,452 square miles)
Capital: Belfast (300,000)
(with adjacent metropolitan area, 500,000)
Other main cities and towns:
Derry (Londonderry) 65,000
Lisburn 41,000
Ballymena 29,000
Government: Part of the United Kingdom of Great Britain and Northern Ireland, a parliamentary democracy and constitutional monarchy. Northern Ireland elects members to the UK Parliament in London.

---

Alternatives are available but it would be perverse to drink any other than **Irish whiskey** while you are here. (To learn about the lore, see page 282.) For the sweeter tooth, there are liqueur whiskeys and the hugely successful 'Irish Cream' mixtures with dairy cream and coffee or chocolate, not to mention the inescapable Irish Coffee made from whiskey, brown sugar, hot black coffee and cream.

# The Scope of This Book

The travel section of this book covers Ireland area by area, beginning in Dublin, followed by the surrounding region. Then we travel roughly clockwise, to the south east, south west, west and north west, finishing in Northern Ireland.

# Taking Time Off in a Land Steeped in History

It may look small on the world map, but Ireland can seem larger than life. And twice as green – the 'emerald isle' is only one of many labels and stereotypes. They can hardly be avoided: Ireland and her people live up to their image, starting with their famous hospitality. 'The Irish are very fond of strangers,' reported a 17th-century French traveller. This remains true today: no people could be readier to help a visitor, or just to stop and chat. There's a timelessness about the place, and the pace. If you devise a rigid schedule don't expect to stick to it. Someone has only to tell you of something you mustn't miss and your plan for the day goes out of the window.

In any case, conversation is one of the greatest pleasures, if you're not in too much of a hurry. Throw in an innocent question and then sit back and enjoy the stream of stories. The people are born raconteurs. Put it down to the oral tradition of the bards, the cadences inherited from Irish Gaelic or kissing the Blarney stone, the effect is undeniable. They're great gossips and humorists and you won't catch all the subtleties. Be warned, as an evening fuelled with drinks wears on, the jokes can get spicier. The talent for giving

*Dubliners: in a young population, women are in the majority, sharp-witted and likely to tell you just what they think.*

and taking raillery and telling tall tales is part of the legendary 'crack' and held in high regard.

New arrivals soon seem to relax and feel at home. All the better if you have any hint of Ireland in your family tree, but no matter where you're from, you'll be welcomed as honorary Irish. Celebrities who are tired of having to evade the spotlight are discovering Ireland too, and not just the country houses and castles that serve so well as luxury hotels, but modest little places in the far west. Not only are the Irish too well-mannered to stare and point, they are genuinely unimpressed by fame and status, so superstars can mix with normal people and pretend they are normal themselves.

The cities and towns are on a human scale, with the old-fashioned virtues:

lively centres, small specialist shops staffed by people who have the time to attend to you. Compared with much of the western world, the difference is that the traditional look has not been lost. It suddenly strikes you that Wexford, Waterford and Galway weren't bombed in World War II like their British equivalents such as Plymouth or Southampton and much of continental Europe. Whole streets of 18th- and 19th-century buildings survived, shabby but complete. And if for long years there wasn't the money to keep them up, there wasn't the money to knock them down either. That began to change in the 1960s and '70s when wholesale destruction was visited on great areas of Dublin. Speculators made a killing by levelling Georgian terraces to build offices for

*Inside information: taking a look at the livestock on market-day morning.*

government and business, and heedless piecemeal 'redevelopment' began to disfigure other historic cities and towns. Not before time, an awareness of what was being lost has dawned and enthusiastic preservation groups have sprung up. The battle hasn't been won yet, but the line is being held.

Life still isn't easy in the rural areas, but the grinding poverty of the past has gone. European Community membership has favoured small farmers, and it shows in up-to-date equipment and better housing. A modern bungalow with double glazing and central heating may not be as picturesque as a draughty thatched cottage, but it's a lot more comfortable. Visitors benefit too, from the guest rooms and bathrooms built on specially as bed and breakfast accommodation. In the south west, the villages have brightened themselves up, with every house painted a different colour, not just polite pastels but vivid lime green, blackcurrant purple and tangerine.

Large families are still the norm, producing an astonishingly youthful population – on average the youngest in Europe. Many of them flee the rural backwaters for the cities. On a Saturday night it sometimes seems as though they are all out roaming the streets of Dublin, Cork and Galway, heading from one pub to another. They don't have to go far: there's such a bewildering number of pubs and bars in every town that you can't see how they can all survive. Once it rains, you'll be glad to duck inside yourself and enjoy a glass with the locals while you wait for it to stop.

You'll probably soon want to get out into the countryside and start exploring. Ireland's scenic beauty is legendary, but everywhere you look there is the imprint of history too. Neolithic tombs, countless ruined abbeys and churches, the patterns of abandoned fields and the tumbled stones of deserted cottages, the great houses and castles of long-vanished landowners, all have their explanations in a past that is still so real that it's almost a burden. People will talk to you of the events of 1922 as if they had occurred yesterday. When it comes to the problems of Northern Ireland today, feelings generally run less high in the Republic, at least on the surface. Most people there are in favour of a united Ireland in principle, but recognize that the majority in the 'six counties' of the North are so set against it that the prospect is remote. A million Protestants and the hard men of the IRA might not be comfortable to live with, anyway. Don't go to Ireland armed with preconceptions. It's full of surprises and paradoxes. Not for nothing do the British call apparently illogical statements 'Irish', only to discover that on examination, they make perfect sense.

# History

Bands of hunters may have roamed across Ireland before the end of the last Ice Age, about 9000 BC, when there was still a land bridge from Britain, and Britain was itself connected to mainland Europe. No trace of them has been found, even in the southern areas that were not covered by ice. The first true settlers didn't arrive until about 7000 BC (for a note on dating, see page 135), and they must have come by boat because by then the land link had been broken.

It was hardly a voyage into the unknown: even today you can see the Irish coast just 19km (12 miles) from southwest Scotland at the nearest point. People had probably been paying summer visits to hunt and fish long before deciding to take their families and move in permanently. Their new home was a land of woods full of game and rivers teeming with fish. They were skilled at making the stone arrowheads, spearpoints, blades and tools they needed; these are the main record we have of this Mesolithic period, along with bones of the wild pigs, birds and fish that they ate.

## The First Farmers
Pollen analysis and other archaeological clues show there was widespread clearance of the woodlands around 4000 BC.

**SNAKE-FREE ZONE**

Ireland has no weasels or moles, fewer sorts of mice than Britain, and the only resident reptile is the newt. Presumably the missing species hadn't made the migration in time before the sea severed the land link – unless you accept the legend that there used to be snakes until they were banished by St Patrick.

41

*I*t looks as if the Bronze Age inhabitants have only just left this
replica of a crannóg or lake dwelling at the Craggaunowen Project.

This seems to have been the work of new immigrants, Neolithic people who introduced the growing of crops and raised domesticated animals. They made decorated pottery and used heavier tools and weapons than their predecessors. Organized field-systems like those discovered near Ballycastle (see Céide Fields, page 250) point to an increased population, and burial monuments – simple at first, but becoming bigger and more elaborate – suggest the emergence of religious ritual and dominant local leaders.

The early tombs were round mounds, usually for one male, presumably a chief. Then came 'court tombs', with an open U-shaped courtyard in front of a covered burial vault formed of large stones. 'Portal tombs' (also known as dolmens or cromlechs) have massive stones weighing up to 100 tonnes, supported by three smaller stones to make a gateway to the burial chamber. 'Passage tombs', of which Newgrange in the Boyne valley is the most famous, have a big, roofed central chamber approached through a narrow passageway.

The emergence of copper and bronze tools around 2000 BC doesn't necessarily mean there was a new wave of mass immigration. Bronze Age technology may well have been introduced by just a few traders. By 1700 BC, copper ore was being mined and smelted in south-western Ireland and cast into axe-heads. Much more spectacular are the later gold ornaments – beautiful collars, bracelets and brooches from 1200-700 BC which you can see in the National Museum in Dublin and the Ulster Museum, Belfast. While you are touring Ireland, you'll come across the landmarks left by the Bronze Age people, great standing stones in circles and rows or just solitary monoliths.

## The Celts

Experts disagree, or admit they don't know. Was the Iron Age in Ireland ushered in by fresh immigrants speaking a Celtic language that developed into Irish Gaelic? Or were the techniques and customs adopted by the existing population? Whichever it was, during the 5th century BC a Celtic culture spread across Europe and into Ireland. Iron Age it may have been, but iron rusts, and it is mostly the stone, bronze and marvellous gold objects that have survived from this period. Big earth and stone forts indicate there was conflict between powerful neighbours. By about 100 BC, great ceremonial sites such as the Hill of Tara and the Navan Fort were the scene of important rituals, perhaps the crowning of kings who feature in the Celtic sagas preserved by story-tellers until the dawn of written history.

The Romans occupied most of Britain in the first century AD, but they seem never to have been seriously tempted by Ireland. Indeed, they had enough trouble trying to subdue the extremities of Britain. By the time they eventually gave up on Scotland and attempted to shut off its recalcitrant inhabitants behind Hadrian's Wall, imperial expansion had run out of steam. Ireland was a source of cattle and slaves, but they could be obtained by trade. The numbers of Roman coins and ornaments found in south-eastern Ireland indicate commerce on a large scale, perhaps even a permanent trading post. The famous geographer Claudius Ptolemy's map of Ireland, drawn in distant Alexandria, must have relied on the experience of merchants or adventurers who had travelled there. Some of the rivers he showed have names that we can recognize today, though his 'cities' can have been no more than settlements, perhaps ritual centres: not even a small town would exist in Ireland until centuries later.

As Roman power declined, the Irish – confusingly called the Scotti by the Romans – began to raid the coasts of Britain, and to settle there, especially in the north and west. When some returned to Ireland, they carried Romano-British ways, wives, goods and slaves with them. It is likely that in this way too, the first adherents of the new religion, Christianity, reached the island. Despite all these contacts, the course of Irish history was set apart from that of its neighbours by the fact that Ireland never experienced, for good or ill, any Roman discipline or culture at first hand.

The island continued as a mosaic of petty kingdoms, grouped into five provinces or 'fifths': Ulster, Meath, Leinster, Munster and Connacht (or Connaught). The king of each province who claimed overlordship demanded, and sometimes received, their allegiance.

## Conversion to Christianity

St Patrick did not begin the process. A reliable record in Rome shows that in AD 431, Pope Celestine I sent a certain Palladius as bishop 'to the Irish believing in Christ'. It doesn't say who these believers were, or how many. They may have come from Britain, voluntarily or not, or perhaps were converted by British Christian missionaries.

The traditional date for the arrival of St Patrick on his mission is AD 432, though it could have been some years later. As he related in his memoirs towards the end of his life, he had been in Ireland before, as the slave of Irish raiders. They had captured him in an attack on the villa in

*The Grianán of Aileach stone fort, on a hilltop in County Donegal. It was in use for at least a thousand years.*

*The ruins of many monasteries and friaries, like this one on the banks of the Eske in Donegal, are still in use as cemeteries.*

Britain where he had been brought up. After seven years spent as a cowherd, possibly in Ulster, he had escaped. It isn't clear whether he returned to Britain first, but he soon made his way to Gaul, where he was educated and ordained.

Although credited in the legends with the near single-handed conversion of the Irish people, he didn't claim as much himself. From his base at Armagh, still the ecclesiastical capital of all Ireland, he travelled widely, however, and he and his successors achieved the spread of Christianity quickly and peaceably: there were no martyrs in the process, in contrast to most of northern Europe.

During the sixth and seventh centuries, powerful personalities such as St Ciaran and St Brigid shifted control of the Irish church to the abbots of the monastic orders, rather than the bishops. Any influence there may have once been from Britain or Gaul had vanished. Even Rome's views were questioned. After all, Ireland was now the torchbearer for literacy and learning, while the western lands of the former Roman Empire were falling to the onslaughts of barbarians. Now Ireland sent out missionaries. Colmcille (St Columba) founded the monastery of Iona off Scotland and monks from there went on to northern England. Columbanus established monasteries in Burgundy, travelled on to Switzerland where one of his followers founded the monastery of St Gall, and ended up at another Irish foundation in Italy.

This was a golden age for Irish art. The 8th-century Ardagh Chalice and the Tara Brooch combine Celtic and imported Anglo-Saxon influences in a dazzling

display of technique and ornament. The Book of Kells (see page 98) was probably produced by Irish monks at Iona around the year 800.

## The Vikings

The sudden eruption of seaborne marauders from Scandinavia at the end of the 8th century, ranging round the coasts and up the rivers of western Europe, can't be put down to a single cause. There may have been poor harvests at home, and more mouths to feed. Better shipbuilding and navigation methods were available. Perhaps above all it was the discovery of rich, tempting targets to be plundered, especially in the form of prosperous monasteries conveniently close to coasts, on islands or next to navigable rivers.

Their raid on Ireland in 795, when several offshore settlements were sacked, was the first of many. Some monasteries were plundered repeatedly. The attacking fleets grew bigger and even places far inland were not safe. The year 840 saw a new development: instead of sailing home at the end of summer, a large party of Vikings camped for the winter by Lough Neagh. Next year they set up a permanent base at the mouth of the Liffey where Dublin now stands. In later years, fortified harbours were built at Wicklow, Arklow, Wexford, Waterford, Cork and Limerick, developing into Ireland's first towns.

The invaders, often referred to as Norsemen (and most were from Norway), didn't have it all their own way. Their set-

*I*rish agriculture is mostly right up to date, but traditional methods of farming survive in the remoter parts.

tlements remained as small enclaves and Irish resistance became better organized. As the local chieftains learned to sink their differences and cooperate, they went over to the attack. Dublin was stormed in 902 and the Vikings there expelled, though they returned in greater strength in 917. Irish forces sacked Limerick in 967 and vanquished a Norse army at Tara in 980.

In the arts, sculpture took over as the prime means of expression, with the carving of the intricately decorated high crosses. Many can still be seen, at the monasteries whose power and influence they were designed to proclaim.

## The Irish Fight Back

In 1002, Brian Boru, the king of Munster, became High King of Ireland, acknowledged by most provincial kings and chieftains. Leading an Irish army to victory over a combined Scandinavian force and their Irish allies at Clontarf, near Dublin in 1014, he was killed at the moment of triumph. It was the stuff of legend. The Irish alliance fell apart soon afterwards and the defeated King Sítríc (Sigtrygg) Silkenbeard still ruled in Dublin, but Viking power was in retreat. The settlements remained as important trading centres; their people became Christians and were eventually assimilated. The influence of Norse art styles is seen in a new flowering of craftsmanship, producing such treasures as the Shrine of St Patrick's Bell (now in the National Museum).

The Irish provinces, reduced to four with Meath demoted to minor status, continued to squabble. The kings of Ulster, Leinster, Munster and Connacht now saw the benefit of alliance with church reformers who were trying to set up a hierarchy of archbishops and bishops (at the expense of monastic power). Together,

47

they made the boundaries of dioceses match the petty kingdoms, to give them both legitimacy. Continental orders were invited to set up new monasteries: the first Cistercian foundation in Ireland was at Mellifont in 1142.

Meanwhile, the expansionist Normans – descendants of Vikings who had settled in France, it might be noted – had taken over in England and were trying to extend their feudal system of control to Wales and Scotland. Perhaps the rulers of Ireland thought they would be immune. After all, they had escaped the attentions of the Romans and the Anglo-Saxons, and tamed the Norsemen.

*T*he Normans began to build churches as soon as they settled in Ireland. This is the 12th-century St Multose Church in Kinsale, County Cork.

## Anglo-Norman Invasion

Just as Rome was extending its influence over the Irish church, land-hungry Normans in England and Wales were looking for new conquests and casting covetous eyes towards Ireland. The only Englishman ever to be pope, Adrian IV (Nicholas Breakspear) gave approval in advance to a Norman invasion, recognizing Henry II of England as 'Lord of Ireland'. For some years Henry was too busy in France to turn the title into reality. Then came an apparently minor event that was to change history. In 1166, Dermot (or Diarmaid) MacMorrough, King of Leinster was forced to flee from Ireland by the High King, Roderic O'Conor. (The dispute between them had begun some years before, when Dermot abducted the wife of O'Rourke, one of O'Conor's allies.) Dermot tracked Henry down in France to ask for aid to regain his lands.

No doubt it would have happened sooner or later, but this was the step which actually began the often tragic, sometimes fruitful, entanglement of Britain and Ireland. Henry did not become directly involved at first, but he permitted his subjects to help. In 1169 an advance party of adventurers landed near Wexford, which quickly surrendered to them. Dermot had also approached the powerful Earl of Pembroke, Richard de Clare, known as 'Strongbow', offering his daughter in marriage and the succession as king of Leinster in exchange for assistance. Strongbow landed near Waterford in 1170 and soon took the town. The promised wedding was celebrated a few days later. The invaders moved on to Dublin, defeating the Norse and Irish defenders there too. With the sudden death of Dermot MacMorrough in 1171, Strongbow inherited his kingdom.

*The ruined Norman castle at Ferns, once capital of Dermot MacMorrough's kingdom of Leinster.*

Alarmed at the prospect of a Norman Ireland outside his control, Henry II now took a hand. Landing at Waterford with an army, he accepted the homage of the Norman lords and most Irish (Gaelic) kings and bishops. Strongbow was confirmed in Leinster and made viceroy; other Anglo-Norman leaders were granted great tracts of land in Ulster and Meath. O'Conor was left in charge of the western kingdom of Connacht. Dublin and the nearby coast Henry kept to himself, the start of the 'Pale' (see page 127).

Now the Norman lords had to establish their rule. Using the same methods as in England and Wales, they seized territory and quickly built castles. Much of the land was granted to their followers as a reward for support, a process that continued down the feudal pecking order, generating land hunger and propelling further Norman expansion. Heavily armed troops compelled the dispossessed to obedience. Later, fortified towns were founded and immigrants brought from England in the first of many schemes of 'Plantation'. The 13th century also saw a wave of church-building in the Gothic style, and the foundation of many abbeys and friaries.

Even so, the 'conquest' of Ireland was far from complete. The Norman lords had never mastered the west and north west, and Gaelic victories there began to roll them back. Especially after the Black Death reached Ireland in 1348 and killed perhaps a third of the population, the Anglo-Norman magnates were constantly short of manpower. This forced them to recruit Irish labour, even as soldiers. They had to enter into agreements with local leaders and make dynastic marriages to preserve their positions. The Normans' ability to assimilate had always been one of their great strengths, and by the 14th century, many had in effect become Irish chieftains. The viceroy vainly tried to reverse the tendency in the Kilkenny Statutes of 1366, forbidding intermarriage and alliances with the Gaelic Irish. Interventions by English kings notwithstanding, Ireland beyond the Pale was in reality ruled not by them, but by the Earls of Desmond, Ormonde and, greatest of them all, Kildare.

## Under the Tudors

The Reformation in England triggered new turbulence in Ireland. Henry VIII, assuming the title King of Ireland in 1541, began the confiscation of church lands, driving the religious orders and most Anglo-Irish into alliance with the Gaelic Irish. When Catholicism was briefly restored under Queen Mary, it soon became clear how little support there had been for the Protestant cause. And when Elizabeth reversed the process again, she trod carefully for fear of making Ireland fertile soil for a Spanish invasion. Spain did make some attempts. A foothold was briefly established on the Dingle Peninsula in 1579, but the most notable advent of the Spanish was when many ships of the Armada were wrecked on the Irish coast in 1588. A succession of failed Irish rebellions marked Elizabeth's reign to its very end. And after each one, the English grip tightened.

The defeat of the last rising, in Ulster, led to the 'Flight of the Earls' (of Tyrone and Tyrconnell) and their supporters in 1607 to exile in mainland Europe. It was followed by the most thoroughgoing Plantation yet, of Scottish and English Protestant settlers on confiscated lands. The effect was to create a Protestant majority in most of Ulster, with results we can see to this day.

## Religious Wars

The outbreak of Civil War in England coincided with another revolt in Ulster in 1641 as dispossessed Irish tried to recover their lost lands. A Catholic Confederacy formed in Kilkenny in 1642 negotiated with Charles I, who was also supported by Protestants led by the Earl of Ormonde. Parliamentary armies from England could not crush the royalists until Cromwell, following the defeat and execution of the king, crossed to Ireland in 1649, determined to finish the job. Drogheda and Wexford were besieged and stormed, their defenders killed or condemned to slavery in West Indies plantations. All those who had opposed the parliamentary cause had their estates confiscated and given to Cromwell's soldiers and to those who had financed his campaigns.

With the death of Cromwell and the restoration of Charles II (1660) there was a limited return to Catholics of a fraction of their lands. The Catholic James II succeeded his brother but before he could proceed far with policies favouring his co-religionists, he was deposed in the Revolution of 1688 and replaced by his son-in-law, William of Orange. Fleeing to France, James was given some troops and money by Louis XIV. Landing at Kinsale in 1689, he received general support and quickly established his government in Dublin. The only armed opposition came from the settlers at Londonderry (Derry) and Enniskillen: the 105-day Siege of Derry (it held out until resupplied by ship) is still celebrated by its Protestant inhabitants.

In June 1690, William landed with a multi-national Protestant army at

*A*lmost every religious foundation in Ireland was destroyed in the wars of the 16th and 17th centuries. Sligo Abbey was sacked in 1641.

Carrickfergus, near Belfast, and marched south to meet a smaller Irish and French force at the Battle of the Boyne on 12 July (now a public holiday in Northern Ireland). William was the clear winner, and James returned to France. The battle, however, did not finish the war, which dragged on for another year. The Treaty of Limerick which ended it was supposed to guarantee the religious rights of Catholics, but these terms were never ratified. Most of the defeated army went abroad, many ('the Wild Geese') to serve in continental armies. A new Protestant parliament of Ireland passed a succession of Penal Laws forbidding Catholics to buy land or take up the professions.

The established Protestant Episcopalian Church of Ireland was still further favoured by the Test Act of 1704. Only its adherents, perhaps 10 percent of the population, had full political rights. Even the more numerous Presbyterians could not hold public office. Rural poverty in Ulster led to the emigration of many to the American colonies; their descendants included several future presidents. The far worse-off Catholics were now confined to the poorest tenth of the land, most of it the bogs and bare rock of Connacht, where people lived in utter penury.

In prosperous Dublin, little was known of this, and in London even less, despite the virulent campaigning pamphlets which Jonathan Swift, Dean of St Patrick's Cathedral, wrote in the 1720s. Famines and disturbances in the west caused hardly a ripple in Dublin's elegant new Georgian terraces.

## Campaigners for Independence

The American Revolution inspired thoughts of greater Irish freedom, especially as many of the colonists were of

*Spared when so much of old Dublin was levelled, the Lord Edward pub is named after Lord Edward Fitzgerald who died in the 1798 Rising.*

Irish descent. Stripped of troops to reinforce the British army across the Atlantic, and with France and Spain entering the war on the American side, Ireland lay open to invasion. Volunteer militia groups sprang up all over the country for its defence; parades and fancy uniforms became all the rage. But soon the volunteer corps, predominantly Protestant though they were, began to rail against London's limitations on Irish commerce and autonomy. Eloquently led by Henry Grattan, they obtained better terms for Irish trade in 1779, and some return of powers to the Irish parliament in 1782. The French Revolution accelerated the process, the British government trying to encourage Catholic loyalty by giving them the vote and also the right to hold many public offices.

In 1791, discontented Presbyterian and Catholic intellectuals led by Wolfe Tone had formed the Society of United Irishmen to campaign for a more representative parliament. It was banned in 1794 after war with France broke out, but regrouped illegally, and Wolfe Tone went to seek French help. He sailed with a French invasion fleet to Bantry Bay in 1796, but it was scattered by storms. Returning with another French expedition in 1798, Tone was captured off the coast of Donegal aboard one the French ships and condemned to death for treason. Rebellions of his supporters on land had already failed, and he committed suicide before the sentence could be carried out.

With a mixture of motives, the British government under William Pitt now pushed through the Act of Union, 1801, joining Ireland with Great Britain in a United Kingdom. Through promises, persuasion and bribery, the Irish parliament voted for its own abolition. With all power and influence concentrated in London, Dublin became a backwater.

A young lawyer, Daniel O'Connell, was an eloquent campaigner for Catholic emancipation. He was elected to the House of Commons in London, but as a Catholic, could not take his seat. The outcry was so great that the law was changed in 1829. As an MP, his next fight was for the repeal of the Act of Union. Although he failed in this, he is honoured in Ireland as 'The Liberator'.

A movement called Young Ireland attempted a rising in 1848. With its failure, the leaders fled or were deported, adding to the anti-British feeling among the emigrants

*Whole books have been published about the Georgian doorways of Dublin, neglected, cherished or turned into an art show.*

which fuelled the next organization, the Irish Republican Brotherhood or Fenian movement. Their 1867 rebellion was crushed, but persuaded Gladstone, in his first term as prime minister in London, to look for ways to defuse the Irish timebomb.

In 1874, more than half the Irish seats in parliament were won by the new Home Rule League, led from 1877 by Charles Stewart Parnell. Back in Ireland, the Fenian Michael Davitt organized the Land League to fight for the rights of tenants. In response, Gladstone's Land Act set up courts to set fairer rents, and eventually led to many tenants actually buying the land they farmed.

## FAMINE AND EMIGRATION

The staple diet of the rural poor had long been the potato. Millions were totally reliant on it, and its success in Ireland's climate had contributed to a population explosion. In 1845 some of the harvest was infected by blight, which caused it to rot in the ground. In 1846, virtually the entire crop was wiped out, and millions were left to face a hard winter with nothing to eat. London was slow to realize the scale of what was happening though it did organize some soup kitchens and work schemes. There seemed to be no shortage of food, since wheat continued to be exported from Ireland – those who were dying of hunger had no money to buy it. Relief sent from England was too little, too late, and bad communications meant it failed to reach the majority. In successive blighted years up to 1851, it is estimated that almost a million people died of starvation and disease. A million more emigrated. Vast numbers sailed to the United States, packed into old ships where many, desperately weak from typhus, dysentery and scurvy when they embarked, died on the voyage. Others went to Canada or Australia, but census figures suggest that no fewer than 700,000 made a shorter journey to Britain, to join the growing numbers of the urban poor, taking any unskilled work they could find.

## Road to Revolt

Eventually Gladstone was converted to Home Rule, but his bills to introduce it were rejected, first in the Commons, then in the House of Lords. With Parnell disgraced as a result of a divorce case (see page 152), and dead not long after, constitutional progress to Irish independence ground to a halt. Nationalist feeling found outlets in the Gaelic League, furthering Irish language and culture, and the Gaelic Athletic Association, promoting the Irish sports of hurling and Gaelic football. Both were fertile recruiting grounds for the revived Irish Republican Brother-

hood (IRB) and the new political grouping *Sinn Féin* ('Ourselves'), led by Arthur Griffith. Trade union militancy in Dublin added yet another strand to the discontent, with the formation of an illegal 'Citizen Army' to defend the workers.

Home Rule was again passed by the House of Commons in 1912, and this time the Lords could only delay it, having lost their power of veto. Led by the dynamic Sir Edward Carson, the Unionists first campaigned against Home Rule in any form, then scaled down their ambitions to a demand that it shouldn't be applied to Ulster. A force of 100,000 Ulster Volunteers stood ready to resist any attempt to do so. In March 1914, British cavalry officers at the Curragh army base declared that they would resign rather than move against this force – a mutiny in all but name despite its label of 'The Curragh Incident'. To counter the Unionist force, Irish Volunteers formed in Dublin and the two militias raced to gather arms.

In September 1914 Home Rule for Ireland finally became law, and was immediately suspended until the end of World War I, whenever that should be. (War had broken out a month earlier.) The British had now achieved the worst of both worlds, incurring the wrath of Protestant Unionists by agreeing to Home Rule, and of Irish Nationalists by setting it aside. The IRB, relying on the support of the Irish Volunteers and the Citizen Army, decided on armed revolt.

*M*any a castle, such as Birr in County Offaly, was gradually turned into a stately home when more peaceful times came in the 19th century.

*Plaque on O'Connell Bridge, one of a series following the legendary footsteps of Leopold Bloom in James Joyce's novel,* Ulysses.

It took place on Easter Monday, 24 April 1916. Scattered buildings in Dublin were seized, notably the General Post Office which became the headquarters of the insurgents. An Irish Republic was declared. But only about 2000 took part in the rising, and although bitter street fighting continued for a week, the remnants were forced to surrender. The British government and most people in Britain saw the revolt as treason, a 'stab in the back' while the nation was at war. Fifteen of its leaders were put before a firing squad in

Kilmainham Jail, including all those who had signed the proclamation of the republic, whether they had taken part in the fighting or not. The effect of this vicious repression was to drive most Irish opinion into the nationalist camp. At the first post-war general election in December 1918, Sinn Féin won a landslide victory except in Protestant Ulster. The moderates who favoured constitutional reform were extinguished.

## Partition and Civil War

Refusing to take their seats in the United Kingdom parliament, the Sinn Féin members led by Éamon De Valéra met in Dublin, proclaiming themselves to be the *Dáil Éireann* (Assembly of Ireland). A provisional government was declared, with the Irish Republican Army formed to protect it. Virtual war broke out as the representatives and symbols of British authority were attacked. Many of the police resigned rather than fight their compatriots, and British ex-servicemen, known from the colour of their uniforms as the 'Black and Tans', were sent to replace them. A pattern of ambush, assassination, reprisal and revenge marked the next two years, until a war-weary Britain realized that it could no longer impose its rule on an ever more alienated Ireland. A truce was called in July 1921, and a treaty signed on 6 December 1921 partitioned Ireland. Twenty-six counties became the Irish Free State, not totally independent but with dominion status, still within the Commonwealth and still owing allegiance to the crown. The six of Ulster's nine counties where there was a Unionist majority were given a sort of home rule. King George V opened the parliament of Northern Ireland in Belfast in 1921.

Partition didn't only divide the island, it split the nationalists too. Denied the

## THE UNSOLVED QUESTION

Many nationalists have never been reconciled to the division of Ireland, and Unionists remain as determined as ever to keep Northern Ireland in the United Kingdom. Sporadic raids by the IRA (an illegal organization on both sides of the border) continued at a low level up to the 1960s. The Catholic minority in the North were unquestionably second class citizens. That was nothing new, but the climate of the time led to the launching of a civil rights campaign in 1968 to demand better housing and a voice in local government. When demonstrators clashed with the police and militant Protestants, parts of Belfast and Londonderry became riot zones. British army troops were sent in to separate the embattled communities. At first they were welcomed by Catholics who saw them as defenders, but the atmosphere soon went sour. When British paratroops shot 13 civil rights marchers dead on 'Bloody Sunday', 30 January 1972, any vestige of goodwill vanished.

In 1971, the Provisional IRA, which had eclipsed the 'Official', more Marxist wing, began a campaign of bombing and shooting, at first aimed at the security forces in Northern Ireland, but extending to civilian targets and to Britain. Its aim appears to be to sicken the British government and people of violence and killing, to the point of abandoning the province. But while a majority in Northern Ireland wishes to stay in the UK, Britain feels bound to support them. Most British people, although weary of the endless carnage, believe withdrawal would lead to a bloodbath. Protestant paramilitaries gave weight to that opinion: in the 1990s the number of Catholics killed by them exceeded the victims of the IRA. Looking for a way to make some sort of progress to a peaceful future, the UK and Ireland signed the 1985 Anglo-Irish Agreement giving the Dublin government a consultative role in the affairs of Northern Ireland. It was and still is bitterly opposed by Unionists.

complete independence for which they had fought, De Valéra and his Republicans opposed the treaty. When the Dáil narrowly passed it, he resigned as president. His replacement, Arthur Griffith, and Michael Collins, the young chairman of the new provisional government, called a general election which gave them broad support. A short but nasty civil war ensued as opponents of the treaty again resorted to arms. Griffith died suddenly, from the strain it was believed, and only ten days later the new state lost a charismatic leader when Michael Collins was killed in an ambush. The provisional government reacted with extreme measures, including the execution of those carrying arms against it. In 1923, armed resistance ceased.

## Free State and Republic

After fresh elections, a government led by William Cosgrave started on the process of reconstruction. De Valéra's republican *Fianna Fáil* ('Soldiers of Destiny') at first boycotted the Dáil, but entered it in 1927, and in 1932 won enough seats to form the government. The oath of allegiance to the British crown was soon abolished, and in 1937 a new constitution was adopted, republican in all but name. The title of Irish Free State was dropped in favour of Éire (Ireland).

The new status was demonstrated in World War II, when Ireland remained neutral, although Northern Ireland was fully involved, Belfast suffering heavy German bombing. In 1949, under the *Fine Gael* ('Tribes of Gaels') government of

John Costello, Ireland declared itself a republic. A generally more outward-looking stance led to participation by Irish troops in various United Nations peacekeeping operations.

Most industry had previously been concentrated in Northern Ireland but the 1960s saw an expansion in the Republic, and joining the European Community in 1973 (at the same time as Britain) brought a foreign investment boom. Dreamland was infected with a fresh pragmatism and the young generation learned new managerial skills. For a while the tide of emigration, reflecting a lack of opportunities at home, was stemmed for the first time since the beginning of the 19th century. In today's harsher world, the outflow has resumed, and now tends to take the trained and educated overseas, where in the past the major export had been of unskilled labour.

**New Beginnings**

In 1979, John Paul II made the first papal visit to Ireland. It was a tribute to a Catholic nation which had kept the faith through centuries of tribulation. He was given a huge welcome and hundreds of thousands attended open-air masses.

In the same year, economic self-confidence in the Republic led to a decision to break the historic link with the pound sterling. At first the Irish pound (or *punt*) floated proudly higher than the British: harder times reversed the position and recently they have been near to

*The Irish President's fine Georgian house on the edge of Phoenix Park was once the home of the British viceroys.*

*The back room at the Brazen Head pub – it claims to be Dublin's oldest – provides a platform for traditional and other music groups.*

parity. Politics in the 1980s were dominated by the controversial Charles Haughey, Fianna Fáil leader and twice *Taoiseach* (Prime Minister). Never quite free of a whiff of scandal, he can be credited with lavish patronage of the arts, and skilful milking of European funds to finance his projects. In 1992, Haughey's name was linked to one questionable deal too many and he had to resign. The drabber Albert Reynolds took over at the head of a coali-

tion with a new force in Irish politics, Dick Spring's Progressive Democrats.

The Irish presidency is largely a ceremonial job, long filled by pensioned-off politicians from one or other of the two big party machines. So the election of Mary Robinson in 1991 was widely seen as a hopeful sign. Brilliant (a law professor at 25), charismatic, the first woman in the office, married to a Protestant, she had aired fresh ideas about thorny old issues ranging from contraception to relations with Northern Ireland.

Perennial problems remain unsolved, but you would hardly know it. The countryside keeps its legendary beauty and even the remotest parts have enjoyed a measure of prosperity. Irish hospitality is as warm as ever and Irish good humour is unquenchable.

## HISTORICAL LANDMARKS

| | |
|---|---|
| c. 7000 BC | First recorded human settlement. Flint and bone implements. |
| c. 4000-2200 BC | Neolithic Era: beginning of farming. Stone tools and simple pottery. Passage tombs such as Newgrange (c. 3000 BC). |
| c. 2200 BC | Dawn of Bronze Age: contacts with Europe bring new metalwork techniques. Gold and bronze ornaments, stone circles. |

**Celtic Era**

| | |
|---|---|
| c. 600-150 BC | Introduction of the use of iron, possibly by Celtic-speaking immigrants. Fine gold and other ornaments. Earth and stone ring-forts. |
| c. AD 150 | Roman geographer Ptolemy draws map of Ireland, at this time split into dozens of small kingdoms. |
| 4th-5th centuries | Christianity arrives from mainland Europe and Britain. |
| 431 | Rome appoints the first bishop to Irish Christians, Palladius. |
| 432 | The traditional date of the arrival of St Patrick on his mission. |
| 6th century | Many monasteries founded. Irish missionaries set out to convert Scotland and the European mainland. |
| c. 800 | Book of Kells |

**Viking Raids and Settlements**

| | |
|---|---|
| 795 | First of many Viking raids. Monasteries plundered. |
| c. 840-920 | Viking settlements established (Dublin, 841, Waterford, Wexford, Cork and Limerick). Disunited Irish unable to resist. |
| 1002 | Brian Boru, king of Munster, becomes high king of Ireland. |
| 1014 | Irish under Brian Boru defeat Norse and Irish force at Clontarf, but Brian Boru is killed. Rivalry of Irish kings resumes. |
| 1142 | First Cistercian foundation in Ireland, at Mellifont. |
| 1166 | Dermot MacMorrough seeks the help of Henry II of England against O'Conor and O'Rourke. Henry has already obtained pa pal approval for the conquest of Ireland. |

**Anglo-Norman Invasion**

| | |
|---|---|
| 1169 | Normans from England and Wales land in south-eastern Ireland. |
| 1170 | Main Norman army under Richard de Clare (Strongbow) captures Waterford. Strongbow marries daughter of MacMorrough. Dublin falls to Normans. |
| 1171 | Henry II lands at Waterford. Anglo-Norman lords, Irish kings and bishops do homage to him. Normans begin to build castles. |
| 1224 | Dominicans and Franciscans establish religious houses. |
| 1348 | Black Death kills up to a third of the population. |
| 1366 | Kilkenny parliament attempts to bring to heel the Anglo-Norman settlers who have become 'more Irish than the Irish'. |
| 1394 | Richard II lands at Waterford with an army, to try and restore control. Warring lords submit, until the army departs. |
| 15th century | Rival Irish and Anglo-Norman lords divide and rule the country. English power restricted to the Pale. |

**Tudor Intervention**

| | |
|---|---|
| 1539 | Monasteries within the Pale dissolved. |

| | |
|---|---|
| 1541 | Henry VIII takes title of King of Ireland, applies English law. |
| 1588 | Ships of the Spanish Armada wrecked on Irish coast. |
| 1592 | Foundation of Trinity College, Dublin. |
| 1595 | Rising in Ulster, led by Hugh O'Neill, Earl of Tyrone. |
| 1601 | Spanish land at Kinsale. O'Neill and O'Donnell attempt to link up with them but are defeated. |
| 1602 | Spanish surrender at Kinsale. |
| 1603 | O'Neill submits, retaining lands and title. |
| 1607 | 'Flight of the Earls'. O'Neill and O'Donnell, Earl of Tyrconnell, and many Ulster landowners leave for exile. |

**Plantation and Civil War**

| | |
|---|---|
| 1610 | Ulster estates are confiscated and 'planted' with Protestant Scots and English. |
| 1642 | English Civil War spreads to Ireland. Catholic Confederation off Kilkenny negotiates with Charles I, fights Parliamentary supporters. |
| 1649 | The victorious Cromwell exacts revenge. Massacres at Drogheda and Wexford. Catholic landowners largely dispossessed. |
| 1660 | Restoration of Charles II. Limited return of some Catholic lands. |
| 1685 | Accession of James II. He begins to place Catholics in positions of authority. |
| 1688 | James II deposed. |
| 1689 | James II lands at Kinsale with French troops, enters Dublin. |
| 1690 | William of Orange lands in Ulster. James II defeated at Battle of the Boyne, leaves for France. |
| 1695-1709 | Protestant-dominated Parliament passes many Penal Laws against Catholics. |
| 1713 | Swift becomes Dean of St Patrick's, Dublin. |
| 1759 | Guinness brewery established in Dublin. |

**Independence Struggles**

| | |
|---|---|
| 18th century | Rural poverty and disturbances contrast with urban affluence. American and French revolutions inspire renewed stirrings for Irish independence. |
| 1791 | Society of United Irishmen formed by Wolfe Tone. |
| 1798 | Rising of United Irishmen. French force lands in support at Killala, but surrenders. Wolfe Tone captured, commits suicide. |
| 1801 | Act of Union with Britain comes into effect. Irish parliament is thereby extinguished, along with Dublin's influence. |
| 1829 | Daniel O'Connell enters British parliament, campaigning for repeal of the Act of Union. |
| 1845-51 | Potato blight and famine. Up to a million die and as many emigrate. |
| 1848 | 'Young Ireland' rising fails. |
| 1867 | Fenian rising suppressed. |
| 1874 | Irish Home Rule League wins half the Irish seats in British parliament. |

| | |
|---|---|
| 1877 | Parnell becomes leader of Home Rule League. |
| 1879-82 | Land League battles for fairer terms for tenants. |
| 1884 | Gaelic Athletic Association formed to encourage Irish sports and activities. |
| 1891 | Death of Parnell. |
| 1903 | Land Purchase Act allows tenants to buy out many landlords. |
| 1906 | First publication of Sinn Féin ('We Ourselves'). |
| 1912 | Home Rule bill passed by House of Commons, but held up by Lords. Ulster Volunteers, a scarcely legal force of 100,000, proclaim their determination to remain united with Britain. |
| 1913 | Eight-month strike and lockout in Dublin. |
| 1914 | The Curragh 'Incident': British officers refuse to move against the Ulster Volunteers. Home Rule bill receives royal assent, but action on it is suspended pending the end of the war in Europe. |
| 1916 | Easter Rising in Dublin is suppressed. Fifteen leaders shot by British. |
| 1918 | Sinn Féin candidates win most seats in general election, but refuse to attend British parliament. They set up the Dáil Éireann (Assembly of Ireland) and declare independence. |
| 1919-21 | War of Independence, assassinations, ambushes and reprisals. |

**Partition**

| | |
|---|---|
| 1920 | Britain splits Ireland. Twenty-six counties are offered dominion status as Irish Free State. The six largely Protestant counties of Northern Ireland stay in the Union. |
| 1922 | Anglo-Irish Treaty narrowly passed by Dáil. Brief civil war between those who accept and those who reject it. Michael Collins assassinated. |
| 1932 | Éamon de Valéra leads Fianna Fáil government. |
| 1937 | Irish Free State, now Éire, cuts link with British crown. |
| 1939-45 | Irish neutrality in World War II. |
| 1949 | Republic declared, ending Commonwealth connection. |
| 1960s | Economic and industrial expansion. Irish participation in UN peacekeeping forces. |
| 1968 | Civil rights marchers and police clash in Northern Ireland. |
| 1969 | British army sent to separate the embattled Catholic and Protestant communities in northern cities. |
| 1971 | Provisional IRA begins bombing campaign. |
| 1972 | 'Bloody Sunday': British paratroopers shoot 13 civil rights marchers dead. Northern Ireland parliament suspended. |
| 1973 | Republic joins European Community. |
| 1979 | Irish pound breaks link with sterling, joining European Monetary System. Visit of Pope John Paul II. |
| 1985 | Anglo-Irish Agreement allows Dublin a voice in Northern Ireland affairs, despite opposition of Unionist parties. |

# *Just the Essentials*

You can't see it all: nobody ever has, and even if you adopt a modest plan, it's liable to change. Distances look short on the map, but in Ireland you're always likely to be diverted or delayed, often in the nicest possible way. However, each region has highlights that it would be a pity to miss, especially on your first visit to that part of the country.

# Dublin

National Museum: the glint of Bronze Age gold

Trinity College: home of the Book of Kells

St Stephen's Green and the Georgian squares

Old Dublin: two medieval cathedrals and the Castle

Along the Liffey: classical buildings and Guinness Brewery

Parnell Square: the Lane Collection and Writers' Museum

Kilmainham: the Museum of Modern Art and the historic Jail

Dublin Pubs: life and soul of the city

# Excursions from Dublin

Malahide: unique castle

Howth: picturesque port and peninsula

The Boyne Valley: megalithic monuments

Monasterboice: superb carved high crosses

Trim: the Normans' biggest castle

Kildare: horse country, the Curragh and the National Stud

# The South East

Glendalough: tranquil valley and monastic site

Johnstown Castle: Gardens and Agricultural Museum

Kilkenny: historic medieval city

Jerpoint Abbey: superb stone carvings

Rock of Cashel: Ireland's Acropolis

# The South West

Cork City: lively capital of the south

Kinsale: historic port and resort

Iveragh Peninsula: the 'Ring of Kerry'

Killarney: legendary lakes and mountains

Dingle Peninsula: scenery and traditions

# The West of Ireland

Limerick: King John's Castle and Georgian city

Clonmacnois: monastic ruins beside the Shannon

The Burren: stony wonderland

The Aran Islands: a life apart

Galway City: cheerful centre of the west

Connemara: wild mountains and coast

# The North West

Westport: pretty town, lively quayside

Achill Island: cliffs, mountains and beaches

Yeats Country: lakes and hills the poet loved

Glencolumbkille: the saint's remote retreat

Glenveagh National Park: Donegal's wilderness

# Northern Ireland

North Antrim Coast: the Giant's Causeway

Belfast: the city that keeps making news

Belfast: the Ulster Museum

The Ards Peninsula: Mount Stewart house and gardens

Armagh: city of two St Patrick's cathedrals

Fermanagh: tranquil and lovely Lough Erne

Omagh: Ulster American Folk Park and History Park

# *Going Places With Something Special in Mind*

Ireland is so packed with sights to see and things to do that you hardly know where to start. One answer may be to specialize a bit and organize your route around two or three particular interests or themes. Here we present some ideas, from following the path of St Patrick to taking a tour of famous Dublin pubs.

## Gardens

The 'soft' climate is just about ideal for gardeners, rarely too hot or too cold, and generous with the water supply. Exotic species which normally wouldn't grow in these latitudes can flourish in the frost-free south and west, but great gardens have been established all over Ireland.

### 1 DUBLIN

The National Botanic Gardens at Glasnevin are two centuries old, with magnificent old glasshouses and a huge

*A*way from it all, on the road through Glenveagh National Park, County Donegal.

collection of trees and shrubs, roses, herbs, vegetables and cacti.

### 2 MALAHIDE, Co. Dublin

The Talbot Botanic Gardens include a walled garden sheltering an unusual number of southern hemisphere plants.

### 3 TULLY, Co. Kildare

An authentic and lovely Japanese Garden might seem an odd companion for the Irish National Stud, but they were both set up by the same eccentric early in the 20th century.

### 4 POWERSCOURT, Co. Wicklow

The great house was burned out but the gardens are still magnificent with endless vistas, flights of terraces and regimented flowerbeds.

**5** ASHFORD, Co. Wicklow
The Mount Usher Gardens occupy the grounds of an old mill. Azaleas, eucalyptus and in all over 5,000 species of plants fill 9ha (22 acres) along the River Vartry.

**6** JOHNSTOWN CASTLE, Co. Wexford
A fairy-tale castle in wooded grounds, reflected in a dramatic ornamental lake, with hothouses, a walled garden and a fascinating rural museum.

*Great gardens to discover wherever you may be in your travels across Ireland.*

**7** NEW ROSS, Co. Wexford
The John F. Kennedy Arboretum at Dunganstown was sent specimens of trees and shrubs from many countries.

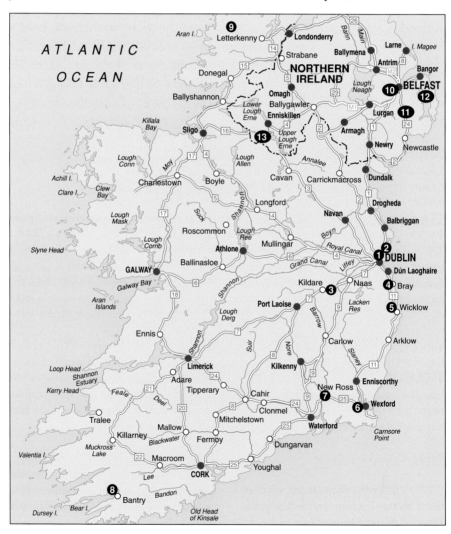

**8 GARINISH ISLAND, Co. Cork**
In the harbour off Glengarriff, an Italian-style garden laid out in 1910. It is usually a riot of colour, with plants from all over the world benefiting from the frost-free winters.

**9 GLENVEAGH CASTLE, Co. Donegal**
Set in superb scenery, beautiful flower gardens and shrubs. Noted for its rhododendrons.

**10 BELFAST**
The Botanic Gardens make a compact but colourful retreat. The restored mid-19th-century Palm House is a masterpiece.

**11 ROWALLANE, Co. Down**
Vast natural gardens, trees and shrubs, walled garden, herbaceous plants and rock garden. Fine displays of spring flowers, rhododendrons and azaleas, roses and heathers. A National Trust property.

**12 MOUNT STEWART, Co. Down**
A National Trust house. The garden designed by Lady Londonderry starting in 1921 is one of Ireland's and the United Kingdom's finest, with an amazing variety of styles.

**13 FLORENCE COURT, Co. Fermanagh**
Spacious grounds of a National Trust house. Georgian pleasure gardens and walled garden.

# Bird-Watching

Cliffs and islands and clean seas alive with fish attract hosts of seabirds. Lonely mudflats and estuaries are perfect for wading

birds, and the lonely mountain skies are patrolled by a wide range of birds of prey.

**1 NORTH BULL ISLAND, Co. Dublin**
A sand spit also known as Dollymount Strand, this is a nature reserve with wintering flocks of geese, many species of ducks, waders and birds of prey.

**2 WEXFORD SLOBS, Co. Wexford**
Reclaimed marshland, now a wildfowl reserve with hides and lookout towers. Thousands of Greenland white-fronted geese and other geese and ducks overwinter here.

**3 SALTEE ISLANDS, Co. Wexford**
Seabirds nesting here from May to July include gannets, puffins, guillemots and kittiwakes.

**4 HOOK HEAD, Co. Wexford**
Migrants pass through in spring and autumn, and rare visitors may arrive at the tip of the peninsula, blown off course in bad weather.

**5 BALLYCOTTON, Co. Cork**
Coastal marshes and lakes attract ducks and waders in winter. Spring and autumn migrants to be seen.

**6 CLEAR ISLAND, Co. Cork**
Hosts of seabirds at all times, and some rare migrants in spring and autumn. There's a bird observatory at North Harbour.

**7 THE SKELLIGS, Co. Kerry**
Little Skellig is a bird sanctuary where thousands of gannets and puffins nest: you can circle it in a boat. Great Skellig is home to many seabirds too.

*B*irds of many species
abound to please bird-watchers of
all varieties.

**8** RIVER SHANNON and
**9** SHANNON ESTUARY
The lowlands around Shannonbridge and
Banagher are good for seeing ducks,

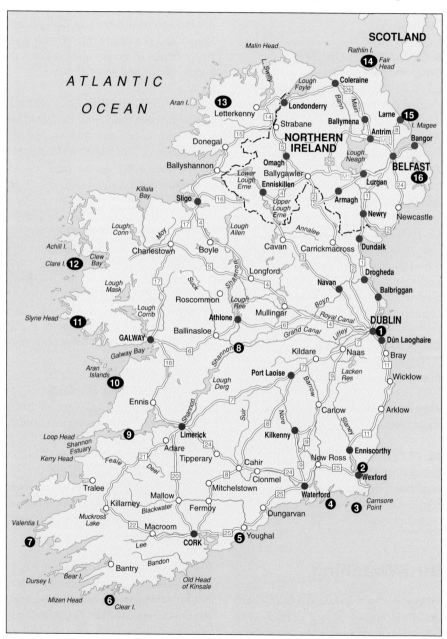

70

waders and corncrakes. Downstream and in the estuary, ducks and geese, seabirds and waders abound, from Limerick to Loop Head.

**10 CLIFFS OF MOHER, Co. Clare**
Choughs, ravens, razorbills, puffins, terns, fulmars and guillemots are among many species to be seen around the towering 200m- (650ft-) cliffs.

**11 ROUNDSTONE, Co. Galway**
You might see a merlin or peregrine over the vast Roundstone Bog. White-fronted geese feed here in winter.

**12 CLARE ISLAND, Co. Mayo**
Corncrakes and corn buntings, choughs and many species of seabirds nest here.

**13 GLENVEAGH NATIONAL PARK, Co. Donegal**
Superb scenery with many species including peregrine and merlin to be seen.

**14 RATHLIN ISLAND, Co. Antrim**
About 10km (6 miles) offshore, this is a bird sanctuary but you can visit and stay. Vast numbers of nesting seabirds – fulmars, kittiwakes and especially guillemots – and birds of prey.

**15 MUCK ISLAND, Co. Antrim**
Reached from Larne or the Island Magee Peninsula, a reserve and breeding site for terns and red-breasted mergansers.

**16 STRANGFORD LOUGH, Co. Down**
Great flocks of wildfowl and waders, especially in winter. Nesting colonies on islands in summer. Collection and hides at the Wildfowl and Wetlands Centre, Castle Espie.

# The Age of Steam

The Irish railway network has contracted but enthusiasts have preserved some fine rolling stock. Several steam engines are in frequent use.

**1 STRAFFAN, Co. Kildare**
The Steam Museum has a fine collection of model engines. Trevithick's Third Model, 1797, is the oldest self-propelled machine in existence.

**2 MALAHIDE, Co. Dublin**
Next to the Castle, in the same building as the remarkable Fry Model Railway, a collection of railway memorabilia.

**3 MULLINGAR, Co. Westmeath**
Two steam locomotives, built in 1880 and 1922, have been preserved and restored. They often pull special excursion trains.

**4 CORK**
The 1847 locomotive No. 36 of the G. S. & W. R. is on display in the station concourse.

**5 BLENNERVILLE, Co. Kerry**
You can travel between Tralee and Blennerville behind the lovingly restored 1892 tank engine of the T. & D. L. R.

**6 SHANNONBRIDGE, Co. Offaly**
The Clonmacnois and West Offaly Railway (no longer steam powered) takes you on an excursion round the Blackwater peat bog.

**7 TUAM, Co. Galway**
The restored 1875 locomotive No. 90 of the G.S. & W.R. is among the rolling stock on show. It pulls excursion trains between Galway and Athenry on Saturdays in July and August.

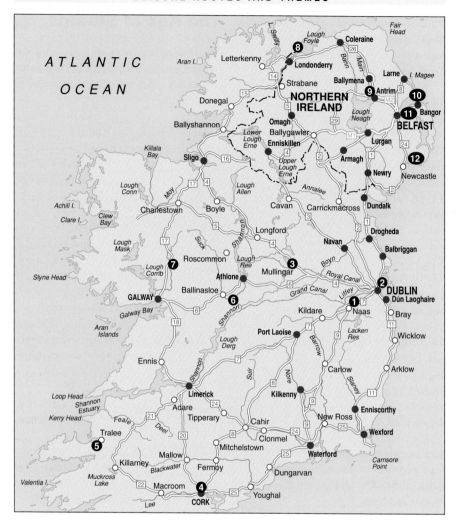

*M*emories of the bygone age of steam engines, some of which are still in use today.

**8 DERRY, Co. Londonderry**
The Foyle Valley Railway Centre preserves the history of the lines which served Donegal and Derry. The 1907 *Columbkille* and the 1912 *Blanche* are on show.

**9 ANTRIM, Co. Antrim**
Shane's Castle 3-ft gauge railway runs between the Castle park and Antrim along Lough Neagh, pulled by a steam locomotive built in 1949 for the Peat Board.

**10 WHITEHEAD, Co. Antrim**
The Railway Preservation Society of Ireland has a unique collection of rolling stock. Historic locomotives haul several summer steam excursions.

## 11 CULTRA, Co. Down

The Ulster Folk and Transport Museum's collection includes the *Maeve*, the biggest steam locomotive ever built in Ireland. There is a miniature railway too, with steam engines in use pulling passenger carriages.

## 12 DOWNPATRICK, Co. Down

The 1919 steam locomotive *Guinness* pulls passenger carriages along a short section of restored standard gauge track, most Sundays in summer.

# Fishing

The best environment in Europe makes Ireland a fishing paradise. Opportunities abound for sea angling from a boat or the shore, all round the coast. Many ports have fully equipped deep sea boats for hire to go after bigger species, shark and rays. Rivers and lakes, large and small, are famous for salmon, trout and sea-trout, or coarse fishing.

## Sea Angling in the South and West

### 1 BALLYCOTTON, Co. Cork

Fishing from the pier or shore for a variety of species, including mackerel, coalfish and flatfish. Small boats and deep sea boats available for hire.

### 2 KINSALE, Co. Cork

Small boat fishing in the bay for pollack, coalfish, skate, bass, etc. Deep sea boat available.

### 3 VALENTIA ISLAND, Co. Kerry

The rocks and shore offer good fishing for pollack, bass, dogfish and many more species. Deep sea boat available.

## 4 DINGLE, Co. Kerry

Fishing from the shore at many points of the peninsula or from small boats in the bay. Deep sea boat available for hire.

## 5 FENIT, Co. Kerry

Excellent fishing from the pier, rocks or strand for flatfish, dogfish, bass and conger. Deep sea boat available.

## 6 KILRUSH, Co. Clare

A great variety of fish is caught from piers and rocks and small boats in the Shannon Estuary. Deep sea boat available.

## 7 DOONBEG, Co. Clare

Fishing from the beaches and exposed rocks to the west for tope, mackerel, dogfish, pollack, etc.

## 8 LISCANNOR, Co. Clare

The end of the pier is good for mackerel and the nearby beaches for flatfish and bass. Deep sea boat available.

## 9 NORTH CLARE COAST, Co. Clare

The limestone ledges of the coast near Black Head are noted for dogfish, rays, mackerel and pollack. Fishing for bass and flatfish from the beaches. Deep sea boat for hire at Ballyvaughan.

## 10 WESTPORT, Co. Mayo

Fishing from the shores and small boats in Clew Bay. Deep sea boat available at Westport Quay.

## 11 BELMULLET, Co. Mayo

Shore fishing and sea angling in the bays. Deep sea boats available to go after porbeagle and blue shark.

## 12 KILLALA, Co. Mayo

The bay is renowned for variety: gurnard,

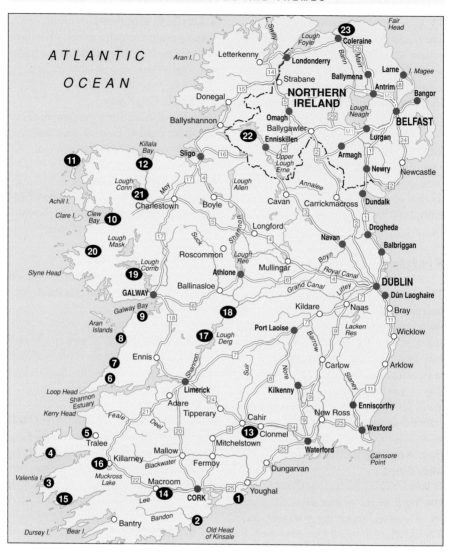

## Lakes and Rivers

*W*hatever the size of catch you are after, Ireland offers you the opportunity to try your luck.

**13** RIVER SUIR, Cos. Waterford and Tipperary

The Suir and its many tributaries are celebrated for salmon and trout. Fishing school at Ballymacarberry.

wrasse, coalfish, dogfish, rays and many more. Deep sea boat for hire.

**14** RIVER LEE, Co. Cork

Salmon and trout. Fishery at Macroom

74

and some fine stretches downstream to Cork City.

## 15 WATERVILLE, Co. Kerry
Sea-trout and salmon in the Waterville rivers and lakes.

## 16 RIVER LAUNE, Co. Kerry
Salmon and trout in the river and in Lough Leane, Killarney.

## 17 LOUGH DERG
Almost an inland sea on the River Shannon. Renowned for coarse fishing: bream, rudd, roach, tench. World record for pike.

## 18 RIVER SHANNON
Salmon and trout. Especially noted for coarse fishing for tench, bream and perch, from stands and banks near Shannonbridge, Banagher and Portumna.

## 19 LOUGH CORRIB, Co. Galway
Famous for salmon and trout and coarse fishing too. There is a trout fishing school at Oughterard.

## 20 RIVER ERRIFF, Co. Mayo
Salmon and sea-trout at the Delphi fishery and Delphi Lodge.

## 21 LOUGH CONN, Co. Mayo
Salmon and trout. There is a fishing school at Pontoon, between Lough Conn and Lough Cullen.

## 22 LOUGH ERNE, Co. Fermanagh
Record-breaking coarse fishing from small boats and piers on the Lower and Upper Lakes. Some salmon and trout.

## 23 RIVER BUSH, Co. Antrim
Long renowned for salmon and trout

fishing in the same waters that go to make whiskey at the Old Bushmills Distillery.

# Walking

Everywhere in Ireland there's a choice of country walks, hills to climb, coastal and cliff paths. Official trails, anything from 20 to 800km (12 to 500 miles) have been signposted. The Tourist Board publishes leaflets for each of them. You can make a full-length expedition or just choose a short stretch.

## 1 THE BOYNE TOWPATH, Co. Meath
From Navan to Drogheda, passing the giant Neolithic passage grave of Newgrange and the river crossing where the famous Battle of the Boyne was fought (33km, 21 miles).

## 2 THE CANAL TOWPATHS, Co. Kildare
For those who don't want to climb hills! The Grand Canal and Royal Canal towpaths head west from Dublin but the most attractive sections actually go west and south from Kildare.

## 3 THE WICKLOW WAY
From Marlay Park in the southern suburbs of Dublin, into the Dublin Mountains, over bleak, eerie moorland in the Wicklow Mountains, Glendalough and Aghavannagh, finishing at Clonegal (132km, 82 miles).

## 4 THE MUNSTER WAY
From Carrick-on-Suir west by paths along the northern edge of the Comeragh Mountains and over the Knockmealdown Mountains by the Vee Pass to Lismore.

## 5 THE KERRY WAY

Take in the superb scenery of the Iveragh Peninsula (the 'Ring of Kerry') while keeping away from the roads and traffic. An extension joins Killarney to the circuit (215km, 133 miles).

*A vast choice of places to walk makes this a rambler's paradise.*

## 6 THE DINGLE WAY

A circuit of the Dingle Peninsula by mountain and coastal paths linking all the main sights (153km, 95 miles).

## 7 THE BURREN WAY

From Liscannor on the Clare coast, past the towering Cliffs of Moher and up into strange limestone terrain. Superb views of Galway Bay on the way down to the sea again at Ballyvaughan (42km, 26 miles).

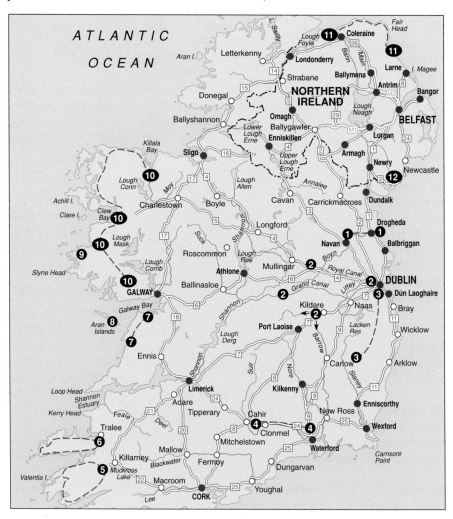

## 8 THE ARAN ISLANDS

Perfect walking country on little Inisheer and Inishmaan and the largest island, Inishmore: distances are short and there's so much to see.

## 9 CONNEMARA NATIONAL PARK

Several trails start from the visitor centre near Letterfrack. The Twelve Bens (or 'Pins') are rewarding but large areas are boggy. Even more than most hill walks, these are for the well prepared.

## 10 THE WESTERN WAY

Some of the finest scenery in Ireland, from Oughterard through the mountains to Leenane and Westport and on to the north coast of Mayo, Killala and Ballina.

## 11 THE NORTH COAST

The Ulster Way, longest of the 'named' trails cuts across the bleak Donegal highlands and around the coast. Wonderful shorter lengths include the Antrim coast from the Giant's Causeway to Fair Head.

## 12 THE MOURNE MOUNTAINS

Compact and beautiful, with few roads, so walking is the best way to see them. Start by climbing from Newcastle on the coast to Slieve Donard.

# Distilleries and Breweries

Learn about Ireland's famous exports and see if you can sort out the facts from the myths. There's a chance to sample the products on most of these visits.

## 1 DUBLIN

The World of Guinness Exhibition in the old Hop Store explains the history and the whole process of producing Ireland's favourite 'extra stout porter'.

## 2 DUBLIN

They don't produce it here any more, but Whiskey Corner at the old Jameson

*Sample your way around some of Ireland's better-known exports.*

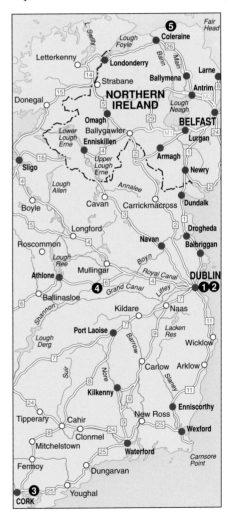

Distillery welcomes visitors, explains the process and invites you to compare the major brands.

### 3 MIDLETON, Co. Cork
The Jameson Heritage Centre, magnificently restored 18th-century buildings with many historic pieces of equipment, tells the story of Irish whiskey and offers a taste of the five brands produced.

### 4 KILBEGGAN, Co. Westmeath
The fine 1757 Locke's Distillery, not currently operating but run as a rural museum including displays on distilling.

### 5 BUSHMILLS, Co. Antrim
'Old Bushmills' claims to be the first licensed distillery in the world: it has been operating legally since 1608. There's a chance to sample the product in the Potstill Bar.

## Dublin Pubs

The life and soul of the city is in its pubs, warm and golden as an old whiskey. Every one is different and yet they couldn't be anywhere but Ireland.

### 1 INTERNATIONAL BAR
At 23 Wicklow Street, with opulent decor of marble, mahogany and classical caryatids. Music from rock groups and others.

### 2 KEHOE'S
A real Dubliners' pub at the corner of Anne and Grafton Streets. Comfortable, with separate snugs – little cubby-holes – for private parties.

### 3 McDAID'S
Behind a bright red and blue façade in Harry Street, a once bohemian haunt where Brendan Behan sat in a corner and railed at his typewriter for failing to produce.

### 4 BRUXELLES
Plush venue in Harry Street, known for jazz sessions on Sunday afternoons and Tuesday evenings.

### 5 DOHENY and NESBITT'S
The traditional local for the *Irish Times* people and occasional politicians at No. 5 Lower Baggot Street. Not for sufferers from claustrophobia or those allergic to smoke.

### 6 TONER'S
Somewhat quieter Victorian pub with private snugs, at No. 139 Lower Baggot Street. Claimed to be the only pub WB Yeats visited – and that was just once. He thought the genre and the Guinness were overrated.

### 7 NEARY'S
Gas lamps and mahogany in Chatham Street, favoured by actors and the rest of the theatre crowd from the nearby Gaiety.

### 8 MULLIGAN'S
At No. 8 Poolbeg Street near Tara Street Station, adherents have long affirmed that it serves the best pint in Dublin. The local for the *Irish Press* reporters.

### 9 DOCKER'S
On Sir John Rogerson's Quay by the Liffey, towards the harbour. The big names in rock sometimes relax here after recording sessions.

### 10 AN BÉAL BOCHT
At No. 58 Charlemont Street, south of St

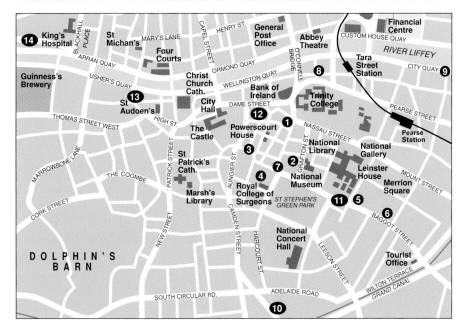

Stephen's Green. Well known for its traditional music programmes.

**11 O'DONOGHUE'S**
In Merrion Row, noted for its traditional and other music, with the crowd sometimes joining in.

**12 STAG'S HEAD**
At No. 1 Dame Court, off Dame Street. Lots of Victorian panelling and glass, and an arty and student crowd.

**13 BRAZEN HEAD**
Claimed to be Dublin's oldest, in Lower Bridge Street, this building dates from the 17th century. It was the meeting place of the United Irishmen in the 1790s. Traditional music in the back bar.

**14 RYAN'S**
Along the Liffey towards Phoenix Park, in Parkgate Street. Something of a private club atmosphere, with the glow of polished

*The very essence of Ireland and the Irish people can be found in the pubs.*

wood and brass. The Guinness has only travelled a stone's throw across the river.

## The Land of WB Yeats

A poet who affected the course of his country's history, his words can read like a prophecy of what has happened since. You can visit the places where he is honoured and those which inspired him.

**1 DUBLIN**
The Writers' Museum in Parnell Square includes a tribute to the poet and his circle, with many memorabilia.

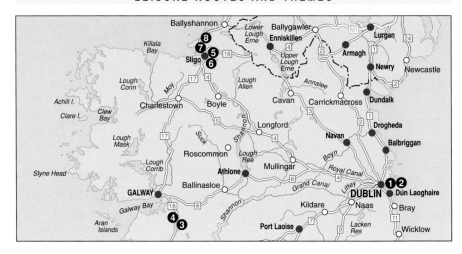

*I*nspiration for WB Yeats, son of Ireland, as well as for his admirers.

## 2 DUBLIN

No. 82 Merrion Square was Yeats's home from 1922-8. There is a memorial to him by Henry Moore in St Stephen's Green. He was born at a house called *Georgeville*, in Sandymount Avenue, Ballsbridge.

## 3 THOOR BALLYLEE, Co. Galway

The old tower house which Yeats restored and made his symbol, and where he lived after his marriage in 1917. It is now a museum.

## 4 COOLE PARK, Co. Galway

The home of Yeats's friend Lady Gregory has gone, but the park remains, with the 'Autograph Tree' bearing his signature along with those of many other famous figures.

## 5 SLIGO

The writer's family home town, with a Yeats statue, Memorial Museum and Memorial Building, the location of the Summer School to study his work.

## 6 LOUGH GILL, Co. Sligo

The tranquil lake the poet loved, with the tiny tree-covered island immortalized in *The Lake Isle of Innisfree*.

## 7 DRUMCLIFF, Co. Sligo

The parish church where his grandfather was rector: the poet's grave stands in the churchyard.

## 8 LISSADELL, Co. Sligo

Classical Revival house, home of the rebellious sisters Eva and Constance (Markievicz) Gore-Booth, much admired by Yeats. In later life he recalled youthful happy days spent there.

# James Joyce's Dublin

Although Joyce left Dublin as a young man and never lived there again, the city is ever-present in his writing. He boasted that if it were destroyed, it could be rebuilt in detail from his books.

## 1 THE BAILEY
2-5 Duke Street, now a pub to be seen in, was the first to honour the great writer. A prized possession is the very door of No. 7 Eccles Street, immortalized as Mr and Mrs Leopold Bloom's house in Joyce's *Ulysses*.

## 2 DAVY BYRNE'S
A few Joycean relics are found at No. 21 Duke Street, where Stephen Bloom once stopped for a gorgonzola sandwich and a glass of burgundy.

## 3 NEWMAN HOUSE
Formerly part of University College, Dublin, where Joyce studied and graduated in modern languages. He later lectured to the Literary and Historical Society here.

## 4 NATIONAL LIBRARY
Where Joyce worked, and where in *Ulysses* Bloom has a close encounter with his wife's lover.

## 5 LINCOLN PLACE
Another site in *Ulysses*, Sweny's Pharmacy has changed little since Joyce's, or Bloom's, day.

## 6 BELVEDERE HOUSE
In Great Denmark Street (near the Writers' Museum in Parnell Square). Joyce went to the Jesuit school here between the

*Follow in the footsteps of James Joyce (1-9) and other writers (10-15).*

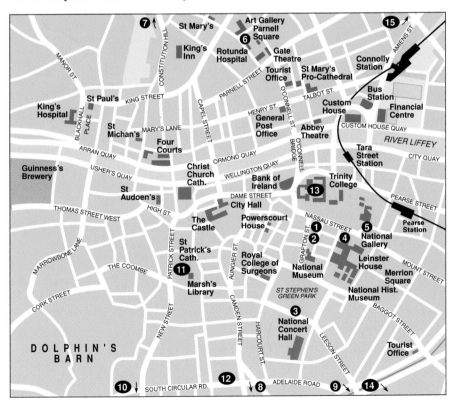

81

ages of 11 and 16. The school figures in *Portrait of the Artist as a Young Man.*

**7** PROSPECT CEMETERY, Glasnevin
Where the day's odyssey of *Ulysses* begins, with Dignam's funeral.

**8** SANDYCOVE, Co. Dublin
The Martello tower ('Joyce's Tower') where he spent a few days in 1904 appears in the first chapter of *Ulysses*. It is now a Joyce museum.

**9** BRAY, Co. Wicklow
Joyce's family home from 1888 to 1891. He was a boarder at Clongoweswood College, Kildare but spent his holidays at Bray. His walks along the shore and cliffs inspired early scenes in *Portrait of the Artist as a Young Man* many years later.

# More Literary Landmarks

So many of Ireland's writers became self-imposed exiles, prophets without honour in their own country, that fewer traces remain than you might expect.

**10** MOUNT JEROME
Dublin's main Protestant Cemetery, where JM Synge, 'AE' Russell and J Sheridan Le Fanu (author of *Uncle Silas*) are buried.

**11** ST PATRICK'S CATHEDRAL, Dublin
Where Jonathan Swift was Dean. His table and chair, bust and epitaph are here and a brass plaque marks his grave and that of his friend 'Stella'.

**12** No. 33 SYNGE STREET, Dublin
The town house where George Bernard Shaw was born in 1856 is open as a small museum.

**13** TRINITY COLLEGE, Dublin
Attended by Swift, Goldsmith, and Burke (commemorated by statues or busts), Wilde and Synge.

**14** DALKEY, Co. Dublin
Torca Cottage on the hill above the seaside village was the boyhood home of Shaw.

**15** SLANE
The Francis Ledwidge Museum just west of the town honours the pastoral poet who was killed in World War I. He wrote the lines carved on a stone outside in memory of the poet Thomas MacDonagh, executed for his part in the 1916 Rising.

# The Love of Horses: Riding and Racing

Ireland has long been famous for breeding and training horses. Race meetings bring countless colourful characters together, and the landscape is ideal for hunting and trail riding. We give only a small selection of the possibilities.

**1** TULLY, Co. Kildare
The home of the Irish National Stud and the Horse Museum. You can see the stallions in their paddocks, and mares and newly-born foals in the springtime.

**2** THE CURRAGH, Co. Kildare
The name means 'racecourse' and these 2,000ha (5,000 acres) of grassland have been used for training, exercising and

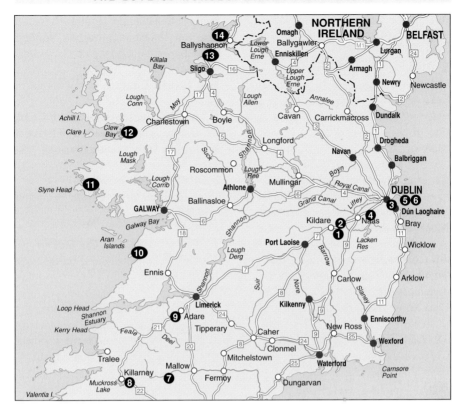

racing horses for centuries. The Irish Derby and other meetings are held here.

*Love and expertise have established Ireland as one of the foremost countries for breeding and training horses.*

**3 LEOPARDSTOWN, Co. Dublin**
Frequent meetings held at Dublin's local racecourse in the south-eastern suburbs.

**4 PUNCHESTOWN, Co. Kildare**
Another favourite racecourse of Dubliners, with a famous spring meeting and international horse trials.

**5 DUBLIN**
The Royal Dublin Society's Horse Show is the great sporting and social event of the calendar.

**6 DUBLIN**
Polo is played at Phoenix Park all sum-

mer, on Tuesday and Thursday evenings and Saturday and Sunday afternoons.

**7 MILLSTREET, Co. Cork**
Big equestrian centre, now also known for hosting the Eurovision Song Contest! International horse show in August. Museum of the Irish horse.

**8 KILLARNEY, Co. Kerry**
Trail rides of up to a week take you

through the lake country and Macgilly-cuddy's Reeks and down the the sea.

## 9  ADARE, Co. Limerick

Riding instruction at every level and daily treks organized. Everything can be provided for you if you want to go out with one of the local hunts (November to March).

## 10  LISCANNOR, Co. Clare

Classes at all levels in the equestrian centre. Trekking along the stunning Cliffs of Moher and in the Burren.

## 11  CONNEMARA, Co. Galway

Trail rides for six days or more, staying each night in a different hotel. Connemara Pony Show at Clifden in August.

## 12  WESTPORT, Co. Mayo

Classes at the riding centre. Three-day trail rides along the lovely beaches of Clew Bay.

## 13  GRANGE, Co. Sligo

Riding holidays either based at one place, or trail rides through beautiful country, staying at a different spot each night.

## 14  BUNDORAN, Co. Donegal

Residential riding centre with all levels of instruction. Six-day trail rides through the glens and mountains or along the coast.

# Golf

Ireland has some of the world's most beautiful and challenging links courses as well as the greenest of parkland courses. They are scattered all over the country but we have picked some in three areas: the south east including Dublin; the south west and Shannon region; and Northern Ireland.

## The South East

## 1  THE ROYAL DUBLIN GOLF CLUB

Links course sharing North Bull Island in Dublin Bay with a nature reserve.

## 2  DEER PARK, Howth

On the hillside of the Howth Peninsula. Superb views.

## 3  PORTMARNOCK, Co. Dublin

World-famous links course on the coast north of Dublin.

## 4  KILDARE CLUB, Co. Kildare

A new 6,400m- (7,000yd-) course designed by Arnold Palmer, in the woodland park of a luxury country house hotel.

## 5  MOUNT JULIET, Co. Kilkenny

At the country house hotel, an acclaimed championship parkland course designed by Jack Nicklaus.

## The South West and Shannon Region

## 6  WATERVILLE, Co. Kerry

Between the mountains and the sea, on the Ring of Kerry, one of the longest links courses in Europe.

## 7  KILLARNEY, Co. Kerry

Two parkland courses in the breathtaking scenery of lakes and mountains.

## 8  TRALEE, Co. Kerry

Practically surrounded by the sea, a challenging links designed with the consultancy of Arnold Palmer.

84

## 9 BALLYBUNNION, Co. Kerry
Two links courses, 'tigers' in a strong wind. The Old Course is rated by Tom Watson as the best in the world.

*Both scenic beauty and a sporting challenge are on offer to the keen golfer.*

## 10 DROMOLAND, Co. Clare
Sculpted out of the wooded park around a lake at the Dromoland Castle Hotel.

## 11 SHANNON, Co. Clare
Lush parkland course next to the Shannon estuary and close to the airport.

## 12 LAHINCH, Co. Clare
On a headland surrounded by sandy

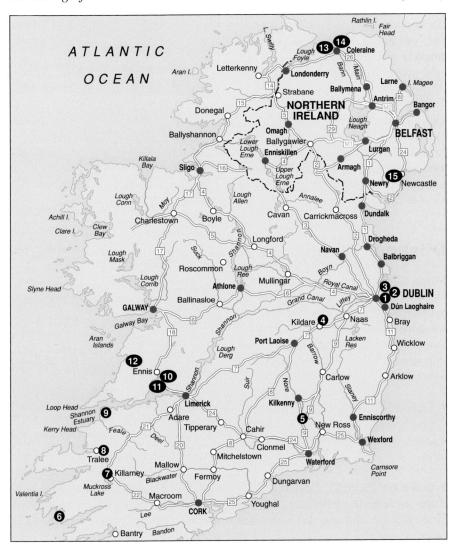

beach, an old-established course built by Scots to resemble St Andrews.

### Northern Ireland

### 13 PORTSTEWART,
### Co. Londonderry
Beautiful links course on the north coast, with great views over the sea.

### 14 ROYAL PORTRUSH,
### Co. Antrim
This celebrated course, that is spectacularly situated over the sea, is the only one in Ireland to have staged the British Open.

### 15 ROYAL COUNTY DOWN,
### Co. Down
At Newcastle, in the shadow of the Mountains of Mourne, a moorland links regarded as one of the great courses of Ireland.

# Offshore Islands

Sanctuaries for early Christian hermits, monastic sites that seemed safe until the Vikings came, islands large and small are sprinkled all round the coast. Some were abandoned in recent times, but many are still inhabited and preserve traditional ways of life.

### 1  CLEAR ISLAND, Co. Cork
For walks and bird-watching, reached by scenic ferry trips from Schull or Baltimore.

### 2  DURSEY ISLAND, Co. Cork
At the end of the Beara Peninsula, reached by a cable car. Hill and cliff walks and superb views.

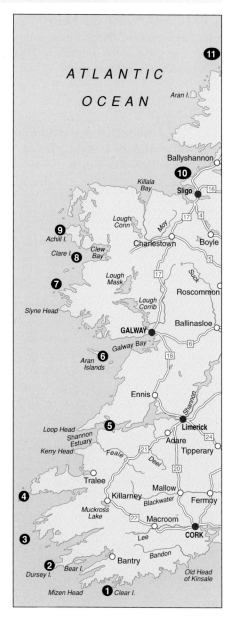

*V*isit the islands of Ireland for the scenery, the bird life, and to experience traditions preserved to the present day.

86

**3** GREAT SKELLIG (SKELLIG MICHAEL), Co. Kerry
A spectacular pinnacle of rock with monastic remains. Boats go in summer from Portmagee and Knightstown on Valentia Island (connected by bridge to the mainland).

**4** GREAT BLASKETT, Co. Kerry
Inhabited until the 1950s, and now with a hostel where you can stay in summer. Boats go from Dunquin near Slea Head at the end of the Dingle Peninsula.

**5** SCATTERY ISLAND, Co. Clare
In the Shannon Estuary, another recently abandoned island, with monastic remains. Good for walks and bird-watching. Boats go from Kilrush.

**6** THE ARAN ISLANDS, Co. Galway
Inishmore, Inishmaan and Inisheer feel magically different but they're all easily reached by flights and ferries. Superb scenery, historic sites and traditional life.

**7** INISHBOFIN, Co. Galway
A gentle place to escape to – there's limited accommodation. Boats go from Cleggan to the island's harbour.

**8** CLARE ISLAND, Co. Mayo
The stronghold of Grace O'Malley, 16th-century pirate-queen, still inhabited and good for hill walks and fishing. Boats go from Roonagh near Louisburgh.

**9** ACHILL ISLAND, Co. Mayo
The biggest of Ireland's islands, connected by a bridge to the mainland. Spectacular scenery of cliffs and mountains.

**10** INISHMURRAY, Co. Sligo
Now abandoned, but boats can take you from Mullaghmore. Important monastic remains and varied bird life.

**11** TORY ISLAND, Co. Donegal
Noted for its group of naive painters, fishing and barren scenery. Boats go from Minlarach, but bad weather can often interrupt the service.

# Neolithic Ireland

Stone Age builders worked on a huge scale, and had an eye for dramatic locations. Equally impressive are the mysterious designs carved on the stones 5,000 years ago – spirals, diamonds, waves and rays.

**1** FOURKNOCKS, Co. Meath
A hilltop mound covering a passage tomb with a large central chamber, lined with carved stones.

**2** NEWGRANGE, Co. Meath
A massive domed mound entered by a long passage, lined with monoliths, leading to a tall central chamber.

**3** KNOWTH, Co. Meath
Many smaller tombs cluster round the big central mound, still being excavated. This site has the greatest collection of carved stones from the period.

**4** LOUGHCREW, Co. Meath
An intriguing group of hilltop and satellite tombs, some with unique markings on the stones.

**5** BROWNESHILL, Co. Carlow
The most colossal dolmen in western Europe: the capstone has a mass of over 100 tonnes.

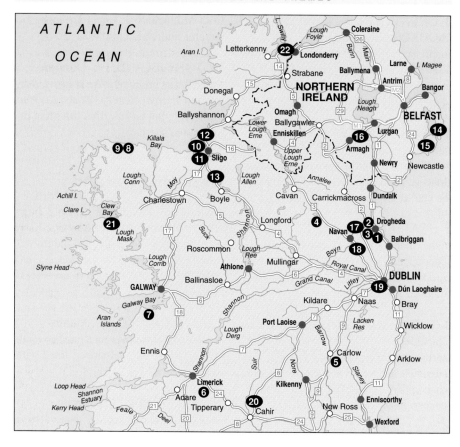

ATLANTIC OCEAN

NORTHERN IRELAND

BELFAST

DUBLIN

GALWAY

$D$ *ramatic sites chosen by Stone Age architects (1-13) or associated with the patron saint of Ireland, St Patrick (14-22).*

**6 LOUGH GUR, Co. Limerick**
A long-occupied and probably sacred site around a lake, with many remains including one of the best-preserved stone circles in Ireland.

**7 POULNABRONE, Co. Clare**
A great dolmen sited spectacularly on the limestone plateau of the high Burren.

**8 CÉIDE FIELDS, Co. Mayo**
Field systems divided by stone walls, preserved when peat bog built up over them, on the cliff tops of Mayo's north coast.

**9 BALLYGLASS, Co. Mayo**
There are three large court tombs and the foundations of neolithic houses which have been excavated, just west of Ballycastle.

**10 KNOCKNAREA, Co. Sligo**
The mountain-top cairn called Queen Maeve's Grave has not been excavated, but it's probably a 5,000-year-old passage grave like Newgrange.

88

**11** CARROWMORE, Co. Sligo
Within sight of Knocknarea, a complex of dolmens, smaller passage graves and stone circles, over 60 in all.

**12** CREEVYKEEL, Co. Sligo
One of the biggest and most complete court tombs in Ireland.

**13** CARROWKEEL, Co. Sligo
More than a dozen cairns, some still roofed and covering passage graves, in the hills above Lough Arrow.

# In the Steps of St Patrick

Captured in Britain and brought to Ireland by raiders, he escaped, returned home and entered the church. Following a vision, he set out on his mission to convert the pagan Irish to Christianity. These are some of the sites traditionally associated with the saint.

**14** SAUL, Co. Down
Soon after returning to Ireland, St Patrick converted a chief who let him set up his first church in a barn here. Modern memorials commemorate the event.

**15** DOWNPATRICK, Co. Down
There's no certainty about the saint's burial place, but some anecdotal evidence favours the hill where Down Cathedral stands. The stone marked with his name is modern.

**16** ARMAGH, Co. Armagh
Here there is little doubt, except about dates. Patrick set up his headquarters here, it became the seat of his bishopric and the ecclesiastical capital of Ireland ever since. It now has two St Patrick's cathedrals.

**17** HILL OF SLANE, Co. Meath
This is where St Patrick is said to have lit an Easter fire in defiance of the King at Tara. Fortunately, the king was converted, so he didn't impose the threatened penalty.

**18** HILL OF TARA, Co. Meath
Tradition says that St Patrick baptized thousands here, at the capital of the High Kings.

**19** DUBLIN
St Patrick's Cathedral was built on the traditional site of a church founded by the saint, who is said to have baptized converts in the nearby well, now buried.

**20** CASHEL, Co. Tipperary
The Rock of Cashel was the stronghold of the kings of Munster and Patrick probably paid a visit. A carving on a worn high cross here is believed to depict him.

**21** CROAGH PATRICK, Co. Mayo
This may have been the place where the young captive Patrick herded sheep. It's also the traditional site of his mountain-top retreat to pray for the conversion of the Irish.

**22** GRIANÁN OF AILEACH, Co. Donegal
Another royal stronghold, a prehistoric stone fortress where the saint preached to the king and his people.

# Abbeys and Monasteries

So many beautiful ruins are scattered across the landscape of Ireland that you might end up by hardly giving them a second glance. We have picked out a few special examples.

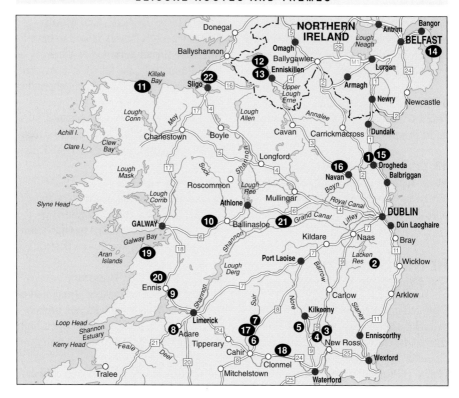

*A* selection of the many evocative ruins of abbeys and monasteries (1-14) and the intricately carved crosses (15-22) to be found scattered throughout Ireland.

**1 MELLIFONT, Co. Louth**
Unusual survival of a high gatehouse and Romanesque arches of the monks' washing house.

**2 GLENDALOUGH, Co. Wicklow**
Lovely valley and extensive ruins of St Kevin's monastery, once one of the most important in Europe.

**3 GRAIGUENAMANAGH, Co. Kilkenny**
Ruins of the 13th-century Cistercian abbey are scattered through the little town.

**4 JERPOINT, Co. Kilkenny**
Admire the magnificent stone carving of tombs and cloisters.

**5 KELLS, Co. Kilkenny**
Uniquely preserved defensive walls, surrounded by green fields. (Note: this is *not* the Kells associated with the *Book of Kells.*)

**6 ATHASSEL, Co. Tipperary**
Another atmospheric, rarely visited site in meadows by a river. See the cloisters and tombs.

90

## 7 HOLY CROSS, Co. Tipperary
An unusual case of restoration of a 12th-century abbey church for modern use.

## 8 ADARE, Co. Limerick
Not one but three abbey ruins are found in this picturebook town.

## 9 QUIN, Co. Clare
Very well preserved 15th-century Franciscan abbey; fine stone tracery.

## 10 KILCONNELL, Co. Galway
Beautiful ruin of a Franciscan friary. Fine stone carving of windows, and tombs.

## 11 ROSSERK and MOYNE, Co. Mayo
Two fine 15th-century abbeys on the shores of Killala Bay.

## 12 WHITE ISLAND, Co. Fermanagh
An important monastic site on an island in Lough Erne. Noted for its curious primitive carved stone figures, probably 8th century.

## 13 DEVENISH ISLAND, Co. Fermanagh
St Molaise's monastery ruins on an island in Lough Erne include a fine example of a round tower.

## 14 GREY ABBEY, Co. Down
A 12th-century Cistercian foundation, the first in Ireland to be built in Gothic style.

# High Crosses

From the 8th to the 12th centuries, the carving of stone crosses became ever more elaborate, and exclusively Irish styles developed. We give a selection of some of the finest of each type.

## 15 MONASTERBOICE, Co. Louth
Three fine high crosses include the superb Muiredach's Cross, covered with beautifully preserved Old and New Testament scenes.

## 16 KELLS (*Ceannanas*), Co. Meath
A cross at the church with complex carvings of biblical scenes, and another in the town centre, broken and said to have been used as a gallows. (This *is* the Kells of the *Book of Kells*.)

## 17 CASHEL, Co. Tipperary
A worn cross depicting a figure believed to be St Patrick has been moved indoors.

## 18 AHENNY, Co. Tipperary
Two early crosses, carved mainly with abstract patterns, and some broken crosses at nearby Kilkeeran.

## 19 KILFENORA, Co. Clare
A collection of high crosses, including a 12th-century cross of the crucifixion-and-bishop type.

## 20 DYSERT O'DEA, Co. Clare
A high cross in a field, with a crucifixion and complex geometric designs.

## 21 DURROW, Co. Offaly
A 10th-century cross, on the site of the Abbey where the *Book of Durrow*, now in Trinity College Library, was written.

## 22 DRUMCLIFF, Co. Sligo
In the churchyard, a worn 11th-century tall cross, with biblical scenes including Adam and Eve, and scrolls.

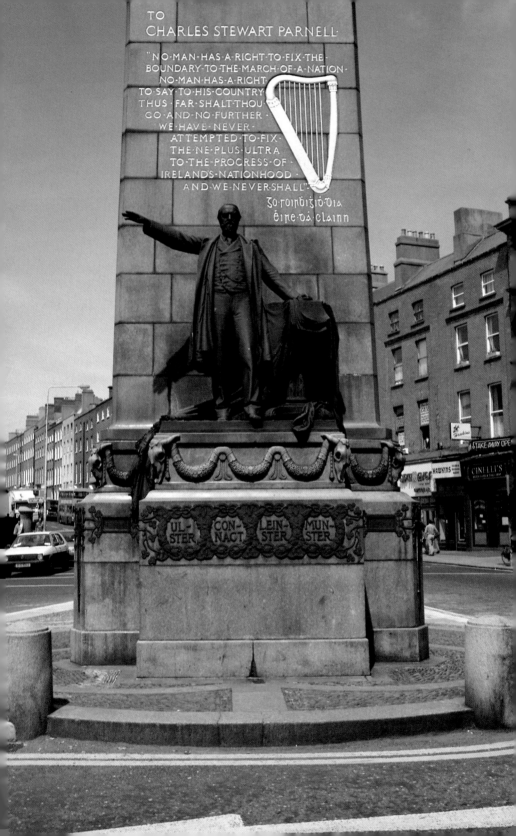

# An Accessible City of Many Faces, Many Moods

The setting is superb. Close at hand to the east is the broad sweep of Dublin Bay, its choppy waters alternating green and grey. Screeching gulls are as common as pigeons in the parks and squares. To the south west the mountains, purple and misty blue, are only twenty minutes' drive away. The outer suburbs sprawl in characterless confusion – name a city where they don't – but in the varied districts of the centre there's fascination round every corner. Gracious classical buildings are reflected in the waters of the Liffey, lively shopping streets and shabby back streets invite you to explore.

A strikingly young population, always on the move, gathering in countless cafés, bars and pubs – to drink, yes, but primarily to talk. This is a village, at least for those in politics, the media, business and the arts. Everyone seems to know everyone else and they love to gossip. The quickest wits in the world are concentrated in the smallest space, mercilessly debunking any trace of pomposity. You want to meet people? Just ask for help or information – if you have time for a chat. Everyone will

*At the top of O'Connell Street, the tragic figure of Charles Stewart Parnell (1846-91), campaigner for Irish Home Rule, and his famous words.*

have a different idea of what you ought to see or do.

In Gaelic she was *Dubh Linn*, the Black Pool, or the name you see on cars' licence plates, *Baile Atha Cliath*, the Town of the Hurdle Ford. The haven of Norse Viking raiders who turned into traders then became an Anglo-Norman stronghold and nucleus of the Pale, the relatively pacific bridgehead controlled by the invaders in an otherwise turbulent island. Then Dublin grew to be the 'Second City of the British Empire' with the institutions, elegant Georgian squares and hellish slums to match. The 19th century began with the Act of Union which abolished the Irish Parliament and moved all important decision-making to London. It took 120 years of agitation and rebellions great and small before the city became the capital of a free nation.

In this book we begin in the area which became the focus of the city in the 18th century and remains so today, with the main shopping streets and Georgian squares, major museums and public buildings. One-way systems, pedestrian-only streets and parking restrictions mean that it's best seen on foot. So if you have a car, you'll do well to find a safe place to park, and leave it there.

# The Centre of the City

When you're ready to begin exploring, any number of spots would make good starting points. We have chosen a central landmark, where the city's most famous thoroughfare, **O'Connell Street** crosses the River Liffey by way of **O'Connell Bridge**. A massive and complex monument to 'The Liberator' himself, Daniel O'Connell (1775-1847, see page 199) stands just north of the bridge. The street was laid out in the 18th century in the form of a wide mall, intended as a desirable residential area, like an elongated Georgian square. It soon became the venue for parades and demonstrations, and was the focus of two dramatic battles on the road to independence. On the west side (the left as you walk away from the

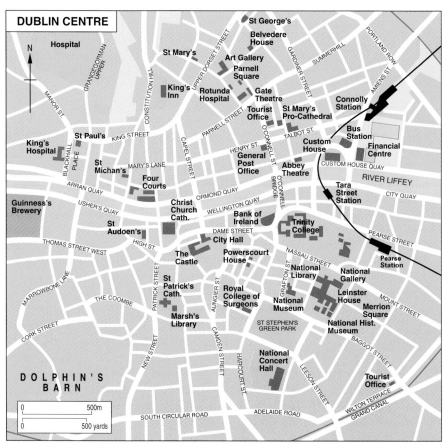

DUBLIN CENTRE

N

Hospital

St George's
Belvedere House
St Mary's
Art Gallery
Parnell Square
King's Inn
Rotunda Hospital
Gate Theatre
Tourist Office
St Mary's Pro-Cathedral
Connolly Station
Bus Station
Financial Centre
St Paul's
King's Hospital
St Michan's
General Post Office
Custom House
Abbey Theatre
CUSTOM HOUSE QUAY
RIVER LIFFEY
CITY QUAY
Four Courts
Christ Church Cath.
Bank of Ireland
Tara Street Station
Guinness's Brewery
St Audoen's
City Hall
Trinity College
PEARSE STREET
The Castle
Powerscourt House
National Library
National Gallery
Pearse Station
St Patrick's Cath.
Royal College of Surgeons
National Museum
Leinster House
Merrion Square
Marsh's Library
ST STEPHEN'S GREEN PARK
National Hist. Museum
DOLPHIN'S BARN
National Concert Hall
Tourist Office

0    500m
0    500 yards

SOUTH CIRCULAR ROAD
ADELAIDE ROAD

bridge) the General Post Office, always shortened to **GPO**, was seized by the insurgents at the start of the Easter Rising of 1916 and became their headquarters. A week later, with the building in flames after shelling, they were forced to abandon it and surrender. These events are commemorated by Oliver Sheppard's dramatic statue inside, *The Death of Cúchulainn*.

*T*he statue, the street and the bridge over the River Liffey all commemorate Daniel O'Connell, 'The Liberator'.

The mythical Irish hero was the subject of a play by WB Yeats, although Yeats himself, hearing of the damage to the GPO dismissed it as no great loss. Much of O'Connell Street was devastated at the same time, and it suffered even worse destruction in the Civil War of 1922-3. Piecemeal rebuilding and commercial development have replaced elegant Georgian and Victorian residences with an ordinary mix of banks and fast-food outlets. Still, the street retains a ceremonial air, helped by **statues** lining the central reservation: notably Father Theobald Mathew (1790-1856), founder of the temperance movement and, at the north end, Charles

Stewart Parnell (1846-91), leader of the parliamentary Home Rule campaign (see page 152). A column topped by a statue of Lord Nelson was so damaged by an explosion set off as an anti-British gesture in 1966 that it had to be demolished. The number was made up by the fleshy figure of Anna Livia Plurabelle, celebrated by James Joyce as spirit of the Liffey and the city, reclining on cushions of water (and inevitably mocked by Dubliners as 'The Floozy in the Jacuzzi').

You'll find the **Irish Tourist Board** (Bord Fáilte) office up the street on the right at No. 14. It's well-stocked with books and pamphlets for sale (little is given away these days). They have information on all aspects of Dublin and the rest of Ireland, as well as a range of souvenirs.

Near the River Liffey along Abbey Street, the famous **Abbey Theatre** is not the original founded by Yeats and Lady Gregory and opened in 1904. It had to be rebuilt in 1966 after a fire. Stop on O'Connell Bridge to look both ways along the river. To the east, you'll see the green copper dome and fine white stone façade of the 1781 **Custom House**, by James Gandon, architect of several of Dublin's finest buildings. It's best viewed from directly across the river, so you might make a diversion along Burgh Quay. The figure of commerce stands on high and the south-facing portico is crowned by four more allegorical statues, Neptune to the right. Seven rounded arches on either side have

*F*acing the Liffey, the Custom House was designed in 1781 by James Gandon. His classical buildings changed the face of Dublin.

keystones of carved heads representing rivers of Ireland – the only female head being Anna Livia as the Liffey. Seen as a symbol of British rule, the Custom House was set ablaze during the 1921 fighting; the original interior and precious historical records were destroyed. The area further along from the Custom House on the north bank of the river to the docks is slowly being redeveloped as the new financial centre and convention centre of Dublin.

Back at the bridge and heading south you'll see on the right the elegantly curved and colonnaded wall of the 18th-century **Bank of Ireland**, started by Edward Lovett Pearce and completed by James Gandon. This was where the Irish Parliament met until it was abolished by the 1800 Act of Union: the Bank saw its chance and bought the handsome building soon afterwards. The old Commons Chamber has disappeared in a welter of offices but it is still possible to take a guided tour, including a look into the former House of Lords. The huge gilded mace on display there used to be in position at every sitting of the Commons.

## Trinity College

Across College Green – a street, not a lawn – from the Bank of Ireland you'll see an imposing gateway. It's the main entrance of Trinity College, the University of Dublin (a mouthful usually shortened to TCD). Founded in 1592 on the orders of Queen Elizabeth I, it was intended, she said, to be a 'counterblast to Popery' and to 'civilize' the Irish. This second objective was at odds with the fact that until 1873 only members of the minority Protestant ascendancy were admitted. Even when the law was changed, the Roman Catholic hierarchy would not allow

its adherents to attend, a restriction which was only gradually relaxed during the 1950s and after.

Over the centuries the college expanded to occupy a fine complex of buildings set around quadrangles paved with cobblestones, green lawns and playing fields, an extraordinary island amid the city streets. The area teems with typical student life, but it's usually open to the public too. The main gate is flanked by statues of the political thinker Edmund Burke and the playwright Oliver Goldsmith who was so poor as a student that he had to clean the cobbled squares and carry dishes to the Fellows' dining room. As famous alumni, their effigies could have been joined by any number of others, among them Swift, Grattan, Wolfe Tone, Berkeley, Oscar Wilde and Samuel Beckett.

Student guides are ready to take you on tours starting at the front gate, or you can make your own way through the interconnecting spaces of Parliament (or Front) Square and Library Square to College Park. Most visitors look round respectfully at the architecture – the 18th-century theatre and chapel, the Henry Moore sculpture on the lawn, and then head for the main attraction, the magnificent **Old Library**. Built between 1712 and 1732, it originally consisted of an open arcaded area, the Colonnades, at ground level and the Long Room upstairs which was the actual library.

In 1801, Trinity was granted the right, which it shares with the British Library and the Bodleian Library, Oxford, to claim a free copy of any book published in Britain or Ireland. Ever since then, the demand for more shelf space has grown inexorably year by year. First the Long Room upstairs, formerly with a flat ceiling, was given its present barrel-vaulted roof and the upper gallery bookcases: it now houses 200,000 of the Library's oldest books. Then the Colonnades were walled in to make still more space. Now, of course, the Library has many more buildings on other sites, and needs half a mile of extra shelves each year to keep pace with the number of books.

The **Colonnades** have been turned into an attractive shop and exhibition area, and here in subdued light is displayed one of the world's treasures, the early 9th-century **Book of Kells**. This pinnacle of Irish art is a Latin manuscript of the four Gospels, embellished with extraordinarily complex designs, scenes, images of Christ, the Virgin and Child, St Matthew, and St John. Initial letters are worked into whole pages of inventive decoration. The book is now bound in four volumes, so you can see more than one page at a time. Its name comes from the vanished monastery of

Kells in County Meath, but that may not have been been where it was written. Kells itself became important when monks retreated there from Iona off the west coast of Scotland, after repeated Viking raids, presumably bringing the precious document with them. If it was written on Iona, does that make it Scottish? Not so, according to the Irish rule book. St Columba's island foundation was well and truly part of the Irish monastic network.

**WORD PROCESSORS**

We know how those patient old scribes worked and how their materials were prepared, from autobiographical pictures they included in some early manuscripts. They wrote on parchment, the cured, stretched and dried skin of animals (in medieval Ireland it was usually calfskin, *vellum*), using quill pens made from the tail feathers of geese or swans. The decorative designs were painted with fine brushes. Cowhorn inkwells held a spectrum of colours. Black was made from iron sulphate and oak apples, or from soot. One kind of red came from red lead, another from kermes insects, and vermilion from mercuric sulphide imported from Spain. A green was prepared by treating copper with vinegar to form verdigris. Blues were made from indigo, woad and precious lapis lazuli brought all the way from Central Asia. The preferred white was from white lead, and a prized golden-yellow was made from arsenic sulphide (orpiment or 'gold pigment').

You'll notice how poisonous many of them sound – and were. Books so perfect that some people thought they could only have been written by angels in heaven were the end product of some remarkably unpleasant and dangerous processes. Tanning the skins to make parchment involved great quantities of excrement and urine, also used in preparing some of the pigments. Several of the inks gave off noxious fumes or were hazardous to touch. Not to mention the wear and tear on eyes and backs caused by years of toil.

*T*he spacious quadrangles of Trinity College, Dublin, with the 18th-century Theatre on the right. The Old Library is behind.

In the same room, the smaller but older **Book of Durrow** from a monastery in County Offaly may date from the mid-7th century, but the Latin script is already characteristically Irish in style, like the *Book of Kells*.

If you emerge at Trinity's main gate opposite the Bank of Ireland and turn left, you'll be in Grafton Street. Just before it meets and crosses Nassau Street, look out for the bronze statue portraying the city's own mascot, **Molly Malone**. With generous cleavage and a barrow laden with baskets of shellfish she has been daringly placed among the pedestrians. Predictably, the statue has been taken over by street traders, musicians and mere loafers: Molly's bronze cockles and mussels are frequently joined on the cart by cheap jewellery and souvenirs.

*In Dublin's fair city*
*Where the girls are so pretty*
*I first set my eyes on sweet Molly Malone.*
*She wheeled her wheelbarrow*
*Through streets broad and narrow*
*Crying 'cockles and mussels*
*Alive, alive, O!'*

(the line that Ireland's rugby supporters sing when their team is winning).

**Grafton Street**, with its offshoots and adjoining lanes, is Dublin's prime shopping area, well supplied with department stores, boutiques and bookshops. In addition, all manner of specialist shops somehow survive here much better than in many capital city centres. South of the Nassau Street crossing, Grafton Street is closed to traffic. Especially at weekends, all sorts of entertainers from professional classical musicians and rock bands to laughably incompetent amateurs compete to engage your ear and solicit your coins. The street leads directly to the north-west entrance of a huge square, **St Stephen's**

---

**THE 'BLOOMSDAY' BOOK**

Even in Dublin, far fewer people have read James Joyce's *Ulysses* than have heard of it. But both sorts are catered for each year on 16 June, the date in 1904 when the events of the novel take place. 'Bloomsday' events include dramatizations and readings, rarely omitting Molly Bloom's erotic daydream ('and yes I said yes I will Yes').

Parties set off to follow the footsteps of the protagonist Leopold Bloom from the site of Paddy Dignam's funeral at Prospect Cemetery in Glasnevin to the banks of the Liffey. They head towards Grafton Street, where Bloom goes knowing that his wife has an assignation with her lover and dreading meeting them. They locate Davy Byrne's restaurant where he has a gorgonzola sandwich and a glass of burgundy, and maybe have the same odd combination themselves before walking on to the National Library. That's where Bloom does catch sight of the lover, Blazes Boylan. Nearby, where Westland Row meets Lincoln Place, Sweny's Pharmacy has probably changed less than most of the sights that figure in *Ulysses*. If you'd like to do the circuit, there's no need to wait for the 16th of June. Just arm yourself with one of the maps sold in bookshops and the Tourist Board's office, showing where the 18 episodes occur and set off. Plaques have been placed in the pavement at strategic points along the way.

---

**Green** ('the Green'), entirely filled by the lawns, flowerbeds, lake and trees of a lovely public park. Once a marsh, then a pasture, it was a fashionable place for Regency beaux to parade. Turned into a private preserve, it was rescued and bought for the people of Dublin by Sir Arthur Guinness, later Lord Ardilaun. His is one of the many statues that stand in the park. Other monuments include a bronze memorial to WB Yeats by Henry Moore

*G*rafton Street is fortunately for pedestrians only. There wouldn't be any room for vehicles in Dublin's best-known shopping street.

and a bust of Countess Constance Markievicz who fought here in the 1916 Rising. An odd statue to (hardly *of*) James Joyce has his legs twisted into a coil and the tribute 'He dismantled the English language and put it together again so that it became music.'

It's 1.5km (almost a mile) round the Green, so you may want to take a short cut and emerge at the north-east corner where the tall, lean bronze figure of Wolfe Tone (see page 53) backed by concrete pillars stands opposite the historic Shelbourne Hotel. The Adam Salerooms, where art and antiques are auctioned, are on the same north side. Elsewhere around the square you'll find on the west side the fine **Royal College of Surgeons** (1806), headquarters of the Citizen Army in 1916, and the big St Stephen's Green shopping centre. On the south side the palatial Iveagh House, once a Guinness family residence, is now the Department of Foreign Affairs.

Conservationists mourn the loss of so many of the fine houses that once lined this and the other squares and streets of Georgian Dublin, although as many still survive – if only as offices or in sad decay. To see what a gracious interior could look like, visit **Newman House** (in fact two 18th-century townhouses, Nos 85 and 86 St Stephen's Green South). It was formerly part of University College, whose campus was south of the Green until a new one was built at Belfield. The extension of the east side of the Green along Earlsfort Terrace leads to the **National Concert Hall**. Leading south east from St

*E*choes of an era of elegance in an age of high-speed travel – touring by open landau past the Georgian terraces of Fitzwilliam Square.

Stephen's Green at the same corner, Leeson Street's basement discos and clubs are where night-owls go when everywhere else has closed.

Keen walkers and enthusiasts for Georgian architecture will want to continue a block east to **Fitzwilliam Square** (1825) which has some of the best-kept houses, many of them now the consulting rooms of members of the medical profession. North along Fitzwilliam Street Lower at No. 29, a largely rebuilt townhouse has been furnished in the way it might have been at the end of the 18th century, and is open to visitors.

**Merrion Square** was for a century and a half the best address in Dublin. Daniel O'Connell once lived at No. 58, WB Yeats at No. 82, the Wilde family at No. 1. You can wander round and inspect the commemorative plaques on the walls, or stroll in the pretty park where there's a big open-air art show and sale every weekend.

# National Treasures

A single city block, between Merrion Square and Kildare Street, is stuffed full of riches. Indeed there really isn't room for all the collections of the National Gallery, National Museum, National Library and Natural History Museum which are concentrated here, not to mention the home of the Irish Parliament which is shoe-horned in as well.

The **National Gallery of Ireland** faces Leinster Lawn on the west side of Merrion Square. You'll see a statue of George Bernard Shaw near the entrance: he left a third of his estate to the gallery, saying he owed much of his early education to the time he spent in it.

Most national collections don't have the space to show even a small fraction of their treasures, and this is especially true of Ireland's. What you can see depends also on which rooms are open, during continuing reorganization. Collect a plan of the gallery at the desk: the staff there are helpful in directing you. As a rough guide, European Art of the 14th to 18th centuries is in the upper floor rooms, the Irish School and most 19th-and early 20th-century works are in the ground floor rooms.

It is hard to pick highlights, but the great names include Fra Angelico (*Saints Cosmas and Damian*), Rubens (*The Annunciation*), Rembrandt (*Rest on the Flight into Egypt*) among many Dutch masters, and a strong Spanish School, including Velasquez (*Maid at the Supper at Emmaus*), Goya (the sensuous *El Sueño, The Dream*) and Murillo (*The Prodigal Son Feasting*). Downstairs, works by Hogarth, Romney, Reynolds and Gainsborough lead the English portraits, but this being Ireland's show, it concentrates on Irish artists. Look for Roderic O'Conor, William Leech (*The Goose Girl* and the vivid *Convent Garden*) and William Orpen's extraordinary *The Holy Well* (1916). John Butler Yeats, father of WB Yeats, Lily Yeats and Jack B. Yeats, painted portraits of his children which hang near one of the biggest collections of Jack B. Yeats's own work, from the exciting *Liffey Swim* to the wild colours and brushstrokes of his mystic late pictures.

White, classical **Leinster House**, originally the Dublin home of the Duke of Leinster, was purchased by the new Free State government from the Royal Dublin Society in 1922 and quickly adapted to be the seat of Parliament (the old Irish Parliament building having become the Bank of Ireland, see page 97). A guided tour of the two houses, the Dáil (Chamber of Deputies) and the Seanad (Senate) is possible when Parliament is not in session. Tickets are issued at the National Gallery's reception desk.

The **Natural History Museum** is near the National Gallery with its entrance also in Merrion Street. It has the full range of Irish and other birds and animals in the form of stuffed specimens, and skeletons, including some examples recovered from peat bogs. The most remarkable are those of the Giant Deer, whose antlers could span well over two metres (over 7ft). It became extinct in Ireland perhaps 10,000 years ago.

*Yes, they do have dinosaurs in the Natural History Museum.*

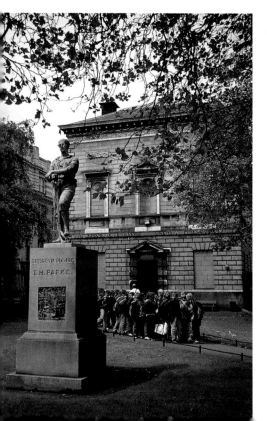

The **National Museum of Ireland** backs on to Leinster Lawn, but its entrance is on Kildare Street. It might not win any prizes for logical arrangement or informative descriptions, but even those who have a resistance to museums ought not to miss this eye-opener. Who is immune to the lure of buried treasure and the glint of gold?

In the **central hall** and the **treasury** leading off it, many of the Irish gold ornaments from the Bronze Age and Iron Age are of a breathtaking beauty. Most were found in hoards: some doubtless hidden to safeguard them in troubled times but others, put in swamps or bogs where they would have been hard to recover, were presumably religious offerings. Spectacular finds were made in the 19th century during excavations for railways and canals or in humble peat cutting. It's certain that many were kept quiet and the precious discoveries sold to dealers and jewellers and melted down. How many more may have been dug up unknowingly in modern times, by the vast machines which harvest peat for power stations?

Look out for the **torcs** from 1000 BC, twisted into perfect corkscrew shapes from ribbons of gold, for huge gold belts, and the 8th-century BC **Gleninsheen gold collar** and armlets. One of the most amazing finds was one of the simplest in conception, a graduated set of large hollow gold spheres, probably components of a huge necklace dating from about 800 BC. Among gold objects from the Iron Age, see the delicate little **boat with 16 tiny oars and rowlocks**, from around 1st century AD, and a gold collar, both from the Broighter hoard in County Derry.

Many other prized exhibits date from the medieval period. The 8th-century **Ardagh Chalice** of beaten silver, polished and decorated with gold filigree, silver and copper, amber and malachite was found under a stone in 1868 by a boy pulling up potatoes. He thought so little of the tarnished and dirty 'cup' that he threw it into a hedge and forgot about it. **The Tara Brooch**, the best example of a whole collection of big ring-and-pin brooches was picked up on a beach. Made of silver with gold filigree and amber, it dates from the 8th century.

The 12th-century bronze **Shrine of St Patrick's Bell** is decorated with gold and silver-gilt in the Urnes style (mesh designs of snake-like animals, named after the Norwegian church where a major example was found, which reached their most elaborate forms in Irish work). The 5th-century iron and bronze bell which the shrine was made to house also survives. The **Cross of Cong**, also 12th century, was designed to display a fragment of the True Cross behind its crystal window.

Less eye-catching to the non-specialist but still fascinating are the flint, bone, stone and bronze tools, weapons and ornaments from the time of the earliest known human settlement in Ireland, around 7000 BC, right up to the modern era. Ogham stones are displayed, with a key to decoding their rudimentary script.

In a gallery adjoining the main hall on the opposite side, the exhibition **In Pursuit of Independence** concentrates on the years from 1900 to 1923. A multi-screen video system shows evocative original film and stills of the 1916 Rising.

The upstairs galleries (displays including Irish Silver, Textiles, Glass, Ceramics and Musical Instruments) are less regularly open than the showpieces on the ground floor. Some of the pressure on space has been relieved by using an annexe in Merrion Row for temporary or long-running exhibitions such as the finds from the excavations of Viking Dublin. Ambitious long-term plans are afoot to restore the magnificent buildings of the Collins Barracks (see page 123) and give the National Museum's collections a worthy setting.

The **National Library** in Kildare Street backs on to the National Gallery. Every famous name in Irish writing seems to have worked under the dome of the first-floor Reading Room since it was opened in 1890. Now *their* first editions are on display along with the works of Swift and Goldsmith. Temporary exhibitions related to Irish literature are frequently set up in the entrance hall.

## Medieval Dublin

The complex of buildings known as **Dublin Castle** scarcely qualifies as medieval any more, being largely an 18th-century reconstruction, in the form of a succession of Georgian squares. Much more recent restorations and additions were undertaken for meetings of European Community prime ministers in the years of Irish presidency.

The original 12th-century Norman castle can only be imagined now. It was in any case augmented in the 13th century and largely superseded by a new one in the 14th century as the threat of rebellion never went away and the expanding organs of government needed the protection of strong walls. The early assaults attempting to dislodge the Normans were echoed in the 1916 Rising when insurgents of the Irish Citizen Army attacked. Failing to break in, they took up positions near the gate in the City Hall (built in the 18th century as the Royal Exchange) until forced to withdraw.

With the crushing of the Rising, the headquarters of British rule seemed secure, but less than six years later, the last viceroy was to hand the keys of castle to Michael Collins, chairman of the government of the new Free State. He and half a dozen colleagues had driven up to the gates in a couple of taxis and walked in to take over 'the Devils' half acre'.

Visitors are free to stroll in the Castle Yards, but if you want to go inside the **State Apartments**, check in at the tour entrance in the Upper Yard. Some rooms (at times all) may be closed, but you can usually see St Patrick's Hall where the Knights of the Order of St Patrick used to be invested, the Bermingham Tower, and the Wedgwood Room with paintings by Angelica Kaufmann. The Picture Gallery houses portraits of British viceroys and the gorgeously gilded Throne Room is where they (or their royal masters on rare visits to Ireland) sat on ceremonial occasions.

Entered from Lower Yard, the **Chapel Royal** is an early example of Gothic Revival, decorated inside with the arms of British viceroys, and outside with 100 stone heads of characters from Irish history, including St Kevin, Brian Boru and Jonathan Swift. They were carved by the Dublin sculptors Edward and John Smyth, responsible for so much fine statuary in the city.

## Temple Bar

One small street has given its name to an area now promoted as Dublin's equivalent of the Left Bank in Paris, although here it's the right bank. Roughly limited by Christ Church Cathedral at one end, the Bank of Ireland at the other and the Liffey on its northern edge, Temple Bar claims a host of wine bars, pubs and

*The Temple Bar area is turning into a lively focus of entertainment with new restaurants, wine bars, discos and small shops.*

restaurants. An increasing number of streets have been designated pedestrian only. The **Olympia Theatre** in Dame Street, almost opposite the gates of Dublin Castle, should not be missed by fans of Victoriana. The interior design dates from the 1870s, and the theatre still stages a varied programme of plays and shows. The Dublin Stock Exchange in Anglesea Street and big bank buildings may not fit the 'fun city' image but they bring welcome daytime business to the food and drink outlets.

## Where Dublin Began

Just to the west of the Castle lies the heart of early Dublin. The Vikings probably first established themselves on the bank of the Liffey where Wood Quay is now: archaeologists discovered the foundations of many of their houses here. The Normans followed suit, and this remained the city's focus until the early 18th century. Then the whole district was neglected when the Georgian streets and squares to the north and east became the fashionable areas to live. In the 19th century it became still more rundown, hardly distinguishable from the once notorious slums called The Liberties which adjoined it on the west (see page 111).

# Rival Cathedrals

It's an oddity of history that the older churches and cathedrals in the Republic belong to the minority Protestant Church of Ireland. Both of Dublin's great medieval cathedrals are 'Church of Ireland'. (The 19th-century Roman Catholic Pro-Cathedral of St Mary is off O'Connell Street.)

**Christ Church Cathedral** was started in about 1038 by the Vikings, but in 1173, soon after the Norman conquest, a new church was begun on the site, by order of Strongbow and Archbishop (later Saint) Laurence O'Toole. Most of the present structure dates from the 12th and 13th centuries but its appearance today also owes a great deal to renovations carried out in the 1870s.

Near the entrance is a tomb still called Strongbow's, although the effigy of a knight with a curiously worn skull is recognized as dating from the 14th century, much later than Strongbow's time. It was probably brought from another church after a roof collapse destroyed the original.

*A footbridge soars across the road from Christ Church Cathedral to its Synod House and the Dublinia Exhibition.*

Beside it lies the top half of a smaller figure, sometimes identified as Strongbow's wife, sometimes his son, perhaps damaged by the same roof-fall.

Behind the high altar in the Peace Chapel of St Laud, a reliquary houses the heart of St Laurence O'Toole. The multi-patterned medieval floor tiles here were the models for the 19th-century copies in the rest of the cathedral.

Don't miss a descent to the **crypt**, with its forest of rough stone pillars and arches supporting the whole massive structure above. It used to be thought that these were the foundations of the Viking church, but it's now accepted that they are 12th-century Norman work. Among many relics stored here are a set of stocks which used to be in Christ Church Yard until 1870, for the punishment of offenders from The Liberties. The statues of Charles I and Charles II used to stand atop the façade of the old City Hall, demolished in 1806.

The **Dublinia** Exhibition across the street from Christ Church (and linked to it by a footbridge) tells and illustrates the history of the city, especially the period from the arrival of the Normans to the upheavals of the reformation of the 1540s.

Just a short walk south from Christ Church along Nicholas Street and Patrick Street, **St Patrick's Cathedral** was consecrated in 1192. It probably stands on the site of successive parish churches, perhaps dating back to the 6th century, soon after St Patrick's own time. Tradition says that the saint baptized converts in a well close to the north side of the tower. The well has long vanished, and a stream that once divided around the site, making it an island, has been channelled underground.

Why was a second cathedral begun so near and so soon after Christ Church? Part of the answer lies in the conflict, already

centuries old, between Ireland's powerful monastic institutions and the separate hierarchy of bishops and archbishops. St Laurence O'Toole's successors as Archbishops of Dublin pushed ahead with building St Patrick's while some influential Norman lords backed Christ Church. The building race developed into a long-running rivalry. The nave of St Patrick's was built in the 1220s, the tower results from a 14th-century rebuilding after a fire, and the spire was completed in 1749.

Immediately to the left of the entrance in the south-west corner, the enormous **Boyle Monument** was erected by Richard Boyle, the first Earl of Cork, in 1633 at the then vast cost of £1,000. The most prominent painted figures represent the Earl and

---

**'BOYLED TO DEATH'**

The Boyle Monument was first placed at the high altar of the cathedral on the orders of the immensely rich and self-important Richard Boyle, Earl of Cork, one of the 'new English' landowners and the greatest plunderer of church property in Ireland. A bishop of Waterford, suffering under his depredations, declared that he had heard of bishops burned to death but never until now of one 'boyled to death'. Charles I's new Lord Deputy in Ireland, Strafford, decided to force the Earl to disgorge some of his gains. He objected to the monument too. Those who attended the cathedral 'could not do reverence to God... without also crouching to an Earl of Cork and his lady... or to those sea-nymphs his daughters, their hair dishevilled, down upon their shoulders.' Strafford ordered it to be dismantled. These dual blows to pocket and pride enraged Boyle. From then on his battles with the Lord Deputy became, literally, a fight to the death which ended with the impeachment and execution of Strafford in 1641.

his second wife who had recently died, with 11 of their children below. The boy in the middle of the lowest tier is taken to be Robert Boyle, who grew up to be a famous scientist (perhaps you remember from school: 'Boyle's Law states that the volume of a given mass of gas at constant temperature is inversely proportional to its pressure'). A similarly grandiose Cork family monument stands in St Mary's Church, Youghal (see page 174).

Also at the west end of the nave stands the famous **chapter house door** with a roughly sawn hole like a large letterbox. The story goes that the Earl of Kildare cut it in 1492. He then reached through to grasp the hand of the Earl of Ormonde, who had taken refuge in the chapter house after a violent argument involving them

---

**INTIMATE RELATIONS**

Swift seems to have first met his 'Stella' in England when she was eight and he was 22. He paid for her education and later asked her to come and live in Ireland. As far as anyone knew, their meetings occurred only when her companion, Rebecca Dingley, was present. Yet their relationship inspired endless gossip and speculation. Some said they had married, but then discovered that they were brother and sister, the illegitimate children of a nobleman (another version says they were uncle and niece). When their remains were examined during one of the reconstructions of St Patrick's it's said that their teeth were found to be identical. In 1728 Stella died, and Swift sat for night after night in the cold dark cathedral, apparently composing letters to her.

---

*J*onathan Swift, author of Gulliver's Travels, was dean of St Patrick's Cathedral from 1713 to 1745. His grave is marked by a brass tablet in the floor.

and their armed followers in the church. By so 'chancing his arm' he gave a phrase to the language as well as restoring peace between them by his gesture.

Jonathan Swift was dean of St Patrick's from 1713 until his death in 1745. The satirist and author of *Gulliver's Travels* wrote many campaigning essays protesting against the appalling conditions of the poor in Ireland. In the nave just to the right of the entrance you'll find his bust and epitaph in Latin ('He lies where savage indignation can no longer pierce his heart. Go, traveller and imitate, if you can, this earnest and dedicated defender of liberty.'). His grave and that of his beloved 'Stella' (Esther Johnson) lie side by side a step away from the wall. Swift's pulpit, table and chair stand in the cathedral's north transept. St Patrick's Hospital for mental disorders was founded with the aid of money left by Swift in his will, with a Parthian shot to the effect that 'no nation needed it more'.

In Swift's time, the cathedral did not look the way it does today. Parts were in ruins, and had been since Cromwell's troopers made their usual gesture of contempt for consecrated ground by stabling their horses here. Others had been hived off for separate use (the Lady Chapel was the Huguenot church). Only massive restoration schemes in the 19th century saved St Patrick's: the chief benefactors, members of the Guinness family are commemorated in statues and in the north transept window by Frank Brangwyn.

The **choir** of the cathedral survives from the medieval building: it is lined with the accoutrements of the Knights of St Patrick as they were in 1870. Over the aisles hang the tattered banners of Irish regiments of the British army who fought for the Empire over the centuries (often against fellow Irishmen in French, American and other armies). The cathedral choir gave the first performance of Handel's *Messiah* in 1742.

*The Tailors' Hall, dating from 1706, is the only surviving guild hall in Dublin. It's now the headquarters of the Irish National Trust.*

Across the little park behind St Patrick's, the low brick building of Archbishop **Marsh's Library**, dating from 1701, was designed as Ireland's first public library, and it still functions as one. The original dark oak bookcases with their carved and lettered gables have been beautifully restored, along with the cages where readers were locked in to prevent them making off with precious volumes.

Across the street to the west of Christ Church Cathedral, the solid **St Audoen's Church** is Norman in origin but extensively rebuilt since. The only medieval parish church still in use in Dublin, it houses an exhibition on Celtic Ireland. In an adjoining alley, the restored St Audoen's Arch is the only gateway to survive from the 13th-century city wall. South across High Street and entered from the cobblestoned Back Lane, the early 18th-century **Tailors' Guild Hall** is likewise the last of many craft guild halls. It is now the headquarters of *An Taisce*, the Irish National Trust.

The narrow streets west from here used to be one of Dublin's more squalid slums. Now partly cleaned up, partly knocked down, the area keeps its old name of '**The Liberties**'. Standing outside the city walls, it was not under the city's authority but that of a now-vanished abbey: until as late as 1860 the enforcement of the law was nominally in the hands of the dean of Christ Church. These days the remaining streets are lined with antique and junk shops, bargain and fly-by-night outlets and street traders' carts.

The celebrated **Brazen Head** in Lower Bridge Street claims to be Dublin's oldest pub: the present building dates from the 17th century but tradition says there was an alehouse on the site long before that. The leaders of the United Irishmen used to meet here in the 1790s, and many of them were arrested here when the organization was declared illegal.

## St James's Gate

West of The Liberties and south of the

*It is claimed there was an ale house on this site 800 years ago: the present Brazen Head dates from the 17th century.*

River Liffey, the Guinness Brewery is one of Europe's biggest. The vast site looks like a refinery, apart from an odd tapering tower which used to be a windmill. More than half the beer drunk in Ireland (including the North) is brewed here, most famously the nearly black stout whose character is credited to Arthur Guinness who first began brewing here in 1759. The idea that he charred some barley by accident and stumbled on the formula is probably a piece of Irish invention: dark porter was known long before. But few dispute that it practically became the life blood of a nation. There's a wide measure of agreement with the hell-raising poet Brendan Behan that 'it has 'atin' and drinkin' in it.'

Plenty is exported around the world, and breweries from London to Lagos produce it to the same formula, although nobody can explain why it never tastes quite the way it does in Ireland. You can't tour the brewery itself, but the World of Guinness exhibition centre is open on weekdays in working hours in the old **hop store** in Crane Street, with a museum of brewing and a video presentation. You're invited to sample a glass of the fabled 'extra stout porter' in the Old Dublin Bar.

Until the 1960s both the Grand Canal, which widens into a harbour just south of the brewery, and the River Liffey were used to bring in supplies of barley and hops. Some of the product went out by the same route, a nice gentle way for it to travel which gave rise to a theory that 'Canal' Guinness was the best of the lot. (If you'd like to know more about the canal and waterway system and its leisure possibilities, go to the **Waterways Visitor Centre** at the Grand Canal basin, Ringsend, east of Trinity College.)

# Kilmainham

West from the centre of Dublin along the south bank of the Liffey, and next to Heuston railway station, the magnificent **Royal Hospital** was built in 1684 as a home for retired soldiers. That was two years before its London equivalent, the Royal Hospital Chelsea. The Duke of Ormonde, Charles II's viceroy, had seen Les Invalides, Louis XIV's home for *his* army pensioners and been inspired to create one like it. Arranged around a spacious arcaded courtyard, the Royal Hospital Kilmainham is the finest 17th-century building in Ireland. It kept its original purpose for almost 250 years and was then used for various official functions, but as its 300th anniversary approached, it had become neglected. The government was stimulated to action and initiated a programme of restoration which was to win several awards.

The high rooms and long, elegant corridors make it a superb exhibition centre, and since 1991 it has been the home of the **Irish Museum of Modern Art (IMMA)**, putting on frequently changing shows of avant garde and often controversial art. Even if that is not your preference, don't fail to see the building, and when they are open, be sure to see the parts not used by IMMA: the Great Hall, Chapel and Master's Lodge. All sorts of events are staged at the Hospital, anything from coin fairs to charity cricket matches on the lawn and state banquets.

Almost adjoining the Royal Hospital, on South Circular Road, stands a building designed for a grimmer purpose, the grey, fortress-like **Kilmainham Jail**. (If you don't mind a walk you can leave the Royal Hospital by the opposite entrance from the main door and head down a long path to an imposing Gothic gatehouse. Through it and across the busy intersection you'll see the forbidding walls of the jail.)

Finished at the end of the 18th century, it was proclaimed as a new and more civilized prison than the stinking dungeons in use hitherto, and many inmates probably did find the conditions better than some Dublin slums. But Kilmainham's place in history has little to do with social reform. From the United Irishmen in 1796 to those who opposed the Free State in the Civil War of 1922-3, it saw the incarceration of Irish patriots ('rebels' to their rulers) in every stage of the fight for independence. Most significantly, for public reaction led to the struggle's eventual success, this was the place of execution of the leaders of the 1916 Easter Rising.

*The Royal Hospital at Kilmainham, built in the 17th century for army pensioners, has been beautifully converted into the Irish Museum of Modern Art.*

The last of its inmates to be freed, in 1924, was Eamon De Valéra, who had been locked up by the Free State government. He had also been imprisoned here in 1916 and would certainly have been shot with the other leaders had it not been for his place of birth – New York. The British wanted to avoid offending the Americans by executing one who held US as well as UK citizenship. Fifty years later, in one of history's great ironies, it was none other than President De Valéra who came to open the partially restored prison to visitors.

For 40 years it had been abandoned to the elements. Parts of the roof had fallen in and the courtyards were as overgrown as a jungle. Then a group of volunteers began the restoration work which still continues. Both a nationalist shrine and a museum, it still feels like a prison and if you shiver when the doors slam shut it may not be only from the cold. You'll be shown where Patrick McCann, United Irishman and stonemason, carved his name in 1798. You'll see the room where those condemned to death spent their last night, and the scaffold where they were hanged. By contrast, the reasonably comfortable room where Parnell was detained for several months in 1881 was usually the warders' sitting room.

In the three-storey cell blocks, the dedicated guides can tell you where most of the famous prisoners were held, particularly the leaders of the 1916 Rising before they were taken out to one of the yards to be shot. There, on the wall, a simple memorial plaque bears their names and the dates of their deaths. The yacht *Asgard*, which ran guns for the Irish Volunteers in 1914, is kept under cover nearby.

Close by at Islandbridge, near one of the gates into Phoenix Park (see page 123), is a memorial garden designed by Lutyens, honouring 50,000 other Irish dead who fell in the First World War.

## Southern Suburbs

South east from St Stephen's Green past Leeson Street's 'disco strip' and across the Grand Canal, **Ballsbridge** is a district of elegant houses and leafy streets. It became the fashionable area to live in late Victorian times, and with most foreign embassies located here, it is now Dublin's diplomatic quarter. The **Royal Dublin Society (RDS),** forerunner of all agricultural societies, has its amazingly extensive grounds right in the middle of some of the most expensive real estate in Dublin. They are the venue of the celebrated Dublin Horse Show in August, equestrian and social event of the season, but the Society's arenas and exhibition space are in use throughout the year for concerts, conventions and exhibitions.

The **Chester Beatty Library** and Gallery of Oriental Art fills a mansion at No. 20 in tree-lined Shrewsbury Road. It began as, and still largely comprises, the collection formed by Sir Alfred Chester Beatty, a Canadian mining magnate who came to live in Dublin in the 1950s and brought his treasures with him. When he died in 1968, he left them to Ireland, and the Library has been an essential resource for scholars in the fields of Near East and Oriental literature and art ever since. Beginning with ancient Egyptian papyruses, his interests had expanded to cover the whole field of manuscripts – Babylonian clay tablets from 2500 BC, Biblical texts, early examples of printed books and Chinese seals. The Islamic collection is justly famous and most admired, especially the superb Persian and Indian Mughal miniatures.

**Donnybrook** was the site of a rowdy medieval fair which survived into the more genteel mid-19th century, when it was shut down for causing too much disturbance. So famous for fighting was it that the name actually became a synonym for a scrap (especially in Irish American parlance). **University College, Dublin,**

formerly crammed into a site adjoining Merrion Square, has its spacious new campus nearby at Belfield. With 10,000 students, 'UCD' is even larger than Trinity College Dublin ('TCD').

**Dún Laoghaire**, pronounced something like 'Dun Leary', and called Kingstown for a hundred years until 1922, became effectively a suburb of Dublin when the railway reached it and all space

*Y*achting centre and port for some Irish Sea ferries, Dún Laoghaire's harbour is protected by two long jetties.

in between the two was built over. It retains a separate character even now, as a fishing port, ferry terminal and yachting centre. Its citizens may commute on the DART to Dublin daily, but they can go home and feel that they're back in a rather exclusive seaside resort. A few good restaurants are clustered around the harbour, including one in the old railway station. The **Maritime Museum** in the former Mariners' Church has some interesting ship models as well as an original longboat left behind by the failed French expedition to Bantry Bay in 1796. On a fine day, take a stroll along the eastern harbour wall for a great view of the port and the bay.

tribute to the Irish-born giants of literature. The first display room deals with the earlier figures: Swift, Goldsmith and Sheridan, Maria Edgeworth who inspired Turgenev, Bram Stoker, creator of Dracula, as well as the two playwrights who count almost as modern, Oscar Wilde and George Bernard Shaw. The second room spans the period from the Irish literary revival of the 1890s onwards: Yeats and his circle, Synge, Joyce, O'Casey and Beckett, among many others. Photographs, letters and memorabilia on show include the typewriter Brendan Behan threw

# The North Bank of the Liffey

At its northern end, O'Connell Street meets **Parnell Square**, four streets that enclose a complex of buildings including the former Assembly Rooms, a fashionable social venue in the 18th century. Part is now a cinema, an extension houses the **Gate Theatre** and the Rotunda Hospital still occupies the site it did when it was founded as the first maternity hospital in Ireland (when there was none in Britain either).

In the north-west corner of the square, the sunken **Garden of Remembrance** honours all those who were forced to emigrate and all who died fighting for Ireland's freedom. They include the original 'Wild Geese' who left Ireland after the defeat of the Jacobite forces at Limerick in 1791. The winged memorial at the end of the garden depicts not geese, but the mythical children of Lir who were turned into swans.

The **Dublin Writers' Museum**, 18 Parnell Square North, with the Irish Writers Centre next door at No. 19, pays

*A pair of 18th-century town houses in Parnell Square have been restored to house the Dublin Writers' Museum.*

through a pub window during a fit of writer's block, among other symptoms. The house is worth a visit on its own account, with original 18th-century plasterwork and 19th-century features added for George Jameson of the whiskey family, notably the salon which is now the Gallery of Writers.

Literary pilgrims will want to walk further in this area, although much of it is sadly run down. James Joyce went to the Jesuit school in Belvedere House just off Parnell Square in Great Denmark Street; Sheridan was born at No. 12 Dorset Street and Sean O'Casey at No. 85 in a house now vanished. Up a side street, the 19th-century St Mary's Chapel of Ease is called the 'Black' Church – because its stone looks so dark when wet. **St George's Church** was brand new and didn't have its elegant spire in 1806 when Arthur Wellesley (not yet the Duke of Wellington) married his childhood friend Kitty Pakenham.

Prominent on the north side of Parnell Square, Charlemont House (1762) was designed by Sir William Chambers for James Caulfield, Earl of Charlemont. He was a founder of the Royal Irish Academy, so it is fitting that the house, extended by the addition of several rooms, is now the **Hugh Lane Municipal Gallery of Modern Art**. It's a long title and perhaps a misleading one: when the man that it honours first had the idea for such a gallery, 'modern' meant late 19th-century.

In the entrance hall is a portrait by Sargent of Hugh Lane himself, only 40 when he died, and a bust of his aunt, the playwright Lady Gregory, by Epstein. There's a massive head of Michael Collins by the sculptor Seámus Murphy and a portrait of Maude Gonne (see page 123) by Sarah Purser. The riches of the collection still reflect Lane's tastes, with great strength in French painting: Monet's *Vetheuil in Sunshine and Snow*, the luminous *Jour d'Eté* by Berthe Morisot, *Eva Gonzales* by Manet and several pictures by Corot to mention just a few. G.F. Watts and Burne-Jones represent the Pre-Raphaelites, and there are varied and vivid Irish scenes by Lavery, Leech, Orpen, John Keating and William Osborne. The gallery's large collection of later Irish art is rotated frequently, and space is found for important temporary exhibitions.

A short walk west of Parnell Square stand the **King's Inns**, another classical landmark designed by James Gandon. His last major building and not finished until 1816, after his death, this is the home of the Irish legal profession. As at the Inns of

---

**DIVISION OF THE SPOILS**

Sir Hugh Lane, art lover and successful dealer, made a will that left most of his collection to the National Gallery in London. After he was tragically drowned in 1915 when the *Lusitania* was sunk by a German submarine, a codicil to the will was found. In it he had made a special bequest of 39 of his most prized pictures (notably works by Corot, Courbet, Monet, Manet and Renoir) to Dublin. But the codicil had not been witnessed and a legal wrangle ensued, the seemingly eternal delays benefiting only the lawyers. The pictures had been taken to London and were held there. Irish resentment mounted, and when the Gallery was opened in 1933, a room was pointedly left empty for the Lane Bequest. At last, by the terms of an interim settlement in 1959, half the pictures went to London and half to Dublin, alternating every five years. By a new – but still not final – agreement in 1979, 30 came to Dublin, 8 to London, and Renoir's *Les Parapluies* shuttled between them.

Court in London, the original 16th-century inns got their name because lawyers actually lived there. A relic of the custom survives: law students are still required to dine at the King's Inns from time to time. **St Michan's Church** was the first to be built north of the river, as early as the Norse period. When Norse inhabitants were forced out of their settlement on the south bank by the Normans, many moved here. (The name Oxmantown, from 'Ostmantown', preserves the memory of a time when most people in the area were of obvious Scandinavian descent.) The present building of St Michan's dates from the 17th century. So, probably, do the part-mummified bodies in its vaults, preserved by some combination of alkaline conditions and dry air and presented as an unpleasant tourist attraction.

**Smithfield**, around the street of the same name, used to be synonymous with markets and distilleries. There's still an early morning traffic jam bringing produce to the Fruit and Vegetable Market in Mary's Lane, but the smell of malted barley and the fumes of bubbling stills have long since faded away. Even the mighty John Jameson and Co. closed in 1972, centralizing production at Midleton, Co. Cork (see page 179). The story is well told in the **Whiskey Museum**, converted from an old distillery building. With relics and models, a film (or 'fillum' as the Irish say) and maybe a little drop to taste, they'll persuade you that whiskey with an 'e' is indeed the king of spirits.

*One of James Gandon's masterpieces, the Four Courts building on the north bank of the River Liffey.*

# Magicians with Words

Ireland is making up for lost time in acclaiming her literary giants. If you haven't noticed, it will soon be drawn to your attention that no other city can equal Dublin's three Nobel prize-winners for literature, so far. George Bernard Shaw, WB Yeats and Samuel Beckett are honoured now as never before in the land of their birth. So is one of the greatest innovators in the English language *not* to have received the prize, James Joyce, whose work was excoriated or banned in Ireland during his lifetime and long after his death. J.M. Synge and Sean O'Casey were world-renowned dramatists, whose plays were greeted by howls of protest in Dublin. In our own day, Seamus Heaney may be the most widely read of living poets in English. Then there are the popular novelists: the prolific Edna O'Brien with timeless tales of rural Ireland and what happens when its children encounter the outside world, and Maeve Binchy, a newspaper columnist whose human stories sell in millions.

The tradition of great writing goes back a long way. The Dublin-born master satirist Jonathan Swift wrote *Gulliver's Travels* (1726) 'to vex the world' and his polemical pamphlets to try to horrify English opinion into a recognition of the appalling plight of Ireland's poor. London was more interested in being entertained than shocked, and Irish-born playwrights were ready with their satires upon English manners: George Farquhar's *The Beaux' Stratagem* (1707) and *The Recruiting Officer* (1706), Oliver Goldsmith's *She Stoops to Conquer* (1773); and Richard Brinsley Sheridan's *The Rivals* (1775) and *The School for Scandal* (1777) are classics of comedy. Born into the Anglo-Irish supremacy, their authors probably never thought of themselves as Irish–they all invented and made fun of foolish, wild or drunken 'stage-Irish' characters. All went to Trinity College Dublin: so did the political philosopher Edmund Burke (1729-97) who in the Swiftian tradition campaigned against the oppression of Ireland, though he is better known for his opposition to the French revolution.

The playwriting vein was continued in the 19th century by the greatest wit of his time, Oscar Wilde (1856-1900) with *Lady Windermere's Fan* (1892) and *The Importance of Being Earnest*. (1895). Born two years after Wilde, George Bernard Shaw was brought up in or near Dublin but moved to London when he was 20. For years his prose skills appeared only newspaper music criticism, but after his first play was staged in 1892, more came in quick succession, including *Arms and the Man* (1894), *Caesar and Cleopatra* (1901), *Pygmalion* (1913) and *St Joan* (1923). He received the Nobel Prize in 1925.

William Butler Yeats, born in Dublin in 1865, went back to Celtic myth for the subject matter of his early plays, intended as part of a revival of a national literature and theatre. To go with it, he and his life-long friend Lady Gregory, a prolific playwright, founded the Abbey Theatre in 1904. As a poet he explored the realms of magic, astrology, mathematics and symbolism, influenced by his editing of the works of Blake. As a campaigner for Irish independence, he was conscious that his writing had influenced events, significantly the years 1916-22. 'Because I helped wind the clock, I come to hear it strike.' In the prophetic *The Second Coming* (1920), he wrote the often-quoted litany for troubled times:

*Things fall apart; the centre cannot hold;*

*Mere anarchy is loosed upon the world,*
*The blood-dimmed tide is loosed, and everywhere*
*The ceremony of innocence is drowned;*
*The best lack all conviction, while the worst*
*Are full of passionate intensity.*

Yeats became a member of the new Free State's senate in 1922 and received the Nobel Prize for Literature in 1923. In later life he was preoccupied with eastern philosophies and the supernatural and looked in history for better times. His poetry became ever more complex but the imagery was never more powerful than in *The Tower* (1928) and *The Winding Stair* (1929), both titles alluding to his tower-house of Thoor Ballylee in the west of Ireland. He died in France in 1939 but his body was eventually returned to his beloved Sligo in 1948 for burial where he had wished, in Drumcliff churchyard.

In contrast to so many of his predecessors and contemporaries, Sean O'Casey came from a poor, Catholic background. His plays are in a strong Dublin dialect, a reaction to the high flown language of the works of the Celtic revival which took their tone from the ancient epics. *The Shadow of a Gunman* (1923), *Juno and the Paycock* (1924) and *The Plough and the Stars* (1926) gave an anti-heroic version of recent Irish history and their first nights at the Abbey caused riots, inside and outside the theatre. O'Casey moved to England and continued to write, but with less impact.

James Joyce (1882-1941) is revered in Dublin now, although he left it in 1904 and never lived there again. His short stories, *Dubliners,* were written in

*The giants of literature are honoured now in the land of their birth as they never were in their lifetimes. This is the Dublin Writers' Museum.*

Trieste the following year and broke previously accepted norms by the exactness of the identifications of living people and actual places. No publisher would dare to bring the book out for nine more years. Joyce went on to revolutionize the novel with *Ulysses* (1922) – a firework display of styles including the first 'stream of consciousness'– and then to destroy it in his *Finnegan's Wake* (1939), where only fragments of conventional sense can be discerned, floating in a soup made of the sum of world literature put through a blender. To quote Seamus Deane, Professor of Modern English at University College Dublin, 'The first thing to say about *Finnegan's Wake* is that it is, in an important sense, unreadable.' Look at the chapter *Anna Livia Plurabelle* which weaves in the names of a thousand rivers. Joyce was the master of plays on words in a dozen languages: does anyone else juggle with *Finnish*? At its most opaque, though, *Finnegan's Wake* is still unmistakeably Irish. It even sounds slightly more accessible read in an Irish accent. And the search is always rewarding: Joyce laced *Ulysses* and *Finnegan's Wake* with inspired and memorable malapropisms: 'Who made these allegations?' says Alf. 'I', says Joe, 'I'm the alligator.'

There are no rules for Irish writers. Indeed, Samuel Beckett wrote mostly in French, the language of his adopted home where he had worked briefly with James Joyce in 1932. When *Waiting for Godot* reached a wide, if puzzled, audience in 1953, he became known for his austere vision of a desperate human predicament, expressed in fractured and exhausted prose and leaden clichés. This may have been unfair: some heard his work as a poetic meditation on life itself. Beckett didn't mind acting up to his image of laconic minimalist. Asked by *The Times* for his resolutions and hopes for the New Year of 1984, he responded by telegram:

RESOLUTIONS COLON ZERO STOP PERIOD HOPES COLON ZERO STOP BECKETT.

The wit of Myles na gCopaleen (born Brian O'Nolan) has acquired cult status, with his columns for the *Irish Times* in the 1940s frequently reprinted in book form. His garrulous creation 'The Brother' speaking the broadest Dublin brogue in conversation with a studiously correct straight man is a comic masterpiece. Under another pseudonym, Flann O'Brien, he wrote the surrealist novels *The Third Policeman* and *At Swim-Two-Birds*.

How has a small island with a population to match produced such an astoundingly rich literature? What makes Dublin, where most of them were born, such fertile ground for writers of genius? To lump them all under the heading of Irish writers is more than a little misleading. Some of the greatest left Ireland as soon as they could and returned only briefly and reluctantly, if at all. You might say they're not Irish writers anyway, reserving the title for writers in Irish Gaelic, a closed book to most of us and to most Irish people as well. But the way they use English is still influenced by the grammar and syntax of Gaelic, almost as if the two had intermeshed. In Ireland they're in love with words and the sound of words, using them like newly forged weapons. The story-telling tradition survives in Ireland too: in some pubs in the west, the going rate can be a pint of Guinness. Necessity is the mother of literary invention too, but perhaps the greatest factor of all is the tradition itself. Every writer has the giants of the past as a model, if not to emulate, at least to inspire.

A landmark on the Liffey's north bank and another superb achievement of James Gandon, the classical **Four Courts** building of 1802, was so named after the courts of law it was built to house. Never mind that there were five of them. It looks its best from across the river, but when it's open, the view of the city from the upper gallery of the domed rotunda is worth seeing too. Seized by anti-Treaty nationalists in 1922, it was shelled by Free State forces on the orders of Michael Collins. The occupiers were eventually dislodged, but not before explosions had wrecked the interior and destroyed the precious archives in the adjoining Record Office.

To the west, facing the river on the way towards Phoenix Park, the magnificent buildings of **Collins Barracks** date from 1704. After long neglect which not all of them survived, they are scheduled for restoration. The plan is eventually to move the National Gallery of Ireland here.

## Phoenix Park

The biggest and best walled city park in Europe, if not the world, could easily hold the entire population of Dublin without the slightest overcrowding. That's an assertion which has been put to the test more than once, for example when Pope John Paul II celebrated mass. The name is probably nothing to do with any phoenix, but a corruption of *Fionn Uisge* (clear water). Notwithstanding, a Phoenix Column was supplied by the Earl of Chesterfield in 1744. Near the south-eastern main gate, you can't miss a colossal **Obelisk**, over 60m (200ft) high, matching the scale of the park itself. Built soon after Waterloo, it commemorates Wellington's victories in India and the Napoleonic Wars which are listed on its faces. Although born in Dublin, the Iron Duke ungraciously

### INDEPENDENT SPIRITS

Maud Gonne (1866-1953), married for a time to one famous independence fighter, mother of another, beloved of WB Yeats, heroine to many, is still a controversial figure in the history of the Republican movement. As the daughter of a British cavalry officer, she might have been an unlikely champion of Irish independence but she never forgot her childhood days at Howth. When she met Yeats he was 22, she 23 and a great beauty, but secretly involved with a French lover by whom she had two children, Georges who was to die young, and Iseult. She was soon campaigning in support of evicted tenants, whose plight deeply moved her, and her impassioned speeches in England and Ireland led to the issuing of the first of many warrants for her arrest.

Yeats was to propose marriage to her many times: always she refused, although later they both felt they were partners in a spiritual union. After going on speaking tours of the United States with John MacBride, a Major in the Irish Brigade which fought with the Boers against the British in the South African War, she married him, though they soon separated and eventually divorced. Their son, Seán was to become as militant a fighter as his father. (Later in life, he was a leading diplomat and a recipient of the Nobel Peace Prize.) John MacBride was a prime mover of the 1916 Easter Rising, and was one of those executed. Banned from Ireland by the British government, Maud Gonne returned there in disguise. Arrested in May 1918, she was imprisoned in London for five months. She worked for Sinn Féin during the war of 1919-21 and supported the Free State government until it began executions during the Civil War which followed independence. Her friendship with Yeats was put to the test and there were periods of estrangement but the two were reconciled before his death in 1939. She died in 1953.

discounted his Irish origins, remarking that a man may be born in a stable, but that doesn't make him a horse! Who knows what he made of the fawning inscription at the base of the massive monument, in Latin but thoughtfully translated for non-classical scholars too:

*Asia and Europe, saved by thee, proclaim*
*Invincible in war, thy deathless name.*
*Now round thy brow the civic oak we twine*
*That every earthly glory may be thine.*

Flower gardens near the same gate rejoice in the name of the **Peoples' Garden**, adjoining the Defence Department and *Garda Siochána* (Police) headquarters. On the northern edge of the park, the official residence of the President of Ireland (*Aras an Uachtaráin*) is the same fine Georgian house where British viceroys once held court, within hearing of the roars and screeches of the animals in Dublin Zoo. In the more distant reaches of the park – and remember it's almost 5km (3 miles) long – only a stone tower remains of Ashtown Castle. The house formerly occupied by the papal nuncio has been demolished, but the stables have been quite tastefully turned into a Visitor Centre (showing a video on the history of the park) and an informal restaurant.

# Northern Outskirts

About 3km (2 miles) north at Glasnevin, Dublin's Botanic Gardens and the vast Prospect Cemetery almost adjoin, but their entrance gates are quite far apart.

The **National Botanic Gardens** were established at the end of the 18th century when expeditions were bringing back seeds and specimens from every part of the globe. The fine cast-iron glasshouses were begun in the 1840s. Separate sections of the gardens feature herbs, roses, cacti, bonsai trees and a dozen more categories. The shady tree-lined avenues are a favourite place for Dubliners to walk on a fine afternoon.

**Prospect Cemetery** (sometimes known as Glasnevin) is the burial place of many of Ireland's heroes, and thus a place of pilgrimage. It's so big that you will need to find one of the staff to help you locate

many of the graves of the famous, but three at least are easily found, close to the main gates. Daniel O'Connell lies in a crypt under the round tower; Charles Stewart Parnell's prominent grave is not far away to the left. Sir Roger Casement was hanged in London for treason: he had landed on the west coast of Ireland from a German submarine just before the 1916 Rising (see page 205). After a long campaign, his remains were brought from London in 1965 and reburied opposite the gate. To the right of the entrance, in the nationalists' plot, you will find the graves of Eamon De Valéra, Maud Gonne MacBride, Constance Markievicz and generations of others who fought for Irish freedom in their various ways, if too often they also fought each other.

*The National Botanic Gardens at Glasnevin were established over 200 years ago and the glasshouses are almost as old.*

# A Region Rich with the Monuments of 5,000 Years

From the Boyne Valley to Kildare lie the fertile lands of the former Pale. Here, the Normans and then the English kept control, even when their grip on the rest of Ireland was broken. Its tranquil meadows contrast with dramatic relics of a turbulent past: the massive burial mounds of Newgrange and Knowth; the Hill of Tara where High Kings of Ireland were crowned; great castles and ruined abbeys. History doesn't have it all its own way. You can enjoy a day at the races at one of the beautiful rural courses, play golf or go fishing or sailing from a picturesque little port.

## North east of Dublin

On the outskirts of Dublin on the road to Sutton and Howth, the **Marino Casino** has nothing to do with blackjack or roulette: the name just signified a little house. This Palladian gem, designed by Sir William Chambers for the extravagant collector Lord Charlemont, was built in the 1760s and '70s to grace the gardens of his magnificent Marino House (demolished in 1921). Much bigger than it looks at first glance, it has three storeys, and furniture of the period is displayed inside. Notice the urns which disguise the chimneys, and the gently bulging window-panes, painstakingly made for the restoration in the old way from blown glass. Near the entrance, don't miss the memorial to a favourite dog, inscribed with a long poem to 'poor Nep':

*Beneath where lilies raise their tiny crests*
*All that remains of faithful Neptune rests.*

The peninsula of **Howth** (the name rhymes with both) stands out like a fortress on the north side of Dublin Bay. And a fortress is what it was to the Gaelic chieftains including, it's said, the legendary Finn Mac Cumhail (Finn

*T he name says it.*
*Sandycove near Dublin is a favourite local swimming place, weather permitting.*

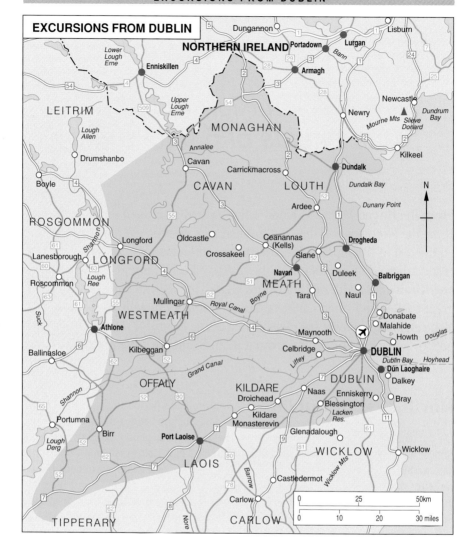

MaccCool). You'll see the commanding view if you take a walk to the top, or to the old lighthouse. Howth, with several restaurants and hotels, is a favourite week-end outing for Dublin families when the weather's fine, and the beautifully shel-tered double harbour is a haven for plea-sure craft. On a calm day excursion boats will take you out to the rocky and unin-habited island called **Ireland's Eye**. Like nearly every other island off the Irish coast, it was an early monastic settlement (Lambay in the distance to the north east was another). Again like the rest, it was sacked by the Vikings. A ruined chapel has been restored and there's also one of the string of Martello towers built along this coast against a possible Napoleonic invasion. Ireland's Eye is a bird sanctuary but visitors can stroll and picnic.

*H*owth is known for its yacht harbour, fish restaurants and trips out to the island called Ireland's Eye.

**Howth Castle**, a largely Georgian house, is occupied to this day by the St Lawrence family, descendants of the Norman lord who took the peninsula in battle with its Viking and Irish defenders. Some of the grounds are now open to the public: part of them has been turned into a golf club. The enthusiasts of the **Transport Museum Society** of Ireland use some of the big outbuildings of the castle to store and restore some of their treasures.

They specialize in working vehicles, so trams, buses and fire engines are packed nose to tail with armoured cars and humble horse-drawn bread vans. Among the prizes is an open-top tram that used to circle the Howth peninsula, now restored so it shines like a jewel. A 1925 Dublin tram, sold in 1949 to a convent, served as a classroom and extra sleeping accommodation until the Society acquired it, and visitors used to ride from Portrush to the Giant's Causeway in an open-sided rail car preserved here. Good explanations of the vehicles' history add to the interest: the museum is well worth a visit.

## Malahide

After Henry II landed in Ireland in 1171, he granted the land in these parts to

129

Richard Talbot, who quickly put up a defensive tower in the Norman style. It was extended and adapted over the centuries to create the present, unique **Malahide Castle**, which remained in possession of the Talbot family until the death of the last Lord Talbot. Then, in 1975, it was bought by Dublin County Council. A lot of the estate was turned into sports fields, but the wooded grounds and vast lawns make a fine park for Dubliners to walk or fly kites with their children.

There may be a short wait to see inside the castle: you have to join one of the guided parties. Tours start in the original tower, in the finest 16th-century panelled room surviving in Ireland, the almost

black wood panels including a Flemish carving of the crowning of the Virgin Mary. The 1812 fireplace with Egyptian motifs is typical of the fashion of its day. You pass into much loftier rooms added in the 18th century and furnished with Irish pieces of the same period. Here and elsewhere in the castle you'll see many pictures on loan from the **National Portrait Collection**, among them a Van Dyck of the children of Charles I, a Romney portrait of his wife, and others by Rubens, Kneller and Lely. A diversion upstairs takes you to the children's room, with dolls, an ancient tricycle and lace robes, and another bedroom with the actor David Garrick's bed. Downstairs again, the

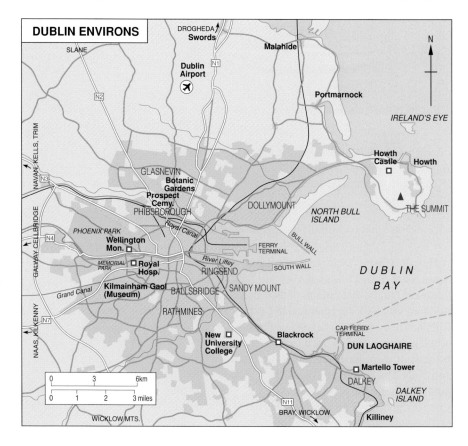

130

medieval **Great Hall**, complete with minstrels' gallery, is the only such hall left in its original form in an Irish house. Paintings include a huge *Battle of the Boyne* by Jan Wyck – the guide tells of 14 Talbots breakfasting here before riding out to meet their deaths in the battle. It's a far cry from that sad gathering to a recent occasion when EC prime ministers dined on Irish oysters, salmon and lamb. Among many portraits there's one, perhaps surprisingly, of Oliver Cromwell. Many of James Boswell's papers were discovered at Malahide, including memoirs of some of his travels with Dr Johnson.

The biggest attraction for children (and not only them) is in one of the large outbuildings. This houses the **Fry Model Railway**, one of the biggest and best setups you'll ever see. Beautiful O-gauge model trains from every era of Irish railway history move endlessly round the enormous network. Model Dublin trams and other vehicles join in, and model barges load barrels of Guinness at a miniature Victoria Quay on the Liffey as they did until 1960.

*M alahide Castle has been adapted and extended over the centuries. Inside, you can see all the stages of its growth.*

131

# North of Dublin

At **Newbridge Demesne** regional park, **Donabate**, you can see how a great country estate of the past could be virtually self-sufficient. The original house was built in 1737 but things were obviously going well for the Cobbe family because they were able to add a new wing 30 years later and double the size of the place. Full of fine furniture and eclectic family possessions collected on their travels, the house is open all year (but closed on Mondays). The ornate Red Drawing Room is a Georgian time capsule, the kitchens seem to have kept every device ever used for cooking in the last 300 years and fine carriages stand in the courtyard. The traditional farmyard, paddock and walled garden have been restored to full operation: there's a herd of Kerry cows, Connemara ponies, hens, ducks and geese and 148ha (370 acres) of pasture and parkland.

Heading north, if you have a few minutes to spare, turn off the main road to the village of **Lusk**. Although the houses are mostly new, it still occupies the land of a former monastery enclosure and you can make out the line of its walls in the present street pattern. The most striking feature is the fortified church tower, formed by adding a keep to a 10th-century round tower. This houses an exhibition on the medieval churches of the area and the fine 16th-century Barnewall effigy tomb.

North again and 10km (6 miles) inland near Naul, the mound of a passage tomb on **Fourknocks Hill** is small by comparison with the more famous Newgrange and Knowth, but superbly sited on a hilltop. The short entrance passage leads to a circular chamber larger than Newgrange's, with three alcoves. The roof has been rebuilt, but original stones decorated with zigzag and lozenge patterns are still in place round the walls inside after more than 5,000 years. (You will need to get the key from a cottage nearby.)

## Drogheda

An unassuming town dating from Viking times, Drogheda (*Droichead Atha*, 'the bridge of the ford') was built in the usual Viking fashion at the first crossing point of the River Boyne, and later walled and fortified by the Anglo-Normans. Former traffic problems have been eased by the building of a new bridge to the west of the town where the viaduct carrying the Dublin to Belfast railway line dominates the view.

Drogheda was the scene of a never-to-be-forgotten, or forgiven, massacre in 1649. Soon after his arrival in Ireland, bent on punishing those who had backed the Royalist cause, Oliver Cromwell and his army besieged the town. When the walls were at last breached, some 2,000 people (by Cromwell's own admission) were butchered. Most of the survivors were transported to work as virtual slaves on the sugar plantations of Barbados. The Lord Protector hoped by these horrors to dissuade other towns in Ireland from defying him. In some cases it worked: others such as Wexford were not deterred and suffered a similar fate.

The chief relic of the defences which faced Cromwell is the twin-tower **St Lawrence's Gate**, not in fact part of the wall but the 13th-century barbican which stood in front of it. Don't confuse Drogheda's two St Peter's churches. The Church of Ireland St Peter's in Fair Street, which is mainly 18th-century, has notable rococo plaster and interesting tombs. In the Gothic revival **Catholic St Peter's** in West Street, the embalmed head and a vertebra of St Oliver Plunkett are displayed in a gold and glass case. He was the Archbishop of Armagh who was hanged in London in 1681 in the aftermath of a so-called 'Popish Plot', and canonized in 1975. Also preserved in the church is the forbidding door of the cell in Newgate Prison where he was held before his execution.

*St Lawrence's Gate, Drogheda, is one of the few vestiges of the town's defences which held out, for a while, against Cromwell.*

South of the Boyne, the Normans built their castle on Millmount, an ancient mound which probably conceals a prehistoric tomb. The tower which stands there now dates mainly from the 18th century, along with the houses of the barrack square below it to the west. These have been cleverly adapted to become the home of the **Millmount Craft and Cultural Centre**, and the excellent local **museum**.

## Monasterboice and Mellifont

Two remarkable sites are found just north of Drogheda, one on each side of the main road to Dundalk and the Northern Ireland border. To the east, St Buithe's Abbey at **Monasterboice** was an early 6th-century foundation. The remains now include a high round tower with a broken top and the ruins of two later churches, surrounded like many such sites by modern graves. If this were all, few would turn aside to see. Monasterboice also has three celebrated 9th- or 10th-century **high crosses**. Arguably the masterpiece among all the surviving works of the Irish stone carvers, the stately **Muiredach's Cross** is covered with Old and New Testamant scenes. It is over 5m (17ft) tall with a top carved to look like a church or perhaps a reliquary. The details of the sculpted panels are remarkably preserved. The hub of the wheel on the west-facing side depicts the Crucifixion and the lowermost panel shows the arrest of Christ in the garden of Gethsemane. On the east, the central scene is the Last Judgement and the four panels below show, starting from the bottom: Adam and Eve (left) and Cain and Abel; David and Goliath and Saul with Jonathan; Moses striking the rock, watched by the Israelites; and the Virgin Mary with the infant Christ receiving the gifts from the Three Kings.

Another fine cross to the west is even taller at over 6m (20ft), although unlike Muiredach's Cross it isn't a monolith but made of three pieces. Again, carved panels of biblical scenes and abstract motifs cover most of the faces but there's been much greater weathering. Paradoxically, they look clearer if you don't stand too close. A simpler cross to the north stands next to a sundial marking the times of the monastic daily routine.

It seems beyond belief that the two finest crosses can have stood undamaged

*One of the finest of all the high crosses of Ireland, the 10th-century Muiredach's Cross at Monasterboice is carved with biblical scenes.*

in what is now a modest country graveyard for 1,000 years, while battles raged and iconoclasts did their worst. The freshness of the carvings on Muireadach's Cross might indicate that it at least has been under cover, perhaps even concealed, for part of that time.

Standing in a tranquil valley west of Drogheda, **Mellifont Abbey** was the earliest Cistercian monastery in Ireland. Dating from 1142, it was to become the mother house of a host of Cistercian foundations in all parts of the island. But its position within the Pale meant that suppression at the time of the Reformation was immediate and complete, unlike some of the others in the far west. The main features now are a gatehouse, a fragment of restored cloister and the pretty lavabo. This, the monk's washhouse, preserves five of its eight sides with their semicircular arches still standing. The five-storey medieval gatehouse is all that's left of what would have been a virtual city wall right around the enclosure. (The only monastic site in Ireland which still has a complete wall is at Kells, the one in County Kilkenny, see page 166.)

## The Boyne Valley

The placid Boyne is far from being the most impressive of Ireland's rivers, but its significance in her history is unrivalled. The region is not as rainy, boggy or mountainous as the rest of the island, so it attracted early settlement. Judging by the scale of prehistoric remains, it supported a big population. Facing east where most incursions came from, the valley acted as a road for immigrants and invaders. It became the axis of the fertile Pale stretching from Dublin to Dundalk, the heart of

Anglo-Norman power. Later, the English clung on when the rest of the country became largely a no-go area for them in the 15th century. And the **Battle of the Boyne** in 1690 was one of the decisive actions of the 'War of the Kings' which assured the Protestant ascendancy for generations (see page 52). The date was 1 July (12 July by the modern calendar, when the anniversary is celebrated by the Protestants of Northern Ireland). The two sides met at the river crossing about 6km (4 miles) west of Drogheda near Oldgrange. James II had drawn up his Irish and French forces, some 25,000 strong, on the southern bank. William's British, Dutch, German, Danish, Irish Protestant and French Huguenot army of 36,000 occupied the north bank. The viewing point signposted there today is the same one their commanders used before the battle.

The course of history was nearly altered the previous day when William was hit by an Irish shot, but it was only a flesh wound. 'It's well it came no nearer', was his laconic response. Next day, he led the assault on the ford with troops from Enniskillen. The fighting was hectic and evenly balanced and William's marshal, the Duke of Schomberg, was killed during a counter-attack by Irish cavalry. Meanwhile, however, detachments of the Protestant army had crossed the Boyne to the east and west of the main engagement. In danger of being outflanked, the Jacobite forces fell back in disarray and retreated beyond the Shannon. James fled and took ship for France.

## Megalithic Monuments

Concentrated into a few square miles west of Drogheda, we have one of the best records left from prehistoric times in Europe. The **Boyne Valley Archaeological**

**Park**, or more romantically **Brugh Na Bóinne** is the collective name for over 30 important Neolithic and Early Bronze Age sites, ranging from massive Newgrange, Knowth and Dowth to many lesser mounds and tombs. Their scale and numbers are evidence of powerful leaders and strong social organization. Clearly the valley supported an advanced civilization.

---

### A WORD ON DATES

With the advent of radio-carbon dating a few decades ago, it seemed that the dates of many prehistoric sites could be pinned down with only a small percentage of doubt.

Then a new method of dating became available, from the study of the patterns of tree-rings in timber caused by seasonal growth and variations from year to year. Ireland was an almost perfect place for this technique of dendrochronology, because of the excellent state of preservation of ancient oak in peat bogs. By looking at older and older samples with overlapping life-spans, it has been possible to make a continuous history of the patterns back through more than 7,000 years!

Now although there are no traces of timber to be found in most very old sites, it is still possible to check one dating system against the other. The key is to take a piece of timber with rings *known* from their pattern to have been laid down at a particular time, for example 3000 BC. Then, a radio-carbon test is done on that piece. Suppose it comes up with a date of about 2500 BC (plus or minus a margin of error). After many such results, the assumption is that the dates given by radio-carbon tests are too 'young'. The difference of 500 years in the example quoted is roughly what is actually found. For later dates the difference becomes less (about 100 years for dates around 700 BC, for example). In this book, we have quoted dates corrected from tree-ring studies where available.

---

If you're impressed by the distant sight of a great dome-topped cylindrical hill with a shining white wall, think what the effect might have been on a visitor 5,000 years ago. The Neolithic passage grave of **Newgrange** close to the north bank of the Boyne averages over 80m (263ft) across and stands up to 10m (33ft) high. Tens of thousands of tonnes of earth must have been moved in its construction. Right in the heart of it all, the cruciform burial chamber is reached by a 19m- (62ft-) long **passage**, the entrance guarded by a huge stone carved with spiral whorls and lozenges. Then as you duck and squeeze along the corridor you'll make out more designs: interconnecting swirls, wave patterns and triangles. Here and in the high **central chamber**, some of the decorated stones appear to have been carved before they were put in position, and may be older than the mound itself. A remarkable and special feature of Newgrange is the rectangular **roofbox**, an opening above the tunnel leading directly to the chamber.

This is so aligned that at the mid-winter solstice, the rays of the sun strike directly along it about an hour after sunrise, illuminating the chamber with a golden light. If you'd like to be there on 22 December, hoping against the odds for a clear sky, you'll need to reserve a place long in advance with the Office of Public Works. As a substitute on ordinary days when the guides have shepherded you into the chamber, they'll plunge it into darkness and then simulate the effect.

Up against the circumference of the mound is a ring of massive **kerbstones**, many of them carved with the same sorts of motif that you see inside the passage and chamber. A few standing stones

*The base of the great mound of Newgrange is ringed by massive kerbstones carved with mysterious patterns 5,000 years ago.*

136

survive from a separate circle that was put around the monument, perhaps some time in the Bronze Age. The forest of posts in front of Newgrange marks the position of a henge monument. For more background, the guides are well-informed and there's a museum and visitor centre near the entrance.

This is understandably one of the most visited sights in Ireland, and the very restricted access to the chamber means that you have to wait to join a party to get in. Try to come early in the day and avoid summer weekends and public holidays if you can.

**Knowth** (rhymes with growth), a mound even bigger the Newgrange, is the subject of an ambitious excavation which has been going on since 1962. Much of the site is still not open to visitors. Not just one but two burial chambers have been found, back to back near the middle of the mound. The entrance passage to the first

is 34m (114ft) long: the other even longer at 40m (130ft) long and so low that it seems unlikely there will ever be public access. Although you can't go inside the main tombs, Knowth is still worth a visit if you have any interest in prehistory. About twenty smaller passage tombs cluster close to the big mound like small mushrooms around a giant one, and some of these have been restored. Best of all, you can see many of the rock carvings on the kerbstones, the most prolific and varied of their period (about 3000 BC) to be found anywhere in the world.

Displays next to the entrance show how Knowth might have looked at various periods in its history, up to the time when the Normans naturally built on top of the great mound, ready-made for them.

Until it is declared safe again for visits, you can only see **Dowth**, the third great mound of the Boyne Valley, from the nearby road. Like Knowth, it contains two passage graves, here with entrances facing west and south west, and it too is ringed by a kerb of large stones. Dug too long ago for expert techniques to be applied, it is admitted by today's archaeologists to be a 'mess'. Until a lot more work is done, there is a danger that the entrance tunnels may collapse, and the site is closed.

The crossroads at **Slane** – all that most drivers hurrying through on the N2 ever see of the place – are notable for the four matching Georgian houses built diagonally across the corners. **Slane Castle** had built up something of a reputation for its restaurant and disco when it was sadly destroyed in a 1992 fire. The grounds are still the occasional venue for rock concerts, at the invitation of the owner, Lord Mount Charles. North east of the crossroads, you can climb the Hill of Slane for the views. You'll also be following in the

---

**WAS IT REALLY LIKE THAT?**

During the excavations at Newgrange, many pieces of glistening white quartz and some big smooth pebbles were found in a line of deposits on either side of the entrance. The quartz has been shown to come from County Wicklow, south of Dublin, and the pebbles from the beaches of County Down, away to the north. Archaeologists decided that this side of Newgrange must have been faced with the quartz, interspersed with the pebbles in a geometrical arrangement. So when the mound was restored after the dig, it was given the present striking – and controversial – appearance. Some insist that it must have looked something like this: others regard the façade as speculative. Outraged opponents liken it to Saddam Hussein's wholesale rebuilding of Babylon according to his own grandiose ideas.

*The Neolithic stone carvings at Loughcrew probably meant something significant, but whatever it was seems likely to remain forever a mystery.*

steps of St Patrick who lit a fire on the hilltop at Easter in 433 to launch his mission in this part of Ireland.

**Kells** bears one of the best-known place names in Ireland, thanks to the famous *Book of Kells*, the sumptuously decorated manuscript of the Gospels produced around the year 800 and now on display in Trinity College Library, Dublin. So it's odd that only the Irish name of *Ceanannas* is given on most road signs, and some maps. Not much is left of the Kells monastery buildings now but there's a **high cross** in the town centre with unusual carvings of deer, two figures wrestling and soldiers with horses. Its top and wheel are

broken – according to tradition it was used as gallows during retributions for the 1798 rising.

You will find more Celtic crosses in the churchyard at the top of town. The best, with particularly fine organic designs derived from Viking art, stands near the 11th-century **round tower** (itself unusual for having five upper windows, each looking towards one of the former town gates). So that those who come expecting to see the famous book won't be too disappointed, there's a good facsimile in the church. Across the street nearby, **St Columba's House** remarkably preserves the structure of a 9th-century church of the high pitched roof type, like Cormac's Chapel at Cashel or St Kevin's 'Kitchen' at Glendalough.

Those with a taste for hilltop tombs should head north west from Kells towards Cavan, turning left after 16km (10 miles), following the signs to **Loughcrew**. Narrow lanes though pretty country lead to the slopes of *Sliabh na Cailli* (spellings vary). Two easily accessible 250m (about 800ft) summits are crowned with a variety of Neolithic cairns: one with stones carved strikingly in ray patterns. The entrances to the most important burial chambers are locked, but the keys can be obtained from a local cottage: directions for finding it are given on a sign by the road at the start of the main path to the cairns.

The markings on the stones and the different alignments of the tombs have led to theories that the whole group acted as a sort of calendar to identify days of the year which were important for religious or agricultural reasons – or both.

Loughcrew itself was the birthplace of St Oliver Plunkett in 1625 (see Drogheda, page 132). North of the Kells–Cavan road, Cuilcagh House was the home of the Sheridan family. Jonathan Swift, a guest here, wrote most of *Gulliver's Travels* during a stay in 1726 and the Dublin-born playwright Richard Brinsley Sheridan (author of *The School for Scandal*) spent part of his childhood at the house.

South east of the busy Boyne Valley town of Navan, the **Hill of Tara** stands over 150m (500ft) above the plain. A Stone Age, Bronze Age and Iron Age site, at various times fortified, it was later the capital of the kings of Tara or Meath and the traditional place where the High Kings of Ireland were crowned. It may have been occupied from about 500 BC to AD 800, with occasional ceremonial use right up to the time of the Anglo-Norman invasions. A rough stone pillar may mark the coronation spot, and a monument honours the dead of the 1798 Rising. Daniel O'Connell (see page 199) symbolically chose Tara for one of his biggest meetings in the campaign for repeal of the Act of Union.

The hill must once have been crowded with wood, thatch and wattle-and-daub buildings (the old tales say 'palaces' but that's a relative term). Nothing of course remains, although traces of their foundations have been identified among the indentations and ridges on the ground. The Mound of the Hostages is better defined; it's the biggest of the mounds and was originally a passage tomb contemporary with Newgrange and Knowth. It was later used for many Bronze Age burials, but all of this happened long before Tara's heyday as recounted in Gaelic legend. Overlapping rings of earthworks and mounds dug up in the distant past make the Hill of Tara a confused and confusing site, and signs like bus stops planted here and there bear debatable names. One solution is just to enjoy the atmosphere, the walk and the views without trying too hard to work out what was what.

The quiet town of **Trim** is dominated – it would have every excuse for being overwhelmed – by the massive remains of its  castle, Augustinian monastery and other impressive ruins. The **Castle** guarding a ford of the slow-moving River Boyne was built early in the Norman period by Walter de Lacy, son of Hugh who accompanied Strongbow to Ireland. The walls punctuated by strong semi-circular towers, the great square keep and main gate are well preserved, but most of the area inside the walls is grass. As long as you keep out of the way of the practising golfers, you're free to stroll down to the river.

Across the river, the 'Yellow Steeple' is the tall remnant of a tower of the 13th-century St Mary's Abbey. You'll appreciate the reason for the name if you're lucky enough to see it lit by the evening sun. Next to it, the much altered 15th-century manor house called **Talbot's**

**Castle** was bought by Jonathan Swift's friend 'Stella' in 1717 (see page 109): he may indeed have paid for it. He had earlier been rector at nearby Laracor, when she was installed in a house in the village. However, when he became Dean of St Patrick's, Trim was too far from Dublin for easy meetings. He bought Talbot's Castle from her and then disposed of it to the church. Later a school, it was attended by Arthur Wesley (the name was later magnified into Wellesley), the future Duke of Wellington. As a young man, he held the Trim seat in the Irish parliament.

# West of Dublin

**Castletown House**, **Celbridge**, the greatest and grandest 18th-century house in Ireland, was built in the 1720s for William Conolly, Speaker of the Irish House of Commons. Land deals had made him the richest man in the country and he was not shy about demonstrating the fact. Alessandro Galilei designed the façade of the main house to look like a 16th-century Italian palace, but the young Irish architect Edward Lovett Pearce supervised the building work. He added the Palladian colonnades and pavilions, the first large-scale use of the style in Ireland and much copied: the house is one of several with a claim to have inspired the Irish-born James Hoban's plans for the White House in Washington DC. Pearce himself went on to design the colonnaded Irish Parlia-

ment building in Dublin which became the Bank of Ireland (see page 97).

Castletown stayed in the Conolly family (a man marrying a Conolly heiress being understandably willing to change his name to hers) until 1965. Then, with a degree of philistinism which now seems unthinkable, a property developer bought the house with the intention of knocking it down. The contents were sold off separately and scattered. In the nick of

*N*ow used only by pleasure craft or for fishing, the Grand Canal goes from Dublin through the heart of Ireland.

time the house was saved by Desmond Guinness (whose venerated ancestor Arthur was born in Celbridge) and became for a while the headquarters of the Irish Georgian Society. Now it is in the care of a charitable foundation which makes it available for dinners, weddings or concerts to help pay for the daunting cost of upkeep. Some of the furniture and many of the original pictures have been bought back or lent by their owners.

Speaker Conolly died in 1729, unfortunately before his palace was completed, and his widow, although employing a huge total of 180 servants, left it in that state. They had no children and it was only when a great nephew Tom Conolly inherited Castletown and married the 15-year-old Lady Louisa Lennox in 1758 that work was renewed. The interior of the house largely reflects her influence over the next 30 years.

The classical entrance hall leads to the extraordinary **staircase hall**. The cantilevered stairs are an engineering feat, set against all-white baroque plasterwork in which the gory painting of a boar hunt by De Vos is something of a shock. Every room has its story. The **State Bedroom** where Speaker Conolly had planned to receive his guests while reclining above them on a high bed was later used for meetings by Lord Edward Fitzgerald, one of the leaders of the 1798 United Irishmen's revolt. The **Print Room**, where ladies pasted their favourite illustrations to the white walls, is a unique survival in Ireland. And the magnificent **Long Gallery** was decorated in the style of Pompeii, with Venetian glass chandeliers, after Lady Louisa's visit to Italy in the 1770s. Her portrait is a copy of the Reynolds now at Harvard. Look in the Blue (visitors') Bedroom for the enchanting portraits painted by 20th-century Irish artist Harriet Hoxley Townsend.

From the Long Gallery windows, you'll be able to look 3km (2 miles) across fields and woods to the north where once were formal gardens to a huge **obelisk** standing on arches and 43m (140ft) high. Built in 1740, it commemorates Speaker Conolly and like many such 'follies' in Ireland, its construction helped to employ the poor during hard times. It's possible to walk or drive to the obelisk, but another weird edifice, the ziggurat-like 'Wonderful Barn' to the east is only visible from the road at nearby Leixlip.

To the north west, **Maynooth** retains the keep and some of the outerworks of its 12th-century Norman castle, a Fitzgerald stronghold for most of the next five centuries. Nearby is the entrance to St Patrick's College, founded in 1795 for training the Catholic priesthood. (The British government saw this as preferable to the previous practice of going to continental schools and picking up revolutionary ideas, but Maynooth too became a cradle of Nationalism.) Now the college is a general university. On the minor roads between Celbridge and Naas (rhymes with 'pace'), hump-back bridges cross the **Grand Canal**, on its way west from Dublin to the Shannon. This section was built in the 1780s but ceased to carry any commercial traffic by 1960. As you'll see, it's open for fishing and cruising: boats can be hired at several points in the area and just west of Sallins, a fine aqueduct takes the canal over the River Liffey.

# Horse Country

Back on the main road west, past Newbridge, you'll suddenly emerge into the green expanses of **The Curragh**, pasture and training area – formerly for the British Army (see page 55), now for the Irish Army, and, above all, for racehorses. A huge grandstand hovers like a mirage in the mist, empty and silent most of the year, but just imagine the scene at the finish of the Irish Derby. Run in May or June, this is one of Europe's richest races.

The quiet little town of **Kildare** is transformed whenever there's a race meeting. The cathedral, probably on the site of a convent founded by St Bridget, has been destroyed and rebuilt many times. Its square tower looks like a castle keep, no doubt for good reason. The old round tower next to it has lost its original top and gained some non-authentic battlements, but it is one of the few that you may be able to climb, if someone is there to let you in. The posted opening hours don't necessarily apply.

The **Irish National Stud** at Tully on the outskirts of Kildare looks like an expensive country club or health farm, but this one is exclusively for horses. Humans are welcome to pay a visit though, and even if you know nothing of horses and regard both ends of them as dangerous, you'll be impressed. Glossy stallions worth millions run up and down the smooth green paddocks and their accommodation blocks rival the best motels.

From February to June, the big attraction is the foaling unit, where you can look in at the latest arrivals, perhaps born just a few hours earlier. You'll be unlikely to see an actual birth – they usually happen between 9pm and 2am – but in one of the stables you can see one in a remarkable video, from the moment the foal's front feet begin to emerge, to its shaky attempts to stand upright only a hour or so later, walking to the paddock when only a day or two old and taking a joyous first gallop, already moving like a racehorse. In the adjoining intensive care unit sick or premature foals can be looked after 24 hours a day. The same yard houses a fully-equipped saddlery workshop where there's often a saddler at work. Next door you might find a farrier heating and hammering horseshoes or giving one of the residents or visitors some hoof care.

The **Horse Museum** at the National Stud traces the evolution of the horse and the history of the partnership of horses and humans, in agriculture, transport, warfare and of course racing. Equine genealogies trace the ancestry of famous winners back to one of the three stallions from Arabia or Turkey from whom all racehorses today are thought to be descended.

The story of the Stud began in 1900 when the eccentric Colonel Hall-Walker bought a farm at Tully to breed horses. He believed the alignment of the moon and stars at the moment of birth predicted racing performance and if he thought a foal's horoscope looked unfavourable, he would sell it. His stables all had big skylights to let in the maximum astrological influences: today's stallion boxes at the Stud preserve the design feature, if not the thinking behind it. For whatever reason, the colonel was highly successful. In 1915, he suddenly decided to give the Stud to the British government. Becoming the British National Stud, it stayed here right through Irish independence and up to 1943 when the property was handed over to Ireland.

The **Japanese Garden** next to the Stud, created for Colonel Hill-Walker at the beginning of the 20th century, is one of the best of its kind outside Japan. You can enjoy it on several levels: as a spectacle of colour and design; for the variety of flowers and shrubs; or as an allegory of the stages of human life from the Cave of Birth to the Hill of Mourning and Gateway to Eternity. (A map and leaflet from the information desk will help you with the interpretation.)

# South West of Dublin

Whether you're making an excursion from Dublin or heading directly for the south coast, to Waterford or Cork, there's a choice of routes, each with sights to see along the way. The rural racecourse at **Punchestown** (some way from the village) sleeps peacefully for most of the year but the April meeting is one of Ireland's big sporting and social events. Local children have a holiday from school, and the countryside is a sea of brilliant yellow gorse flowers. In a field next to the main gate, a sharply pointed prehistoric

**standing stone** looks like a huge spear head. Made of granite and 7m (23ft) high, it is the tallest in Ireland.

Just beyond the nearby village of Blessington, **Russborough House** is a fine 18th-century Palladian mansion with famously exuberant plasterwork. Bought by Sir Alfred Beit (heir to a mining fortune), it's filled with furnishings and art from the Beit Collection. The house gained an unwanted place in the news in 1974 when some of the most valuable paintings were stolen in a raid organized by Dr Bridget Rose Dugdale to raise funds for the IRA. They were soon retrieved, although some were taken again in a 1986 theft (apparently non-political this time) of 18 pictures. Most of these, including a priceless Vermeer, *Lady Writing a Letter*, have also been recovered. Some prime pictures have been donated to the National Gallery in Dublin but you can still see major works by French, Italian and Dutch masters and portraits by Reynolds and Gainsborough among many others. Check up on the visiting times before setting off (tel. 045-65239): Russborough is generally open at weekends from Easter to October, and daily in July, August and September. Opposite the house, Blessington Lake is a reservoir open for all sorts of watersports.

**Ballitore**, on the road to Carlow, was an 18th-century settlement set up by Yorkshire Quakers. The political thinker Edmund Burke went to their school from the age of 11 to 14. The village museum tells the history of the Quakers in Ireland and gives you an idea of the way they lived. On the same road, **Castledermot** sprawls through an area of extensive ruins, including a 9th-century monastery with high crosses and an early round tower. A 12th-century Romanesque door survives from an old church, but instead of being incorporated in the modern church on the site, it stands free and is merely echoed in the new building. At the edge of the Pale, **Carlow Town** (in the small county of the same name) was an Anglo-Norman

*D*alkey Island, now a bird sanctuary, with another of the chain of Martello towers built to fend off a possible Napoleonic invasion.

fortress and the scene of frequent raids and sieges. The castle is a poor relic now, long abandoned, but you can learn about the area's turbulent history in the local museum. About 3km (2 miles) east of Carlow on the road to Killerrig, look across the fields to the south for the the the giant **Brownshill Dolmen**, largest of its kind in Ireland and perhaps Europe. The mass of the capstone has been calculated at over 100 tonnes. Don't march straight across the field: a special path leads to the dolmen from a point just along the road.

## South of Dublin

Almost adjoining Dún Laoghaire on the south side of Dublin Bay, **Sandycove** has become a commuter suburb of Dublin but still feels like the seaside village it was. The birthplace of Roger Casement (see page 205), its fame now derives from a very brief visit by James Joyce in 1904. At the invitation of the poet Oliver St John Gogarty, Joyce was staying in the Martello tower (one of many built along the coast against a possible French land-

ing during the Napoleonic wars). He understandably left in a hurry after another guest and his host fired off a gun inside the tower following a night's drinking. The few days he spent there would scarcely justify the name of Joyce's Tower which became attached to it, but he made the tower the setting of the first scene in *Ulysses*, with Gogarty transformed into the character of 'Buck Mulligan', and his publisher Sylvia Beach set it up as a Joyce museum in 1962. At first the exhibits were sparse, but they have grown in number and significance over the years, with first editions of his books, the special edition of *Ulysses* illustrated by Matisse, copies of letters between Joyce and Nora Bar-

nacle, his guitar and walking stick, photographs and curios, such as a tie he gave to Samuel Beckett.

**Forty-Foot Hole** next to the tower is neither 40 feet deep, nor wide: it may have been named after the British regiment (the 40th Foot) who were once stationed here. It's a sheltered cove used by hardy swimmers. Formerly only male and mostly nude, now they are still mostly male and, despite signs calling for a cover-up, include some traditionalists holding out against such prudery.

At the attractive little resort of **Dalkey** pronounced 'Dawky'), Dublin Bay ends and the coast turns south. Houses are scattered up the steep hill behind the town, keeping the walking part of the population fit. Direction signs and a plaque outside mark George Bernard Shaw's boyhood home on the hill, Torca Cottage. A private house which you can't visit, it might charitably be called unassuming, apart from the view, and that's even better from the adjoining Killiney park on the hilltop. Offshore, you can see Dalkey Island, with a bird sanctuary, the usual ancient monastic ruins and Martello tower.

Next down the coast, **Bray** has a little harbour where you can hire a boat for some excellent offshore fishing. The town itself is messy and rundown, an unexciting resort with seaside hotels and holiday apartments, and is primarily a commuter dormitory for Dublin.

*The Martello tower at Sandycove is now a James Joyce museum with a growing collection of objects donated by his admirers, although he only spent a few days there.*

*T*he sea cliffs can be a
rock garden, providing a vivid
splash of colour to delight the eye.

The road inland leads to the chocolate-box picturesque village of **Enniskerry**. It was never more than an appendage of **Powerscourt**, the great 18th-century house it grew up to serve. The house has been a shell since it was devastated by fire in 1974 but the gardens are a triumph of grand terraces, balustrades and statuary, borders and lawns. A flight of steps flanked by two superb winged horses stretches down to a lake and fountain, and all this tamed version of nature is contrasted against the scenery of the wild Wicklow Mountains. The highest waterfall in Ireland is 5km (3 miles) to the south, reached by a woodland walk or from the road.

# Historic Towns and Romantic Ruined Abbeys

With marginally more sunshine and less rain than the rest of Ireland, the south-eastern counties are agreeable, accessible and just as green. The varied landscapes of placid rivers and pastures, long sandy beaches and rounded hills don't have quite the drama of the west. The layers of history are evident everywhere: the ancient monastic sites such as Jerpoint; the old ports of Wexford and Waterford built on Viking foundations; and picturesque inland towns which grew up around Norman castles. We cover the area county by county, but that may not correspond to your planned route. Consult the maps!

## County Wicklow

Filling the horizon south of Dublin, the dark shapes of the Wicklow Mountains looked like a menace to the city-dwellers in the old days. From the very beginning, the tribes in the hills had never been reconciled to the foreign presence. In countless raids and several major assaults they tried to throw the aliens out. Gradually their power to disrupt the life of the capital declined, and the tribes were forced or tricked into moving away to the west, but

*Hook Head Lighthouse has stood here since Norman times, marking the entrance to Waterford harbour.*

right up to the end of the 18th century 'rebels' and outlaws could hide here: there were no roads and only local experts could pick their way through the bogs.

Now, with only the weather to fear, the **Wicklow Mountains** are a magnet for walkers. A designated route, the Wicklow Way, links many of the beauty spots. The whole route might take a week or more to walk but you can pick out shorter sections: an information leaflet is available from Tourist Board offices. For a scenic drive from Dublin, take the R115 road through the Sally Gap or go via Blessington through the Wicklow Gap (R756). Either way will lead you to one of the most idyllic spots in Ireland.

### Glendalough

Walking or driving, you shouldn't miss

this hidden valley with two lakes (which gave the place its name), chosen by St Kevin in the 6th century as the site for his monastery. If he had any idea of escaping the outside world, he may have been disappointed. Glendalough became rich and famous and eventually attracted Viking raiders who looted it more than once. The monastery went into a decline after being wrecked by an army from Dublin in 1398, and the enforcement of the Reformation in the 16th century finished it off.

On arrival, you'll come first to the visitor centre. It's not essential to enter that way, but the photographs, displays and video are useful and well presented. Guided tours also start from here. Further along the road, you can still use the original gateway, the best preserved of any of its kind in Ireland. (If you go in through the visitor centre, be sure to come out this way.)

Glendalough is an extensive and complicated site, scattered with the ruins of seven churches. The nearest (to both entrances) is the roofless **Cathedral**, probably begun in the 9th century. Just down the slope is the still older oratory, labelled '**St Kevin's Kitchen** because the round bell-tower, an afterthought, looks like a

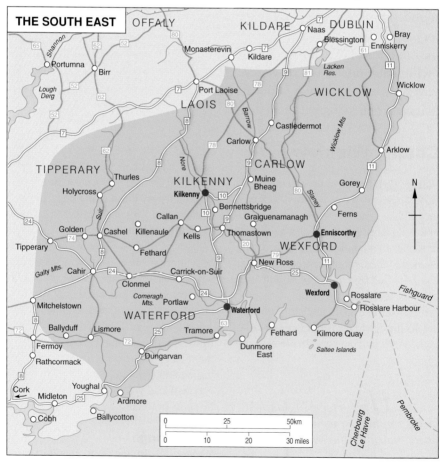

---

**NO PLACE TO HIDE**

Fanciful old theories about Egyptians and druids have been discarded, but the long debate about the purpose of the Irish round towers isn't over. Some think they were intended as places of refuge, during Viking raids for example, although most towers are later than the period of the Viking threat. Others hold that they were belfries built to show off church power, like cathedral towers and spires. Perhaps they *were* built as belfries, but doorways high above the ground back up the refuge theory, even if such a chimney-like structure scarcely looks like a sensible place to be when raiders are looting and burning. Church records tell of disasters such as happened at Monasterboice, when those who retreated up the tower perished in a fire, together with all the books and treasures they had taken with them.

---

chimney. The steeply pitched roofs of early churches such as this hide one or more upper rooms above their barrel-vaulted ceilings. The separate **Round Tower** was added much later, but is such a symbol of this and other great Irish monastic sites that Glendalough can hardly be imagined without it now.

*The tranquil valley of Glendalough, where St Kevin founded a monastery in the 6th century.*

Weather permitting, take the time to stroll along the south shore of the lower lake to the upper lake. An information centre for the **Wicklow Mountains National Park** which includes Glendalough stands between the two. Open in summer, it can give you details of walks in the area; some guided walks are arranged from here. A short climb up a signposted path through the woods leads to the traditional site of St Kevin's Cell, but only a ring of stone foundations remains. Continue up the main path nearby for a fine view of the whole valley. On a cliff above the upper lake, 'St Kevin's Bed' is a cave that cannot be reached by walking, and has no regular boat service – the authorities decided the precipitous spot was too dangerous.

Down the wooded valley of the Avonmore and through the village of Rathdrum, you'll reach the birthplace and home of one of Ireland's heroes. Set in a beautiful forest park and its own landscaped gardens, **Avondale House** is restored to the decor (and bold colours) of the 1850s, when Charles Stewart Parnell was growing up here, and furnished in the style of his time. It was opened as a museum to

## HOME RULER

Charles Stewart Parnell (1846-91) was a Protestant landowner who entered the British parliament in 1874. A charismatic campaigner for the restoration of self-government, he was soon elected to head the Irish Home Rule League party in the House of Commons. At the same time, he joined up with the Fenian Michael Davitt to fight for the rights of tenant farmers who faced bankruptcy and eviction every time prices fell or crops failed. The Land League they organized gained mass support and developed the tactic of ostracizing vicious and unfair landlords and their agents, called the 'boycott' after a notable example (see page 250). A general election in 1880 confirmed Parnell as the leader of a militant Irish party. Gladstone as the new prime minister went some way towards meeting the Land League's demands, but not far enough. The League continued its agitation, and its leaders were arrested, Parnell spending several months in Kilmainham jail. Gladstone implemented the concessions, and more followed: the land battle was on the way to being won. Yet Parnell saw this only as a first step in the struggle for Irish home rule. In the 1885 election his party won almost all the Irish seats. Gladstone saw this as evidence of 'the fixed desire of a nation', a just cause which he too would now support. He introduced a Home Rule Bill, but it split the ruling Liberal Party, the defectors joining the opposition to defeat the measure.

Parnell fought on, gaining increasing respect in Britain as well as overwhelming support in Ireland. Then in November 1890 came disaster, in the shape of a revelation in the divorce court of Parnell's adultery with the wife of Captain O'Shea, a former colleague in the Home Rule party. Some in Ireland, and many in the Liberal Party whose backing was vital, turned against him. Gladstone asked him to stand down as a temporary measure, to avoid injury to the cause, but Parnell refused, splitting his own party. When Kitty O'Shea's divorce came through, they married, but soon after, on 6 October 1891, in the midst of his struggle to retain the leadership, he died.

The Home Rule cause was damaged, but Gladstone did not give up. In 1893 at the age of 84 he brought the issue before the House of Commons again, and this time the bill was passed, only to be defeated in the House of Lords. What might have happened if Parnell had not fallen? Could he have achieved self government for all Ireland? It's one of the many "If onlys" of modern Irish history.

honour the memory of Parnell in 1991, the centenary of his death. Press cuttings, posters, documents and tributes are on display and a video history of his life is screened. Most moving are his poems to Kitty O'Shea, and their wedding ring which he fashioned from gold mined on the Avondale estate.

Along the pretty valley on the way to Avoca and Woodenbridge, the hillsides have been churned up by the old gold mines. **Avoca** is a long-established weaving village producing colourful wool fabrics – you can see the weavers working at hand looms. The road reaches the coast at **Arklow**, a port since Viking times and still a boat-building centre. If you are heading back to Dublin up the coast, you can take a look at the equally old but nondescript county town of Wicklow, but our route takes us south.

*E*ndless sands along the coast of County Wicklow, with only the birds to enjoy them for most of the year.

# County Wexford

The south-eastern corner of Ireland attracts a lot of local holiday-makers who head for the sandy beaches and dunes: Courtown is a favourite resort. Easy-going Wexford Town becomes a magnet for music lovers at festival time, and Rosslare Harbour sees a constant flow of visitors coming off the ferries from Britain and France. Too often they rush out of the county and miss its highlights.

## Ferns

On the road into Wexford from the north, this was once the capital of Leinster and a stronghold of Dermot MacMorrough, the man who invited the Normans to Ireland and then conveniently died. The round tower and chapel of the impressive 13th-century castle that the invaders built still stand today. In fact, the whole town is strewn with the ruins of a thousand years, the cycle of destruction and rebuilding all too evident. Even the most ardent fans of history in stone will get a surfeit here.

## Enniscorthy

The rivers of Ireland were her best roads, almost until modern times. River ports were built at the points where the larger vessels could get no further upstream and had to unload. The settlement then became the obvious place to build a bridge, and a castle to defend it. Enniscorthy on the River Slaney is a perfect example.

It's a short drive or a vigorous walk to the top of **Vinegar Hill**, across the river from the town and castle. The panoramic view alone would make it worth while, but history turns this into a place of pilgrimage. For the hilltop was the main encampment of the United Irishmen in the

1798 Rising, and the scene of the greatest although not the last battle of that campaign. Hundreds were killed by a much larger government force, although some were able to slip away to fight another day. The stump of the windmill which served as a lookout post still stands near the rocky summit, and a new memorial of

engraved stones gives a detailed explanation of the events.

Back in the town, the four-towered **castle** guarding the river crossing is now the county museum, with relics of the 1798 battle, sections on folk life and voluptuous figureheads of ships which foundered on the Wexford coast.

*At Enniscorthy, County Wexford, a new bridge shares the traffic with the old. The castle which guarded the river crossing is now the local museum.*

155

## Wexford Town (*Loch Garman*)

It's clear why the location appealed to the Vikings, with its big, almost land-locked harbour linked to the wide estuary of the River Slaney. The vanguard of the Norman invasions landed not far away at Bannow Bay and Wexford was the first town they captured. Their first fortification in Ireland was built on the hill above the river estuary. As an English garrison town it was ringed by walls and towers, and held out briefly against Cromwell in 1649, despite the example he had just made of Drogheda for daring to do the same. Here too, when his forces took the town, he ordered a massacre of the defenders.

The long **main quay** is only used by fishing boats and pleasure craft now: the harbour is too shallow for today's bigger ships. The line of seafront houses is interrupted by the curve of **Crescent Quay**, centred on a statue of John Barry, a local man who became first commodore of the US Navy in the American War of Independence. In the middle of the crescent, you'll find the tourist information office in a fine Georgian house. Narrow streets lead up to the town behind, not much more than one long twisting street, roughly parallel to the quays. It's rather like a friendly village, with small old-world shops and innumerable pubs and bars. Among the limited landmarks, a tower survives from the town wall's old west gate. Selskar Abbey at the northern end of town, inland from the railway station, is just a shell.

This may seem an unlikely place for it, but the annual International **Opera Festival** in October is known as one of the most creative and enjoyable on the circuit, for audiences and artists alike. Every space the small town can offer for accommodation and performances has to be pressed into service.

### Near Wexford

Close to the main road north (N11), the **Irish National Heritage Park** at **Ferrycarrig** features full-sized replicas of ancient sites. Collect a map from the reception desk and you can move through

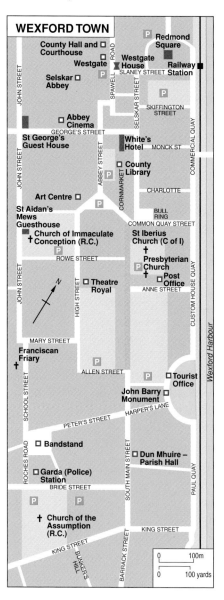

WEXFORD TOWN

County Hall and Courthouse
Westgate
Selskar Abbey
Abbey Cinema
St George's Guest House
Art Centre
St Aidan's Mews Guesthouse
Church of Immaculate Conception (R.C.)
Theatre Royal
Franciscan Friary
Bandstand
Garda (Police) Station
Church of the Assumption (R.C.)

JOHN STREET
SPAWELL ROAD
GEORGE'S STREET
ABBEY STREET
CORNMARKET
ROWE STREET
HIGH STREET
MARY STREET
ALLEN STREET
SCHOOL STREET
ROCHES ROAD
PETER'S STREET
KING STREET
BUNKER'S HILL
BARRACK STREET

Redmond Square
Westgate House
Railway Station
SLANEY STREET
SELSKAR STREET
SKIFFINGTON STREET
White's Hotel
MONCK ST
COMMERCIAL QUAY
County Library
CHARLOTTE
BULL RING
COMMON QUAY STREET
St Iberius Church (C of I)
Presbyterian Church
Post Office
ANNE STREET
Tourist Office
John Barry Monument
HARPER'S LANE
CUSTOM HOUSE QUAY
Dun Mhuire – Parish Hall
SOUTH MAIN STREET
PAUL QUAY
KING STREET
Wexford Harbour

0    100m
0    100 yards

156

*Looking out over Wexford harbour, the statue of John Barry, first commodore of the young U.S. Navy in the War of Independence.*

9,000 years of history, from the first Stone Age camp to tombs, a ringfort and a monastic site. The setting is something of a nature reserve, of swamp and woodland. A replica of a 9th-century horizontal water mill grinds flour beautifully. Back near the entrance, a thatched *crannóg* (lake dwelling) and a riverside Viking settlement and shipyard complete with a Viking longship start the second half of the tour. Visiting all the sites in the park involves about 2km (over a mile) of walking.

Widespread dismay and derision greeted the replica Norman motte and bailey on a prominent hilltop when it was painted brilliant white, although the experts cited historical evidence in support. Close by, a real Norman fortification has been excavated. It was probably the first in Ireland, built in 1169 by Robert FitzStephen. The round tower inside the old rampart is another replica, but one built in 1857 to honour the dead of the Crimean War. Walk to the end of the park for a view down to the 16th-century passage tower guarding the narrows of the River Slaney.

In the 19th century, mudflats on the north and south sides of Wexford Harbour were partially drained to provide rough grazing for cattle. Known by the unlovely name of the Slobs, they also attracted great numbers of migrating birds, especially several species of geese. Now, 190ha (470 acres) of the North Slob has become the **Wexford Wildfowl Reserve**. You can see dozens of species of waders, ducks and some geese at any time of year, including occasional rarer species. The greatest activity occurs from October to April, when spectacular numbers of geese and swans from more northern latitudes take up residence. Remarkably, these include more than one third of the world population of the Greenland White-fronted Goose; over 10,000 birds. Farmers often resent the way geese graze on their crops, but here, special fields of cereals are planted just for them.

South of Wexford beyond Murrintown, the early 19th-century neo-Gothic **Johnstown Castle** is a confection of fairy-tale towers and battlements, set in magnificent gardens and romantically reflected in an ornamental lake. You can wander at will in the grounds, looking at the walled garden, the hothouses and shrubberies. The house isn't open to visitors: it is scheduled to become the headquarters of the National Environmental Protection Agency and the estate is an agricultural research centre and working farm. Fine buildings round the old farmyard make an ideal home for the **Irish Agricultural Museum**, a superb collection of farm tools and machinery, country furniture, ingenious domestic inventions and intriguing bric à brac: almost anything to do with rural life is here. Replicas of the workshops of a blacksmith, cooper, wheelwright and saddler are fully and accurately equipped.

Down some narrow lanes but signposted off the road from Wexford to Rosslare Harbour, search out the fortified tower house dated 1451 at **Rathmacknee**. Although unrestored, it has sound walls and typically Irish stepped battlements like broken teeth. A later farmhouse nestles inside the bawm (walled enclosure) which makes a fine sheltered garden.

**Rosslare**'s holiday homes and hotels spread along the coast behind sand dunes and a long beach teeming with birdlife at dawn and dusk. The ferries from Fishguard, Pembroke, Le Havre and Cherbourg dock just along the coast at breezy **Rosslare Harbour**, which took over from Wexford when modern shipping called for a deepwater port. Plenty of bed-and-breakfast and hotel accommodation is available for late arrivals and those with early morning departures.

New arrivals tend to rush out of the area, either heading west to Waterford or up to Dublin. Not many discover the peninsulas pointing south and the convoluted coastline in between. The south-east corner is not particularly dramatic, but the thatched windmill at **Tacumshin** is a unique survivor – other mills have been rebuilt but this is the original. **Kilmore Quay**, on the south coast, is a charming little fishing village and harbour, home to an old lightship converted into a maritime museum. Trips are run to the offshore Saltee Islands, a sanctuary for seabirds and particularly active during nesting time in spring or early summer.

Further west, the sandy beach of Bannow Bay saw the landing of the Norman vanguard in 1169. They were followed the following year by another group of a hundred knights and archers who came ashore not far to the south at **Baginbun**. Although vastly outnumbered, they defeated a Norse and Irish force sent to expel them. When Strongbow landed soon afterwards with the main party, across the harbour at Passage East, the combined Norman army moved to assault the walls of Waterford.

*The holiday beach near Baginbun Head, where the second party of Norman invaders landed in 1170.*

## The Hook Peninsula

The southernmost point in County Wexford, Hook Head, actually marks the entrance to Waterford harbour. The building of the **Lighthouse** is credited to the first Normans: if so, it has stood for 800 years and ranks as Europe's oldest. What's more, an ancient tradition says that some sort of warning light has been maintained here for most of the last 1,500 years.

Nearby **Slade** is a quiet little fishing port: notice the old salthouses on the quay where seawater was evaporated to obtain salt. **Fethard**'s sheltered sandy beach and good fishing from shore or boat make it a favourite Irish holiday resort. Bannow, on the bay where the first Normans landed, was so silted up by shifting sands that it was abandoned long ago, although it continued to 'elect' two MPs until the demise of the Irish Parliament. So did tiny Fethard and several other 'rotten boroughs', which were thick on the ground in this area. **Tintern Abbey** (named after the Welsh original) was built on the orders of William the Marshal in about 1200, after he vowed to endow an abbey if he survived a particularly rough crossing of the Irish Sea. After the Reformation, it was granted to the Colclough family, who turned it into a fortified house. **Ballyhack Castle** has been restored and commercialized recently, putting on displays of costume, weapons and regalia.

If you have been exploring the Hook Head peninsula and want to head west to Waterford, there's no need to drive all the way north to New Ross to the first bridge over the River Barrow: a convenient and frequent car ferry runs between Ballyhack and Passage East. (As the latter name suggests, some kind of ferry has operated here since early times.)

Inland, up the Barrow, **New Ross** was once an important river port rivalling Waterford. Now it is rather rundown, but cruise boats ply the Barrow and its tributary the Nore, as well as making the trip to Waterford on the River Suir. They can even serve you lunch, tea or dinner on board. About 6km (4 miles) south of New Ross, the little village of **Dunganstown** is the ancestral home of President John F. Kennedy's family. The 240ha- (600 acre-) Kennedy Park and Arboretum was established in his memory, and many of the 4,500 species of trees and shrubs were donated by contributors all round the world. Not far south, near the banks of the Barrow, the 12th-century Cistercian **Dunbrody Abbey** is a big, impressive but plain ruin. The castle next to it sets out to attract visitors, with a complex yew hedge maze, pitch and putt course, tea shop and museum.

## County Waterford

Small but with a prosperous air, the county is defined by its rivers. The Suir (pronounced 'Shure') marks the northern and eastern border, and its sheltered estuary attracted both Viking and Norman landings. The fertile valley of the broad

*Reginald's Tower on the quayside at Waterford, built by the Normans, probably on Viking foundations.*

Blackwater flowing out of Cork makes up most of the west. Rounded uplands in the north hardly rate the title of mountain, but they make for good walking country. West of Waterford, a few more harbours are dotted along the coast, combining the roles of fishing port and holiday resort.

## Waterford City

At the very east of the county, the city is some way from the sea, but the broad River Suir made it a significant port from the time the Vikings sailed in to settle, early in the 10th century. The long quayside on the south bank is still its most striking feature, with the sturdy cylinder of **Reginald's Tower** as a waterfront landmark. This stands on the site of a fort built by the Vikings and taken by the Normans when they captured Waterford in 1170. Tradition says that the marriage of Strongbow to MacMorrough's daughter Aoife (Eva) took place here soon after the battle. Some of the stonework at the base looks venerable enough to be Viking work, but the upper parts are Anglo-Norman. After functioning as a mint, prison and police station, it is now the Civic Museum.

Plenty of other survivals are scattered around the area of the old walled city, including parts of the wall itself. Call at the Tourist Office (41 The Quay) for a street plan. When in 1987 a site was cleared for a new shopping centre, between Peter, Arundel and High Streets, archaeologists were able to excavate part of the earliest settlement. As many as sixty Viking houses were identified, and eventually over 200,000 objects from the Viking period were recovered, from humble

*You can see the glass-blowers, cutters and polishers at work on a tour of the Waterford Crystal Glass Factory.*

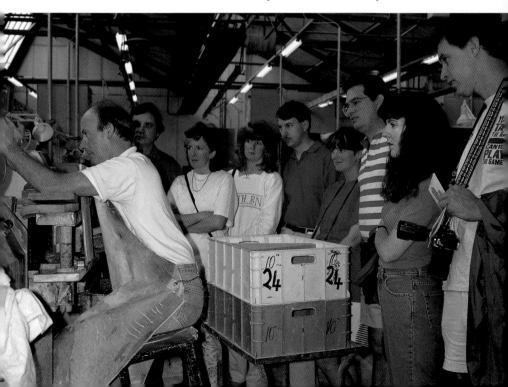

potsherds and bone implements to jewellery and weapons. Some are on display at the **Heritage Centre** in Greyfriars, next to the ruined Franciscan friary called the French Church. The foundations of St Peter's Church were revealed: the Vikings had become Christian in the 11th century. Up Keyser Street from The Quay, over one crossroads, you'll find on the left the doorway and wall of another Viking church, St Olaf's.

Waterford's two cathedrals date from the late 18th century. The architect of both, John Roberts, lived in the attractive **Cathedral Square**, opposite one of his creations, the Catholic Cathedral of the Blessed Trinity. The same Georgian era saw the creation of the elegant Mall and of City Hall, whose chandelier is naturally Waterford glass. The famous glass factory is at **Kilbarry**, 3km (2 miles) south west on the road to Cork. Glass production first started in 1783, but ceased in 1851, when a swingeing tax was put on Irish exports by the government in London to stop the factory competing with English manufacturers. The industry was revived in 1947, when master craftsmen came from the continent to teach a new generation of apprentices. There are tours, on weekdays only; not all the processes are on view but you might see glass-blowing or cutting and engraving. Ask at the Tourist Office if you want to visit: you may have to make a reservation.

In summer, you can take a teatime or dinner cruise and see Waterford and the country around from the river.

## South Coast

There could hardly be a greater contrast between the two seaside resorts due south of Waterford. Pretty little **Dunmore East**

*The little resort of Dunmore East near Waterford has a fishing harbour and sheltered beaches.*

*Sculpted biblical scenes and Romanesque arches from an even earlier building, in the wall of the 12th-century St Declan's Cathedral at Ardmore.*

was immensely fashionable in the 19th century, and its discreet charm still has plenty of devotees today. The harbour at its west end, where steamers from Britain once docked, is now an active fishing port. To the east, three small beaches, two of them sandy, face a sheltered horseshoe cove.

**Tramore** is anything but discreet. Its huge stretch of sand is exposed to wind and weather, and the brash but rundown seafront buildings face a funfair. The first stage of redevelopment, 'Celtworld', is an indoor attraction in the latest shiny mould, excitingly retelling Celtic myths and legends in comic-book style, using animated figures, lasers and 3D effects.

The substantial port of Dungarvan has a fine sheltered harbour and beach and not much of interest otherwise. South and west of the harbour, an isolated pocket of the Gaeltacht (Irish-speaking community) somehow flourishes. Called **Ring** (*An Rinn*), an area of scattered cottages and farms, its small population have their own radio station. If you're driving, you will pick it up loud and clear on your car radio and perhaps hear some traditional music, even if you can't follow the talk.

In the south-western corner of County Waterford, the little resort of **Ardmore** was the site of the 6th-century St Declan's monastery. Today, it is notable for a nearly complete round tower and the 11th- and 12th-century cathedral's strong Romanesque lines. Boldly sculpted but well-worn carvings below the west window show Adam and Eve, the Judgement of Solomon, the Adoration of the Magi and the Last Judgement. Nearby, a re-roofed stone building is thought to preserve the walls at least of St Declan's Oratory. Walk to the east up the hill to St Declan's Well, marked by some old crosses standing by a ruined temple. If you have had enough ruins for the time being, take the cliff walk from Ardmore Head, round Ram Head to Whiting Bay. There's a short cut back along the road, making about 13km (8 miles) in all.

# County Kilkenny

Broad rivers flowing through lush green meadows, sheep grazing round the spectacular ruins of medieval monasteries, these are the quintessence of the beautiful and historic inland county of the south east. Jerpoint Abbey has some of the finest stone carving to survive, and Kells has miraculously kept its ancient walls. We begin in one of the most picturesque and delightful little cities in all Ireland.

### Kilkenny

**Kilkenny Town** as it is called locally to distinguish it from the county, was once *Cill Chainnigh* (the Church of Canice), the capital of the ancient kingdom of Ossory. Then it came into the possession of the Norman Earl, Strongbow. His son-in-law, the indomitable William the Marshal (he had married Isabel de Clare, Strongbow's daughter by Aoife MacMorrough), built the first stone fortress, predecessor of the palatial castle which dominates the city to this day. Kilkenny gave its name to the 14th-century parliaments which met here. In 1366, one of them passed the statutes which were intended to stop the Anglo-Normans assimilating – by adopting Irish ways,

language and laws, taking Irish names or wearing Irish dress. Marriages between Anglo-Normans and Irish were declared to be treason. This attempt at apartheid led to bitter divisions between those who accepted the laws and those who rebelled. The chief mediator as the dust settled had been James Butler, 1st Earl of Ormonde, and the 3rd Earl acquired Kilkenny Castle at the end of the 14th century.

From 1642-8, it was the headquarters of the Catholic Confederation, which tried to restore the rights of the Gaelic Irish lords and the Catholic aristocracy descended from the Anglo-Normans, and negotiated with Charles I to that end. This inevitably attracted the wrath of Cromwell, and the town was stormed and taken by his troops in 1650. The people were spared the massacre which befell Wexford, but many were expelled or deported.

Ireland's best preserved medieval city is a perfect size for exploring on foot, with plenty to see. You can orient yourself at the Tourist Office in the historic **Shee's Almshouse** (1584) in Rose Inn Street, the oldest such foundation in Ireland. They were much needed after dissolution of many monasteries meant there was nowhere for the destitute to go for help. The Cityscope Exhibition is a clever presentation of how Kilkenny would have looked at the pinnacle of its influence in the 1640s, using a scale model of the town at the time and picking out the historic sites with dramatic lighting.

**Kilkenny Castle**, dominating the crossing of the River Nore, was held by the powerful Butler family for over 500 years until it was donated to the state in 1937. On a tour you'll see the impressively long picture gallery, with Butler family portraits by Van Dyck, Kneller and others, and many tapestries – there was a tapestry-weaving workshop here in the 17th century. Everything is on an outsize scale, including the massive **kitchens** which are put to use every summer running a restaurant for the visitors. The **Butler Gallery**, converted from former servants' rooms, houses the Pennefeather Collection of 20th-century Irish art and changing exhibitions. Converted stables across the road from the castle are the home of the **Kilkenny Design Centre**, a group established in the 1960s and dedicated to improving the quality of craft products: glass, ceramics, fabrics, knitwear and jewellery.

High Street and its extension Parliament Street are lined by colourful shops and Georgian houses. You'll pass the 18th-century Town Hall (Tholsel) with its octagonal clock tower and, further along on the opposite side, **Rothe House**, a fine Tudor townhouse which is now a local museum with a costume collection. Just beyond, Abbey Street leads through the only surviving town gate to Black Abbey, wrecked by Cromwell's troops but partly restored as the Dominican Church.

The lower end of Parliament Street leads to **St Canice's Cathedral**, with Norman tombs and a much older round tower, which you can climb by special arrangement – it isn't always open. Many Ormond tombs are in the south transept, most notably those of the 16th-century 8th and 9th Earls. Across the bridge below the Castle, **Kilkenny College** claims Dean Swift, Bishop Berkeley and the Restoration dramatists Congreve and Farquhar as old pupils (although all of them attended when the school was on its former site next to St Canice's Cathedral).

**Dunmore Cave**, about 11km (7 miles) north, is actually a series of caves which have been known for at least a thousand years. Ancient records tell of a massacre by the Vikings of people who had taken refuge inside, and modern excavations certainly turned up human bones from that time as well as Viking coins. These and other objects found in the caves are displayed at the entrance. Steps lead down and walkways take you through interlinking caverns past calcite formations with the usual fanciful names, shining in the powerful electric lights.

### Jerpoint Abbey (Thomastown)

In Ireland you will gaze at dozens of ruins, impressive from a distance but often lacking in interesting features when you get up close (except to specialists in medieval architecture). Cistercian Jerpoint

*Inside the shell of a typical Cistercian building, Jerpoint Abbey is full of fine stone carving.*

*Many remarkable stone carvings at Jerpoint Abbey were the work of one family, the O'Tunneys, during the 15th and 16th centuries.*

by contrast is full of wonderful details, so be sure to buy the visitor's guide leaflet at the entrance. Beneath the tower lies the tomb of the first abbot, Felix O'Dullany who died in 1202. His well-worn effigy shows him holding a crozier with a serpent biting its end. Later tombs have fine sculptures of apostles and other saints and archangels, carved by the local O'Tunney family in the early 16th century. There's an extraordinary and mysterious life-size picture incised in stone depicting two knights called 'The Brothers': perhaps they were crusaders or Templars. The partly restored cloisters include many

vignettes in stone: look for the frowning 14th-century Butler knight, the lady in her pleated dress and the unexpected little figures of imps and devils in odd places. Just north of Thomastown, in Kilfane church, the 13th-century effigy of an armed knight is worth stopping to see.

West of Jerpoint, near Stonyford on the main Kilkenny–Waterford road, the 18th-century mansion of **Mount Juliet** is now a luxury hotel with a championship golf course. Continue to head west along a narrow country lane and you'll suddenly come upon a sight like a mirage. Amid grazing sheep, protected by grey stone towers and massive protecting walls big enough for a whole city, is the ruined priory of **Kells** (but not the one which the Book is named after). Unlike Jerpoint, it does not have much carved detail now, but the lonely splendour of the setting and the amazing preservation of the defences make it well worth a detour and a stroll across the fields to see.

# County Tipperary

The biggest inland county stretches from the banks of the Suir in the south east to the Shannon in the west. Look down from the surrounding hills into the Golden Vale on a clear day, and you may think you have seen the land of milk and honey. The major sights are in the southern half of Tipperary, led by the historic Rock of Cashel, its heights crowded with magnificent medieval churches and towers.

## Carrick-on-Suir

This little place in the south-east corner of the county is said to be the birthplace of Henry VIII's second wife, Anne Boleyn (1507-36). Although there is no reliable record of this, family connections make it a possibility. If true, she would have been born in one of the 15th-century towers of Ormonde Castle, not in the adjoining Tudor mansion which was added some years after Anne lost her head. Because there was still a pressing need for fortification in most of Ireland, houses in this style are extremely rare, and none can match this one, with its array of stone-mullioned windows and pointed gables. Inside, there are some pieces of original furniture, finely restored plasterwork ceilings, medallion portraits of Elizabeth I and Edward VI and a carved chimneypiece dated 1565. The Elizabethan long gallery is unique in Ireland.

**Ahenny**, 8km (5 miles) north of Carrick-on-Suir, has two fine 8th-century high crosses, with generally simple, abstract geometric motifs on the shafts. The north cross has what looks like a funeral procession carved on the base. In age and development, they come between the plain early crosses and the later high crosses

*E*lizabethan houses like this at Carrick-on-Suir are rare in Ireland: in the 16th century most landowners still needed the protection of a castle.

with figures of Christ, saints or bishops, and densely carved panels showing biblical scenes.

Another town that grew up beside the River Suir, **Clonmel** was the birthplace of Laurence Sterne, author of *Tristram Shandy*, in 1713. Old warehouses along the water show how much river trade there once was, and relics of fine Georgian public buildings and quaint back streets make this a pleasant place to stroll round, although there is no notable landmark. Meetings at Clonmel's race-

*A*t *their best, Irish country towns such as Clonmel retain an agreeably traditional look, with gracious houses and old shop fronts.*

course liven things up with an influx of the horse-racing community.

If you are travelling between Clonmel and Cashel, it's worth going slightly out of your way to see **Fethard** (not to be confused with the one on the Hook peninsula). It isn't on the main road to anywhere and does not attract many visitors, but the town is highly unusual in retaining long sections of its Anglo-Norman town walls. These are up to 5.5m (18ft) high in places, and some hard work is currently going into restoring and even rebuilding them, especially along the river.

### Cashel

The Rock of Cashel stands out dramatically, 80m (260ft) above the plain, so it was a natural site for a fortress of the kings of Munster. Now, crowned with as fine a collection of ancient and sacred buildings as you will see anywhere, it has become one of the most visited sites in Ireland. Don't let the possibility of crowds put you off, but for the best atmosphere, light and a chance of peace and quiet, try to time your visit for early morning or evening (it stays open from 9am to 7.30pm in summer).

Once through the gatehouse, look for the exact reproduction of a worn **high cross** depicting Christ and a figure presumed to be St Patrick, probably dating from the 11th century. It stands in the open, south of the nave of the cathedral, the largest of the buildings on the Rock. You can see the original under cover in the restored 15th-century **Hall of the Vicars Choral**, adjoining the present entrance. Legends about St Patrick have inevitably grown up around the Rock. One has it that he said one of his first masses in Ireland here, and a more reliably recorded visit is dated to 450, when he is reported to have converted Aengus, king of Munster. His explanation of the Trinity with the aid of a shamrock is sometimes placed at Cashel, among other claimants.

The first Irish-Romanesque church, **Cormac's Chapel**, named after the king-bishop Cormac MacCarthy, was consecrated in 1134. It looks at first sight to have been built at an odd angle into the south-east corner of the much larger cathedral. In fact, the chapel is at least a century older, and it's the *cathedral* which was added, aligned east-west as had become the norm by then. The chapel's elaborate north door with its multiple columns and decorative arches was blocked off in the process. Its very steep roof is a feature in common with early oratories like St Kevin's at Glendalough: otherwise it represents a remarkable departure from anything previously seen in Ireland and may well have been designed by architects (probably monks as well) trained in Europe. Inside, the broken 12th-century sarcophagus, which may be Cormac's own, is decorated with deeply cut carvings of entwined snakes and tendrils, in the Scandinavian Urnes style (see page 105).

The Irish-Gothic 13th-century **cathedral** must have been a fine sight in its day. A 15th-century archbishop felt the need to tack a castle on to the western end of the nave and to fortify the whole building but this did not save it when the Earl of Kildare set fire to it in 1495. (He offered the impudent excuse to an angry King Henry VII that he had 'thought the archbishop was inside'!) Even now, roofless since the 18th century, it is a majestic ruin. Take note of the double walls, with passages, stairways and galleries between them. If there are only a few visitors about, the staff in charge may open the gates to let you climb up inside.

Like Cormac's Chapel, the 11th-century **round tower** abuts the cathedral, in this case at a corner of the north transept. Plain but sturdy and complete, this one is unusually fitted with a range of windows at different heights.

It is worth a walk, even a muddy one, on the rough slopes immediately to the west of the Rock for some dramatic views of the tight cluster of buildings and the countryside around. The ruins of Hore Abbey in the fields below are picturesque at a distance but less interesting close up.

At the foot of the Rock on the other side, near the car park, the Brú Ború Heritage Centre stages traditional music and dance performances in summer, when it also runs a restaurant offering banquets with entertainment. The souvenir shop operates most days, and you can get help with tracing your Irish ancestry, if you have any, from the genealogy computer.

Set back from the town's one main street, the elegant 18th-century Georgian bishops' house known as **Cashel Palace** is now a hotel. The Archbishop Bolton who had it built also left his collection of ancient manuscripts, maps and priceless early printed books to the Protestant cathedral. It formed the basis of the Bolton Library, across the road from Cashel Palace.

On a sunlit summer evening, Golden Vale seems a good name for the rich Tipperary countryside west of Cashel, but there is actually a town called **Golden** on the River Suir, with a fortified tower guarding the crossing. If the crowds have invaded Cashel, turn south a short way from Golden and retreat to the tranquillity of 12th-century **Athassel Priory**, amid meadows running down to a stream. It's a beautiful spot for a picnic, though you may have to share the solitude with some fishermen.

'*It's a long way to Tipperary*', goes the old British army marching song, but from Cashel, or Golden, it's not. Even so, there are far more interesting places in the county than this quiet town which shares a name with the county. You might pass this way if you are cutting across to Limerick and the west. **Thurles**, north of Cashel, has few sights to detain you today, but it had its moments in history. In 1174 O'Conor and O'Brien stopped the advance of Strongbow's Normans here. And this is where the Gaelic Athletic Association was formed in 1884. An organization of far more than sporting significance, its greater purpose was to promote the revival of a separate Irish culture as a step towards the recovery of independence. Beside the River Suir about 6km (4 miles) south, the 12th-century Cistercian **Holy Cross Abbey** took its name from the fragment supposed to have come from the True Cross of Christ which was kept here. Rebuilt in the 15th century, the abbey

*M*odern bronze in the restored Holy Cross Abbey.

church fell into ruin after the Reformation, like so many others, but unlike most of them, it has been re-roofed and restored in modern times to serve as the parish church. Not everyone approved of all the changes: for example the graves which had typically been sited inside the church walls were removed. The great east window, the ribbed stone vaulting of the roof and beautifully carved sedilia (canopied seats for the priests) all remain to be admitted. An unusual survival, traces of medieval wall paintings of a Norman hunting scene can be seen in the north transept.

### Cahir

The little market town is dominated by its mighty 14th-century **castle**. A Butler family stronghold on a rocky island in the Suir, it has now been thoroughly restored and is sometimes used as a film set when something medieval is called for. You can either tour on your own or wait for the guides who explain the details: the castle is a textbook of medieval military architecture. An audio-visual show tells you about this and other sights of the region. The castle is not the only attraction that brings visitors to Cahir: it has parks, golf and riding too.

The 1817 Protestant church is credited to John Nash, and a unique house called **Swiss Cottage** is presumed on circumstantial evidence to have been designed by him too. South of the town, across the Suir from the castle but still in its grounds, this thatched retreat was built for Lord Cahir so he and his wife could get away from the formality of the castle and play at being happy rustics. Simple life or not, servants were naturally needed, but they could enter unseen by the same tunnel that you will use to get to the cottage. When

*Y*<sub></sub>*ou have probably seen Cahir Castle as the setting for some film or television series. This is the refectory.*

the estate was sold off in the 1960s, Swiss Cottage was bought by the water bailiff who lived in it until 1980. Then, shamefully, it was allowed to fall into disrepair and many original details were lost or damaged, although it has now been meticulously restored. The guides can tell you some strange stories about this Lord Cahir who was illegitimate and was spirited away to France as a child, by relatives who hoped to inherit. Somehow he was discovered, brought back and educated and married to Emily Jeffereys of Blarney Castle. His mother, a poor woman of the town, became the dowager Lady Cahir! Tiny **Ballyporeen**, south west of Cahir, was suddenly identified in 1984 as

the ancestral home of Ronald Reagan's family. Cynics said that researchers were under orders to find *somewhere* that his forebears might have come from. Whatever the truth of the matter, the village experienced all the hullaballoo of a whirlwind presidential visit.

From Cahir to the south coast, the most direct route is also the most scenic. Called the **Vee**, after a particularly extreme bend, it zigzags through the heather and over the ridge of the Knockmealdown Mountains by way of a pass called the Gap. On a clear day, stop at the Vee itself and near the top of the pass for the views or a walk – this is a favourite Sunday outing for local people too. Now you're in County Waterford, and the road quickly descends to **Lismore**, dominated by its turreted stone castle. This one is largely the result of 19th-century rebuilding to comfortable standards, but an earlier building was owned by Richard Boyle, Earl of Cork (see page 174), whose son Robert Boyle the scientist was born there.

# Cork and Kerry: Rivals Sharing the Magic

From the Dingle Peninsula to Roaringwater Bay, ragged fingers stretch into the Atlantic amidst a scattering of islands. Ireland's highest mountains are here, rejoicing in the name of MacGillycuddy's Reeks. The Lakes of Killarney and the Ring of Kerry have been celebrated since tourism began in earnest with the arrival of the railways. So much is crammed into this corner of the country that a lifetime isn't enough to experience it, although plenty of escapists have decided to try, adding a newly cosmopolitan touch to some of the remotest fishing villages.

## County Cork

Ireland's biggest county cannot be summed up quickly. It straddles the meandering, roughly north–south line which marks the end of the rich rolling farmlands to the east and the beginning of the rocks and bogs, picturesque but hard to scratch a living from. History and major attractions are concentrated near Cork City: the ports of Cobh and Kinsale, Blarney Castle, Midleton the whiskey capital. Going

*The Old Head of Kinsale, reserved for walkers and seabirds. It was off this promontory that the liner* Lusitania *was sunk in 1915.*

west, fields, farms and villages are smaller. The coast grows wilder and more barren, but its convolutions conceal pretty fishing ports on sheltered bays and some good beaches. In the city people speak of West Cork as if of a different country. In an hour's journey you can feel as remote as the moon. We start at the county's eastern border, at a charming and historic little port.

### Youghal

The coast road crosses into County Cork over the broad estuary of the Blackwater river. On the sheltered western side, the little fishing port of Youghal (pronounced 'Yawl') used to be known for its lace but only a few enthusiasts can make *point d'Irlande* (or Youghal lace) nowadays. The town centre retains a nicely old-

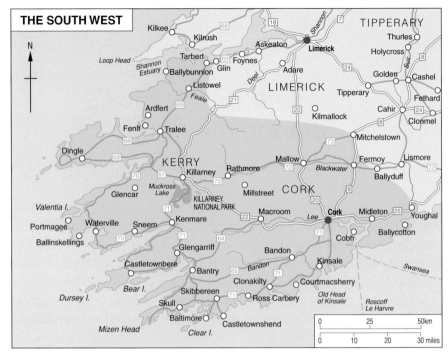

**THE SOUTH WEST**

N

Kilkee
Kilrush
Loop Head
Shannon Estuary
Tarbert
Ballybunnion
Foynes
Glin
Askeaton
Limerick
Adare
Shannon
TIPPERARY
Thurles
Holycross
Golden
Cashel
Listowel
Feale
LIMERICK
Tipperary
Fethard
Ardfert
Fenit
Tralee
Deel
Kilmallock
Cahir
Clonmel
Dingle
KERRY
Killarney
Rathmore
Mallow
Blackwater
Mitchelstown
Fermoy
Lismore
Ballyduff
Muckross Lake
Glencar
KILLARNEY NATIONAL PARK
Millstreet
CORK
Valentia I.
Macroom
Lee
Cork
Midleton
Youghal
Portmagee
Waterville
Sneem
Kenmare
Cobh
Ballycotton
Ballinskelligs
Glengarriff
Bandon
Castletownbere
Bantry
Bandon
Clonakilty
Kinsale
Courtmacsherry
Swansea
Bear I.
Skibbereen
Ross Carbery
Old Head of Kinsale
Dursey I.
Skull
Roscoff
Le Harvre
Baltimore
Castletownshend
Mizen Head
Clear I.

0    25    50km
0    10    20    30 miles

fashioned look despite the often heavy traffic passing along its two parallel one-way streets. In one of them, Main Street, the traffic has to pass through the archway of the solid four-storey **Clock House**, built in the 1770s and now housing a local museum.

As Main Street heads north (the way the traffic goes) it becomes Tallow Street. Near some fine restored almshouses dated 1610, and vestiges of the old town walls, Church Street leads to **St Mary's Church**. Notable for its separate old round belfry and 13th-century tower, it was in a state of dilapidation before restoration in the 19th century. Fortunately, the cleaning-up process did not go too far and the interior is agreeably filled with remarkable tombs and carvings. Most striking is the elaborate, full-colour monument to Richard Boyle, the 'Great Earl of Cork', which he designed himself

in about 1620. Painted effigies of his two wives, praying, and nine of his children surround the reclining figure of the earl in his armour and robes. (A similar piece of self-aggrandisement in Dublin led to a clash with the viceroy – see page 108).

It was the same Richard Boyle who in 1602 purchased great tracts of confiscated land which Elizabeth I had awarded to Sir Walter Raleigh. Local legend claims that Raleigh brought the potato to Ireland and planted the first crop, and that this was where he was smoking tobacco when a servant threw water over him to put the fire out. There's no evidence for either story, but his ship certainly called at Youghal on more than one occasion and he may have spent some time at the Elizabethan house called Myrtle Grove, near St Mary's Church.

West of the port, the vast stretch of broad sandy beach is called the Strand.

*M*ain Street, Youghal,
County Cork. It was traditional in
the south west to paint houses in
bold bright colours and the
fashion is returning.

(Irish beaches often are: the word comes from old Norse and was presumably introduced by the Vikings.) It has made Youghal into something of a summer resort.

### Cork City

The Republic's second city, though very much smaller than Dublin, doesn't see it-self that way. The unofficial southern capital has loads of confidence to go with its friendly small-town feeling. The streets buzz with activity and people, and like the crowds in every Irish city, the average age looks to be about 19.

The Irish name, *Corcaigh*, means a marsh, and Cork grew up on low-lying islands in the River Lee. Some of today's main streets once carried water traffic: the curve of St Patrick's Street follows the line of one arm of the river, and the broad Grand Parade was another until it was covered over at the end of the 18th century. Enough waterways remain for the city to keep its special atmosphere: you will be constantly crossing bridges until you reach the outskirts. Then you're climbing hills, seven of them according to the local count, to match Rome's.

Cork's foundation is credited to St Finbarr, who set up a monastery south of the main branch of the Lee in the 6th century. Easily reached by the Vikings, it was repeatedly sacked in the 9th century until the raiders decided to stay and build a settlement themselves. The tortured course of Irish history found Cork on the 'losing' side in many rebellions and sieges, but by the 18th century it was becoming a prosperous trading and manufacturing centre, and the focus of a rich agricultural region. In the 1919-21 troubles, the city was especially ardent for independence. It suffered vicious retaliation and destruction at the hands of the 'Black and Tans' (see page 56) who murdered the Nationalist lord mayor, Thomas Mac-Curtain. The damage took a long time to repair, and the effects of the depression

and decline of Cork's commerce and industry can be seen to this day in the derelict quayside warehouses and factories. It took the boom of the 1970s to get things moving again with the growth of light industry and the service sector.

Heavy traffic, a confusing layout and difficult parking mean that the best way to see the main sights is to walk. The tourist office at the southern end of **Grand Parade** will give you a map, and also sells a booklet of walking tours. Don't miss the finely restored **English Market** nearby, leading off Grand Parade. Then you might

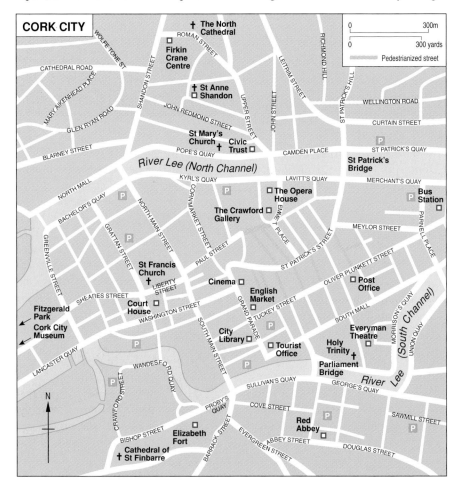

follow St Patrick Street as far as the north channel of the Lee, and Cork's most famous meeting point, the statue of Father Theobald Mathew, indefatigable 19th-century campaigner for temperance. Along Lavitt's Quay, the **Opera House** is a modern venue for touring productions, variety shows and theatre: the Cork Theatre Company specializes in the Irish dramatists. Close by on the south side, on Emmet Place, the **Crawford Municipal Art School's Gallery** concentrates on Irish painters and sculptors such as the eccentric Harry Clark as well as some historic portraits of characters in Irish history. It is also noted for having an excellent restaurant. The pedestrian area around Paul Street has some of the best small shops and cafés.

On a steep little hill across the river from the Opera House, Shandon is one of

*C*ork City grew up along *its waterways and on its hillsides. The church in the background is St Ann's, Shandon.*

the oldest parts of the city: **St Ann's Church** (1722) with its curious steeple, salmon weathervane and famous bells is a landmark. Across the street, the restored Old Butter Market and neo-classical Firkin Crane building used to trade in Cork and Kerry meat and dairy produce. Now the latter building houses a craft centre with fabric, leather and glass studios.

Across the southern arm of the Lee from Grand Parade, **Red Abbey** is one of the few medieval relics, surviving from an Augustinian monastery. To the west of the old abbey, you can see the spire of **St Finbarr's Cathedral**, a fairly standard example of 19th-century Gothic revival with a highly decorated but rather stilted interior. On the western edge of the city centre, Fitzgerald Park is the location of **Cork City Museum**, mainly a commemoration of the struggle for independence but with archaeology, geology and local history sections too. For a view of Cork and its superb harbour, take to the water on an excursion or go by boat to Cobh.

## Excursions from Cork

**Blarney Castle**, 8km (5 miles) north west of Cork, is a particularly impressive example of a 15th-century tower house, built for defence at a time when the threat was not reckoned to be of a kind to justify the expense of a curtain wall. There are hundreds of ruined castles in Ireland, so why does this former seat of the MacCarthys attract visitors in their thousands? Elizabeth I of England started it by adding a word to the language. Tired of the sweet talk – unaccompanied by action – of the MacCarthy, Lord of Blarney of the time, she is quoted as complaining 'This is all Blarney: what he says he never does!' The legend that those who kiss a certain stone will be endowed with similarly fluent and persuasive tongues is probably a 19th-

*The contortions required to kiss the Blarney Stone won't break your neck, just bend it.*

*T*he old distillery at
*Midleton is now the Jameson
Heritage Centre, telling the story
of Irish whiskey.*

century concoction – Victorian travellers
reported that the castle guides were not really sure *which* stone had the power. It
seems as though they picked one suited to
the agility, or lack of it, of each gullible
visitor. There is no such doubt today. High
on the battlements, one by one the tourists
lie on their backs and bend their necks still
further backwards until their lips reach the
spot and the requisite photo can be taken.
Iron railings ensure they won't fall.

The spiral stairs up the tower are con-
gested in summer, and there may be a long
wait in the kissing line. There are other
distractions at Blarney: the castle grounds
include Rock Close, an example of 18th-
century romantic landscaping. Blarney

village has hotels, a restored wool mill
given a shot in the arm by the tourist trade
and shops selling Irish souvenirs.

Nearby **Blarney House** is a 19th-
century mansion with conical turrets in
Scottish baronial style, also open to the
public in summer. It is finely furnished
and decorated, if not particularly exciting.

### The Whiskey Capital

At **Midleton**, 21km (15 miles) east of Cork
City, the **Jameson Heritage Centre** presents the story of Irish whiskey, in the beautifully restored old distillery buildings
where it was made from 1825 until 1975.
There's a short audio-visual show, a tour,
and a chance at the end of it to sample five
Irish brands plus a Scotch and an American
bourbon for comparison. If you aren't converted, it won't be the fault of the en-
chantresses who act as guides. They tell the
facts, the legends and the fairy stories so
well that you'll hardly notice you don't get
to see any actual production going on! That
happens in the new buildings nearby.

Both the road and the railway from Cork City to Cobh go by way of **Fota Island** (Foaty on some maps). At one time the whole island was a private estate – even the railway station was restricted to the owning family and their entourage. The fine neo-classical mansion, Fota House, contains an important collection of Irish landscape paintings. It used to be open to visitors but is now closed for long-term major repairs. You can still walk in part of the grounds, including an arboretum. From April to October the main attraction is the **Fota Wildlife Park**, which is about as far removed from the traditional zoo as it is possible to go. Just a few

*T*he waterfront of the historic port of Cobh on Cork harbour is dominated by St Colman's Cathedral.

*A* long way from home, the king penguins at the Wildlife Park on Fota Island. Most of the birds and animals here can mix freely with the visitors.

animals such as the breeding cheetahs have to be kept in spacious enclosures, and some others are separated by water barriers. Most are free-range so you will be strolling among giraffes, zebras, wallabies, friendly ring-tailed lemurs and countless exotic birds. Fota has had great success in breeding rare and endangered species for release into the wild or to supply other parks.

## Cobh

Halfway down the long inlet that leads from Cork to the open sea, the port of Cobh has seen its share of drama, tragedy and glamour. A perfect sheltered harbour,

## WHAT'S IN A NAME?

Cobh, the name of the port since 1921, is just the Irish rendering of the old name of Cove (or The Cove of Cork) and pronounced the same way. British sailors jokily called it Cob-H when the Royal Navy retained a base here for some years after Irish independence. And it was known as Queenstown from the occasion of a visit in 1849 by Queen Victoria. 'The day was grey and excessively "muggy", which is characteristic of the Irish climate', she grumbled.

it grew in importance when ocean-going vessels became much too big to reach Cork itself.

A ship carrying convicts to Australia sailed from here in 1791: by the time the practice was stopped decades later, a total of 39,000 had been transported, usually in appalling conditions. Troopships embarked soldiers at Cobh for the Napoleonic, Crimean and Boer Wars, and the port saw the mass departures of emigrants fleeing famines and depressions from the 1840s until well into the 20th century. Cunard and White Star liners called regularly, on their way between Liverpool and New York. Little boats used to come out to where the great ships were moored, selling souvenirs, Irish linen and lace. This was the last port of call of the ill-fated *Titanic* on her maiden voyage in 1912, and when on 7 May 1915 the *Lusitania* was sunk by a German submarine off the Old Head of Kinsale not far from the harbour entrance, the lucky survivors were brought here. Some of the 1,198 who were drowned are buried in the old churchyard to the north of the town. Many were Americans, and the attack lit a slow fuse that eventually triggered the United States' entry two years later into World War I.

The fine Victorian railway station on the quayside has been beautifully restored, after years of neglect when it was used as a coal store. Now it houses an exhibition called **The Queenstown Story** which relates the port's history, cleverly using models, paintings and sculpture, rare archive photographs and newsreel film, and dramatic sound effects.

There is a list of the 187 passengers who joined the *Titanic* when she put in here. Almost all were poor emigrants, in the cheapest berths: almost all were drowned. Poignant notices put up by passengers rescued from the *Lusitania* ask for news of lost relatives. Happier pictures evoke the heyday of the luxury transatlantic liners in the 1920s and '30s when film stars and royalty came ashore for a quick tour or a civic reception.

Above all, the exhibition tells the story of the three *million* Irish who sailed from this quayside to seek a better life. From just a few thousand in the 1830s, emigration jumped to 239,000 in the famine years of the 1840s, reached 305,000 in the 1860s and peaked at 390,000 in the 1880s. In the early days, cooped up in unseaworthy 'coffin ships', half-starved and ill when they came on board, seasick from the moment they sailed, fed on stale biscuits and tainted oatmeal, many failed to survive the 4-6 week voyage. The Queenstown Story will give you some idea of what it was like – don't miss it.

Outside the station and exhibition, a statue depicts a woman and her two children. They are a particular family, but the memorial honours all the emigrants. Another, in the town centre, commemorates those lost in the *Lusitania*. On the steep hill above the harbour, the spire of the 19th- and 20th-century Gothic **Cathedral of St Colman** is a landmark.

# Born to Leave – Irish Emigration

The statistics tell part of the story. Ireland's population in 1840 was over 8 million. By the 1880s it was only 4 million. In spite of high birth rates, it continued to fall until in the 1930s it was about 3 million. Today the figure is close to 5 million, counting both parts of Ireland. Compare that with the multitudes throughout the world who say that they are of primarily Irish descent, estimated at 60 million (and twice that number in America on St Patrick's Day).

All this mobility has rarely been from preference, and emigration is no recent phenomenon. In the 14th century, the Black Death drastically reduced the work force in England. Although Ireland had suffered just as greatly, many Irish were induced to move to England by the higher wages on offer, or the chance to earn any wages at all. More departures were driven by persecution of Catholics after the Reformation in the 16th century and by discrimination that continued into the 19th. Every failed rebellion generated a new wave of emigration when its supporters went to seek help abroad, or just gave up hope of any change. Frequently their lands were confiscated and 'planted' with English yeomen, Cromwellian or Williamite soldiers, and in parts of Ulster, many Scottish Presbyterians. Ironically, *their* descendants in turn joined the outflow during economic depressions in the 18th and early 19th centuries. In the United States the 'Scots-Irish' produced no fewer than eleven presidents (including Monroe and Jackson), countless business magnates, explorers and generals on both sides in the Civil War.

## Wild Geese

Serving under other nations' colours had become an Irish tradition even before the 'Flight of the Wild Geese' in 1691, when 14,000 of the defeated Jacobite forces chose exile. First they joined the Spanish and French armies *en masse* as special Irish brigades. Eventually no self-respecting army from Russia to Turkey was complete without its Irish colonels and sergeants; Italian princes and Indian sultans appointed them to train and command their soldiery. Often they found themselves fighting the British army, which also recruited heavily in Ireland. Thus was repeated the oldest story in Irish history, one lot of Irishmen pitted against another. Sensitive to injustice in their new homes as their forebears had been in the old country, Irish emigrés were in the forefront of independence movements in Latin America – the first head of state of a free Chile was Bernardo O'Higgins, son of an Irish officer in the Spanish army.

## Fleeing the Famine

The greatest and saddest of the emigrations was still to come. The result of a natural disaster that was waiting to happen, its origins lay in the 17th century with the introduction of the humble potato. The new crop seemed like manna from heaven. Cereal harvests in the past had often failed and left the poor hungry. Now even the wet and stony west could grow plenty of potatoes and feed ever-increasing numbers. There was a population explosion and the vast majority depended entirely on the potato. In 1845 potato blight, a fungus disease, hit parts of Ireland. The following year the crop was virtually destroyed, everywhere (see page 54). Now there was a stark choice: emigrate or perish. Over the next six years almost a million died. More made their way somehow to the ports to find a ship to take them away. Many took the traditional voyage, to Britain. Smaller numbers went to Canada (Ireland providing more than half of all Canadian immigrants over the next twenty years), Australia and a dozen other destinations. The greatest magnet by far was the United States.

Families held an 'American wake' the night before the emigrants left home, sometimes dancing until dawn before bidding farewell to children, brothers or sisters they knew they would never see again. Friends and relations brought small gifts of money, perhaps only a few shillings, to help them on their way. All too often they were relieved of it by hucksters selling mementoes of Ireland at the dockside. Cheap lodging houses multiplied at the departure ports,

*Last of the many, the restored working windmill at Blennerville near Tralee. Thousands of emigrants left from the quayside nearby.*

where there was sometimes a long and unpredictable wait for a ship. At Queenstown (now Cobh), for example, would-be emigrants had to gather at the quayside each morning to hear a clerk call out the names of those who had been allocated a berth on that day's sailing.

## Workers of the World

The tide scarcely slackened for the rest of the 19th century, but gradually the motivation was less the fear of starvation, more the opportunities that beckoned. Word came back from those who had gone before: there were lands of opportunity out there. Most of the emigrants were illiterate, through no fault of their own, but if they were prepared to work, they made a living, and often spectacularly more than a living.

Absence has never diminished the love the Irish have for their moist island. It only made the heart grow fonder and increased the appetite for traditional music and sentimental ballads. In remote parts of Georgia, the Carolinas and Louisiana, Irish communities descended from early settlers preserve the Gaelic language. A succession of independence movements was backed and financed by emigrés and even today, controversy surrounds fund-raising activities for the support of nationalists in Northern Ireland. Fulfilling the dream of seeing the ancestral home again drives a large part of the tourist industry.

Even after Irish independence, great numbers continued to go to Britain, and still do. As a hangover from the imperial past, anyone from the Republic of Ireland has the full rights of a UK citizen, the vote included. Now with European Community membership and free movement of labour, you are likely to meet Irish people working from Amsterdam to Athens, especially in the hotel business. It must have something to do with that legendary hospitality. Travel is in their blood. Perhaps it always has been. Long before the famines made it imperative, people were used to the idea of moving. Children as young as eight or nine were sent or taken to hiring fairs all over the country and engaged to work for a farmer or family for nine months. Frequently they would earn no more than their keep but it meant there was a mouth less to feed at home. Men went to dig canals or build railways or gather the potato harvest in Scotland. Priests spent years training with hardly ever a visit home; and then they might be sent anywhere in the world.

## Educated to Travel

Since the 1840s, only one generation has expected to stay in Ireland: those brought up in the late 1960s and '70s when the economy was expanding and investment was booming. Since then, the exodus has resumed: *half a million* left during the 1980s. The stimulus is the same as it was in the beginning: the search for employment, and for the more ambitious a bigger theatre in which to display their talents. Neither rural Ireland nor her cities can generate enough opportunities for her children. Today there are enormous differences. Past emigrants were largely uneducated, willing to do any sort of job but ill-equipped for most. Today's leavers include many highly trained specialists, the product of one of the best education systems in the world. There is less sadness about their departure these days: they always mean to come back for frequent visits and cheap air travel makes it possible. Many also hope to return to their home for good – eventually.

A row of elegant houses faces the quay, and the former Cunard office is a bank.

Cobh is still an important fishing port. Irish boats shelter in the harbour in winter and a cosmopolitan fleet – French, Spanish, Dutch, Norwegian and East European – can often be seen taking compulsory rest-days. It's also one of the south coast's main yachting centres: you can hire boats and sailboats (windsurfers) at the International Sailing Centre, East Beach.

### Kinsale

On its own fine sheltered inlet south of Cork City, this little port looks like a transplant from the Mediterranean. It's a holiday centre for fishing and yachting, with cobbled streets, colourful houses and picturesque old shop fronts. Above-average restaurants support Kinsale's claims to the title of 'gourmet capital of Ireland', against admittedly mediocre opposition.

*A monument at Cobh commemorates more than a thousand who were drowned when the* Lusitania *was sunk in 1915.*

*The beautifully sheltered harbour of Kinsale has seen some dramatic events. Now it's a centre for sailing, fishing and good eating.*

The port's past includes more than its fair share of momentous events. A Spanish expedition landed here in 1601 to aid the Irish rising against the English, only to be besieged for ten weeks by English troops. The forces of the Earls of Tyrone and Tyrconnell marched south from Ulster to relieve their allies but were heavily-defeated in the kind of set-piece battle they were untrained to fight. The Spaniards were forced to surrender. The ultimate re-

*The massive bastions of the 17th-century Charles Fort were built to guard Kinsale harbour against a French or Spanish attack.*

sult of the Battle of Kinsale was the downfall of the Gaelic Irish lords and the extinction of their world.

James II came ashore at Kinsale in 1689 with French arms and money in his attempt to regain his throne from his son-in-law William. And it was from here too that he left the following year after losing the Battle of the Boyne.

On a peninsula standing out from the west side of the harbour, you can see the ruins of **James Fort**, a star-shaped redoubt built after the 1601 Spanish invasion to deter any similar threat. Much more is left of the fine buildings of **Charles Fort**, across the harbour on the eastern side. Started in the 1670s, it housed a British garrison right up to 1921

but was wrecked in the Civil War which followed. Only limited preservation work has been attempted so far. Tours are run in summer, but you can walk round at any time although some of the buildings are off limits because of their dangerous state.

The tourist information office in the town centre near the harbour will give you a map with the main sites marked. The church of **St Multose** is partly Norman. **Desmond Castle** is a 16th-century tower house where French prisoners were kept during the Napoleonic wars. The Queen Anne-style **old town hall** houses a small museum – notice the long list of tolls and duties payable by market traders and importers in the entrance.

Take the road towards the **Old Head of Kinsale** for some spectacularly giddy clifftop views. You can't drive to the end of the peninsula, which makes walking there particularly enjoyable.

Meandering along the coast from here can be pleasant but time-consuming. Most people will want to head for the southwest, and there's not much on the main road from Cork City to detain them. At the market town of **Bandon**, founded early in the plantation (see page 50), the old stocks and whipping post are kept in the church.

## West Cork

The main road meets the sea at **Clonakilty**, a lively little town during its summer music festival. Just west of here, the hamlet of Woodfield was the birthplace of the Free State leader Michael Collins in 1890, and he was killed not far from here, near Crookstown, during the Civil War in 1922.

At the seaside village of **Castletown-shend** steep streets run down to the harbour, where Jonathan Swift used to visit

*I*rish towns are full of colourful, old-style shops like this pets' paradise in Clonakilty, County Cork.

and write. Much later, it was the home of Edith Somerville, who with her cousin Violet Martin wrote the cult comic stories they called *Some Experiences of an Irish RM* (meaning Resident Magistrate) in 1899 and a follow-up in 1908. In the 'big house' tradition of the ascendancy, on the face of it laughing at the ways of Irish servants, they subtly satirize the fox-hunting squirearchy too. The books gained a wider audience when some of the episodes were televised. The authors are buried in adjacent graves in St Barrahane's churchyard.

Mysterious straight rows of standing stones are found all over Cork and Kerry, perhaps dating from the early Bronze Age. There's a fine example at **Gurranes** near Castletownshend.

South west of the market town of Skibbereen, the tiny port of **Baltimore** is doubly sheltered by offshore islands and its harbour wall. The home base of a few fishing boats, it is almost deserted for most of the year, but in high summer its narrow streets lined with brightly painted houses can be a bottleneck for traffic. American visitors might think Baltimore in Maryland was called after this town. Not so, the Maryland town name honoured the Lord Baltimore of the time, who wasn't from here. There's another possible American connection: President George Bush believes this was his ancestral home. There are still Bushes living in the area, although half the people you'll meet bear the name of O'Driscoll, the clan who ruled these parts and grew rich on the proceeds of piracy until the 16th century.

Speaking of pirates, opposite the ruined fort stands a pub called the Algiers Inn. The name commemorates an event that seems as unlikely today as it no doubt did to the hapless villagers at the time. The year was 1631, and out of the blue came Barbary pirates all the way from the Mediterranean coast of Algeria, to descend on Baltimore and carry off over a hundred of its inhabitants into slavery. It is rather strange to imagine all those O'Driscolls in the galleys and harems of North Africa. (Several Cornish villages met with the same fate around this time: the raiders had been forced to range further afield as the coasts of Spain and France improved their defences.)

A daily ferry – more often in summer – serves **Sherkin** (or **Sharkey**) **Island** and **Clear Island**, carrying the residents, their coal and beer supplies, occasional visitors and birdwatchers. It takes about 15 minutes to reach Sherkin Island, another 15 to Clear Island and it is worth

*T he convoluted coastline of south-west Ireland: Baltimore Head and Sherkin (or Sharkey) Island.*

going for the boat trip alone, even if you don't plan to go ashore and walk, swim or birdwatch.

The islands mark the outer limits of **Roaringwater Bay**, liberally peppered with many smaller islets and rocks. **Ballydehob**, near the head of the bay, is a little town of brightly painted houses, a scattering of bars and cafés but few places to stay. **Schull** with its well-protected harbour is a watersports and sailing centre, with equipment for hire. There is plenty of bed-and-breakfast accommodation in and around the town. Oddly enough, it has a planetarium, a rarity in Ireland, installed by an enthusiast. It gives you something to do when the weather is wet. If you're hungry, visit the Courtyard complex in the middle of town, which combines a traditional bakery, bar, restaurant and delicatessen as well as craft shops. In summer, boats make daily or more frequent trips to Clear Island (see above), across Roaringwater Bay.

### The Mizen Head Peninsula

On a long narrow inlet facing east, **Crookhaven** is a sheltered little fishing harbour and holiday retreat for caravanners and campers. One or two restaurants and bars serve some good local seafood. **Mizen Head** itself is a panorama of black rocks, breaking white surf and a lighthouse reached by a bridge over the chasm which separates its island site from the mainland: it remains closed to anyone not on official business. East of the head, **Barley Cove**'s white sand beaches are a favourite with surfers. When the sea calms down, swimmers take over, assuring each other that the water's really not cold, on account of the Gulf Stream.

### Bantry

Bantry Bay is the biggest deep-water inlet in Ireland, but facing south west, it fails to give much shelter from the prevailing winds – which are often full-blown gales. Few fishing villages grew up along the shores. The only two of any size are each protected by separate islands: Castletownbere (see page 192) on the north by Bear Island, and Bantry by Whiddy Island. Remoteness from major markets meant that the port of Bantry stayed small,

*T*he great natural harbour of Bantry Bay, site of a failed French invasion attempt in 1796.

but the same remoteness drew an attempted French invasion in 1796, during the Napoleonic wars. Whiddy Island was a busy oil terminal but it hasn't been active since the tanker *Betelgeuse* exploded and sank in 1979, killing 50 people. When divers were looking at the wreck, they also discovered the remains of the French frigate *La Surveillante*, scuttled by her crew almost two centuries earlier.

The town of **Bantry** can offer a wide choice of bed-and-breakfast accommodation but few good places to eat. Like so many sea loughs on this coast, the bay is full of mussel and oyster beds, but you may not find these on local menus. There's one notable seafood restaurant, relatively expensive as usual. To be honest, the town itself is not of great interest but it could be a base for touring the coast and mountains.

**Bantry House**, built in the 18th and 19th centuries, has a lived-in look, because the White family who have owned it since 1739 are still here, battling to keep up the great mansion. They run part of it as a hotel – guests stay in modern, comfortable rooms, not the palatial ones on show. You'll see some striking tapestries and French furniture, rare old Waterford glass and Russian icons as well as the sort of family jumble that makes the place look like a home, not a museum. The magnificent dining room is a riot of blue and gold, under the gaze of enormous portraits of George III and Queen Charlotte by their court painter Allen Ramsay, given to Richard White, along with a title as a mark of gratitude for loyalty to the crown in 1796 (see below). The Georgian mahogany dining table is set with French porcelain and antique glass. Outside, the Italian gardens are a bit run down, but it's well worth climbing the

---

### KEEPING THE FRENCH AT BAY

When the British government banned the United Irishmen and at the same time went to war with France, Wolfe Tone made his way to Paris to persuade the Revolution's leaders that the time was ripe for cooperation. If they would make common cause with his movement and launch an invasion, he predicted that the Irish people would rise against their rulers.

It took six months to organize, and there were countless setbacks. At last the expedition was as ready as it would ever be, and 14,000 men in 47 vessels, including 19 ships of the line, sailed from Brest in December 1796 when winter storms were all too predictable. They duly materialized, the fleet was scattered over hundreds of miles of sea and some ships were sunk. The flagship carrying the brilliant young French commander, Hoche, was blown far into the Atlantic, and never made it to Bantry Bay. The ships that did were unable to carry out a landing in the wild weather. Wolfe Tone, aboard one of them, seethed with frustration. After a few days, with the element of surprise lost and no sign of their commander, the depleted fleet sailed back to France. Almost two years were to pass before Tone could return to Ireland on a similar mission: it resulted in his arrest and death.

---

multiple flights of steps for a fine view of the house and bay.

In the extensive stables of Bantry House, the **French Armada Exhibition** on the attempted invasion of 1796 is open from May to October. A one-sixth scale model of the *La Surveillante* is on display, with cannon and a few other objects so far recovered from the wreck, found under the waters of Bantry Bay in 1985. Excellent descriptions and illustrations explain the background and tell the story of the whole ill-starred expedition. Extracts from

Wolfe Tone's diaries are particularly moving. In the long term, there are plans to raise and preserve the ship and eventually put her on display here.

At **Ballylickey**, at the head of Bantry Bay, you'll be faced with a choice of three routes, all of them enticing. When visibility is good, the scenery along the inland road over the Keimaneigh Pass towards Macroom is dramatic. Lough **Gougane Barra**, the Holy Lake below on the left, is surrounded on three sides by precipitous rocks where a hundred waterfalls tumble after rain. The lake in turn is the source of the River Lee, which flows down to Cork City. A little island in the middle was the site of St Finbarr's church and oratory before he too moved downstream to found his monastery at Cork.

If your destination is Kenmare or Killarney in County Kerry, the Ballylickey to Kilgarvan road has the most spectacular views. Alternatively, the third choice is to stay in County Cork for a bit longer, continuing round the shores of Bantry Bay.

**Glengarriff**, at the head of an inlet off the bay, is hemmed in on three sides by odd-shaped mountains and rocks. The garden town of Victorian houses is lush with vegetation. It became a genteel year-round resort in the mid-19th century, and the palm trees are there to let you know how warm and sheltered it is. These days, many tour buses stop, although this is hardly what their passengers have come to the 'wild' south west to see.

The same mild and moist climate favours Ilnacullin or **Garinish Island** in Glengariff Harbour: apart from a martello tower the whole island is an Italian garden, laid out in 1910. Boats are ready to take you across, at a price, and then there's an admission charge to pay on landing.

At Glengarriff more route options are on offer: over the mountains and through the tunnels direct to Kenmare, or the long way round the coast of the **Beara Peninsula** (also written Bheara, Bere or Bear, depending on the degree of Anglicization of the spelling). Promoted as the 'Ring of Beara', it is less travelled and exploited than its famous counterpart the Ring of Kerry and has the advantage that you can cut across the peninsula at several points if you want to shorten the trip. (The first of these, a turn to the right signposted to Healy Pass, comes before you have reached the most interesting parts of the peninsula.)

Looming above the road, the peak of Hungry Hill, 686m (2250ft) is often shrouded in cloud. Then, just when you might think you have reached as remote a part of Ireland as could be, the next bend reveals the sizeable and cosmopolitan fishing port of **Castletownbere**. You can sometimes hear as much Russian spoken in the town as English, or Irish, and when one of their factory ships (with an on-board cannery) is in harbour, the town is full of Russian women doing their shopping. Compulsory days in port for the fishing fleets, a conservation measure, mean that you might see Spanish, Portuguese, French and Belgian trawlers tied up at the quay. The Irish boats based here travel widely too, sometimes sailing as far as the Azores. The desolate ruins of Dunboy Castle, a former O'Sullivan stronghold, lie to the south west of the port.

If the weather's good, and you have the time, continue to the end of land. Otherwise, take the shortcut from Castletownbere to Eyeries and head north east along the Kenmare estuary with its massed mussel farms and salmon pens. Just out of Eyeries, look out for a tall Ogham stone standing on an outcrop of rock.

# County Kerry

If you're looking for the Ireland of lakes and purple mountains, wild coasts and pretty fishing villages that you've seen in a dozen films, you are probably thinking of Kerry. It's as far west as you can go in Europe, unless you count Iceland or Madeira, but that remoteness doesn't keep crowds away. Three of Ireland's most visited areas are conveniently concentrated here: Killarney, the Ring of Kerry and the Dingle Peninsula. Don't make the mistake of looking at the map, deciding the distances are small and allocating a day to each. If you only *have* three days, pick one to visit properly.

*Jaunting cars driven by jarveys have carried visitors to the sights of Killarney since its fame began to spread 200 years ago.*

In summer, the roads and towns can be busy, even choked with holiday traffic, but you only have to walk a little to find some solitude. Tourism has brought prosperity to what was one of the poorest parts of Ireland. Long the butt of 'Kerrymen' jokes by other Irish implying that they're slow-thinking peasants, the locals can enjoy the last laugh.

## Killarney

The town is largely dedicated to the leisure business – in the Irish Tourist Board's Accommodation Guide it boasts as many pages as Dublin! Next to the railway station where the first rush of visitors disembarked in the mid-19th century, the hotel built to house them still flourishes. Horse-drawn 'jaunting cars' just like the ones which carried those early tourists are still around, waiting at various vantage points. If you would like to take a trip in one, establish just where you're going, how long it will take and the price, *first*. If you feel shy about negotiating with the

drivers (known as jarveys), the tourist information office, at the end of Main Street opposite St Mary's Church of Ireland, can tell you the going rates. Souvenir shops, cafés, some reasonable restaurants and innumerable pubs line Main Street and its continuation, High Street. None of this commercialization quite spoils Killarney, which remains an agreeable enough place, and a great centre for exploring the wonders on its doorstep.

The spire of the **Catholic Cathedral**, another St Mary's, in Gothic Revival style

*There's no secret about it. Killarney's main business is tourism, and the town is no less agreeable for that.*

by Pugin, marks the western edge of town. The simple, bare stone walls inside result from problems with the plaster which had to be removed, but the result is still effective.

The **National Museum of Irish Transport** in the middle of town next to Scotts Hotel Gardens is privately owned, despite its name. Packed into a crowded space are some real treasures: the 1907 Silver Stream built at Kilcurran in County Kildare was a one-off; there's a rare Belgian Germain of 1904 by famous coachbuilders Van den Plas; a magnificent monster Mercedes 540K of 1938 and many more, plus penny-farthing bicycles and babies' prams. If you are in the market for old cars yourself, check the 'For Sale' board in the museum. Other diversions in Killarney include horse-racing and Gaelic football, Kerry's favourite spectator sport. Especially at weekends, the pubs and bars may put on traditional music nights: look for the monthly *Killarney Entertainment Guide* booklet to find out where and when. Most visitors aren't here to stay in town, however: they have come for the scenery of lakes and mountains.

### Around Killarney

Of the famous Lakes of Killarney, **Lough Leane** (or Lower Lake) is the nearest to town and the largest. The ruined **Ross Castle** on the lake shore is undergoing a prolonged restoration: it has been closed to the public for years. It was once a stronghold of the O'Donoghue chieftains: legend says that one of them rides in spirit across the water every May Day morning. The castle held out for months against Cromwellian forces, until their commander heard of a tradition that it would never fall until ships sailed on the lake. So he

*A tranquil scene of rural beauty in Killarney National Park.*

had some dragged up from Kenmare, and the fortress duly surrendered. Today, waterbuses – glass-topped against the chance of rain – wait here to take you on a tour. Inisfallen, the biggest of many islets in the lake, was the site of a famous 7th-century abbey where Brian Born is said to have been educated. Nothing remains of it now: the ruins you see date from the 12th century and later: the publicity-minded Earl of Kenmare who first promoted tourism turned some of them into a banqueting suite for entertaining influential guests. It, too, has reverted to ruin. The waterbuses only circle the island. If you would like to land, hire a rowing boat at the castle landing stage.

## Muckross

The main road south from the town soon reaches the gate to the Franciscan **Muckross Abbey**, wrecked by Cromwell's troops in 1652. Like many such ruins, it's now a tranquil graveyard. From the abbey, or from a second gate on the main road, it's a few minutes' walk to the early Victorian **Muckross House**, built in 1843 in Elizabethan style. In 1911 William Bourn bought it as a wedding gift for his daughter and her husband, Arthur Vincent, later a member of the Irish senate. In 1932, the house and its 4,400ha- (11,000 acre-) estate was presented by the family to the nation. Known as the Bourn-Vincent Memorial Park, the land became the nucleus of today's much larger **Killarney National Park** which takes in all the lakes and most of the mountains around. You are free to stroll in the superb gardens and vast lawns stretching down to Middle Lake, but there's a lot to see in Muckross House as well. The magnificent furniture in the dining room includes 12 Chippendale chairs, and the curtains were specially woven for a visit by Queen Victoria and Prince Albert (which naturally made Killarney even more fashionable). **Exhibitions** in some of the rooms include a needlework display and a collection of bog oak carvings, made from the hard black wood preserved for over 2,500 years in peat bogs. Another traces population changes through the famines and emigration of the 19th century, combining the bare statistics with a study of the way in which people lived.

The **basements** are like a craft village, with workshops and displays of basketry, stone-cutting, printing, shoemaking and bookbinding. In the summer months, the artisans work here, and some of their products are sold in the unusually good craft shop. The great kitchen is still fully equipped, and you can take a look at the dairy and wine-cellar. Notice the bells in the corridor: a different note called each servant. Not much use if they were tone-deaf.

The **Kerry Country Life Experience** in the grounds of Muckross House goes in for much more than replicas of traditional buildings and their contents. It's a working farm as well, reviving methods used before mechanization to demonstrate the self-sufficiency of remote communities.

*Lakeside Walks*
A footpath from Muckross House leads along the peninsula separating Lower and

*On foot, horseback or wheels, a trip through the Gap of Dunloe is a must when you visit Killarney.*

Middle Lakes to the '**Meeting of the Waters**' where the two adjoin. The path passes through lush vegetation: the frost-free climate allows some species to flourish that aren't usually seen north of the Mediterranean. The arbutus or strawberry tree, perhaps brought from Spain by the monks of old, is practically Killarney's symbol.

Bridges link the islets at the end of the finger of land where a river flows from the

Upper Lake, so walkers can make a circuit of about 10km (6 miles) in all, returning by the south shore of Middle Lake (Torc Lake or Muckross Lake on some maps). This second half of the walk parallels the busy road, but a path passing under the road leads to the impressive **Torc Cascade**, with the option of climbing the steep slopes of Torc Mountain. A lot of the traffic on the road is heading for **Upper Lake**, in particular to the parking spot at

**Ladies' View**. This looks out across all three lakes, and is said to have been named in honour of Queen Victoria's ladies-in-waiting, who went into ecstasies at the sight.

*The Gap of Dunloe*

West of the lakes, a beautiful gorge slices through the mountains for 6km (4 miles), and a trip through it is one of the 'musts' of a visit to Killarney. That can

mean a crowd, but you should avoid most of them by making an early start, or waiting until late in the day. Starting from the car park at Kate Kearney's Cottage, you can ride part of the way by horse or pony, or take a jaunting car, or just walk – at a steady pace it will take you about three hours to the head of the gap and back. If you're not a walker, consider taking one of the tours offered in the town. Some of them return a different way, linking up with a boat trip on the Upper Lake and down river to Lough Leane.

A sign at the start says the road is unsuitable for cars, but they are not generally banned (although there are many who think they should be). In fact, the road to the head of the gap is adequate, if you don't mind having to reverse to allow jaunting cars to get by. South of the gap it becomes very narrow and rocky, first climbing and then descending into **Black Valley**, where the organized excursion boats to Killarney leave from near Lord Brandon's Cottage. If you are driving, continue south and, despite some confusing and some missing signs, it's not too hard to find your way back to Killarney past Ladies' View (see above, page 197).

**MacGillycuddy's Reeks** are the memorably named mountains that line the horizon to the south and west of Killarney, sliced through by the Gap of Dunloe. **Carrantuohill**, the highest peak in Ireland at 1,041m (3,416ft) can be a fairly easy day's hill walk, rather than a serious climb. Even better views can be had from **Mangerton**, 840m (2,756ft), standing apart from the Reeks due south of Killarney. On a clear day, a couple of hours' aerobic ascent will progressively reveal the lakes and town, the Reeks and then the Kenmare estuary and the Atlantic. Even if the weather looks to be set fair, it can

change suddenly, so take rain gear and windproof clothing and a good map (the Ordnance Survey 1:50,000 *The Reeks* is useful).

## The Ring of Kerry

The name, whoever thought of it, was a stroke of genius. Ask someone about the **Iveragh Peninsula** and the chances are that they won't have heard of it unless they live there, but the Ring of Kerry rings a bell with people around the world who have never been to Ireland. Now you're here, and unless you are on a package tour, some decisions have to be made. Which direction to travel, and how long to take? In this book we follow a clockwise route. That puts you on the seaward side of the roads, for marginally better views. How long? Plenty of people drive around in a day but we don't recommend it: there's too much to see and you want to be able to make frequent stops. (In July and August you will need to book accommodation in advance.)

Kenmare, at the head of an estuary 37km (23 miles) long, makes a convenient starting point. An estate village which grew up in the 18th century, it's a centre for walking, climbing and fishing, with some good hotels and a fine golf course. Compared with what is to come, a gentle coastline brings you to Parknasilla, a quietly luxurious resort ever since the railways promoted this coast as the 'Irish Riviera'. Seals are often seen offshore, no doubt enjoying the good fishing. Sneem, backed by the Caha Mountains, with houses all brightly painted in different colours around a village green, sets out to entice passing tourists into its souvenir shops. At Castlecove, look for the sign to the right pointing to Staigue Fort, 4km (2.5 miles) inland, a remarkable

## THE LIBERATOR

You can't fail to notice that half the cities and towns of Ireland have an O'Connell Street, if not an O'Connell Bridge as well. When independence was won at last in 1922, the leaders of the new Free State lost no time in honouring the man who had achieved the first step a century before. Born in 1775, Daniel O'Connell was the son of a small landowner in County Kerry. He was called to the bar in 1798, one of the first Catholics to enter the legal profession after a change in the law allowed them to do so. Many other restrictions on Catholics were still in force, and they could not hold any high public office. O'Connell became a successful lawyer, but he also embarked on a political career, with Catholic emancipation as his goal. He formed the Catholic Association, using the clergy as organizers to achieve a mass membership. In the 1826 general election the Association mobilized enough support to elect several members who backed emancipation. A by-election in County Clare in 1828 gave another opportunity and this time the idea was put forward that O'Connell himself should stand. As a Catholic, he could not sit in parliament, but the law didn't forbid him from being a candidate. Amid wild excitement, he was elected by a 2 to 1 majority. The British government under the Duke of Wellington and Sir Robert Peel recognized the new situation. To exclude the victorious O'Connell might produce riots or worse. They reluctantly introduced a bill removing virtually all remaining restrictions against Catholics – in Britain as well as Ireland. The bill was passed, and a triumphant O'Connell entered the House of Commons in 1829.

Now he turned to the second great campaign of his life, its objective the repeal of the Act of Union of Britain and Ireland. His weapon was the mass meeting, for example when he spoke to hundreds of thousands at the Hill of Tara in 1843. Although the majority in Ireland was again with him, there was a vital difference from 1829. This time, he had only a tiny party of supporters in the House of Commons. Peel, now prime minister, was utterly opposed to repeal of the union, labelling it 'the dismemberment of this empire'. O'Connell's huge meetings were banned and his movement seemed to lose momentum. It split between those who, like him, wanted to stay within the law and others who were prepared to go outside it. By the time of his death in 1847, it was clear that his second struggle had failed, but he had aroused the masses to political action as never before, and thus set the course which led to independence.

prehistoric ring-fort on a hillside overlooking the Kenmare estuary. The dry stone walls are up to 4m (13ft) high, terraced internally and with two small chambers in the walls. Elaborate double stairways lead to the 'mezzanine' level. These stone constructions are notoriously hard to date. One expert estimate puts the building of Staigue Fort at about 500 bc but it would have been in use for many centuries and often repaired.

The little village of **Caherdaniel** has a couple of friendly old pubs and a good restaurant. A loop off the main road down to the sea leads to **Derrynane House**, the home of Daniel O'Connell, the campaigner for Catholic rights (see box above) who inherited it in 1825 and lived here on and off until 1847. The estate is now designated Derrynane National Historic Park and includes Abbey Island, only accessible at low tide. Even the direct road to the house is cut when tides are exceptionally high, but there is an alternative route. It's extraordinary to learn that Derrynane House was neglected and left open for years after the last of the family died. Some of Daniel O'Connell's books and possessions which had been kept safe for over a century were lost, but a lot survived and more have been donated. You can see an informative audio-visual programme on the life of O'Connell, and tour the modestly elegant rooms of the wing which he added to the house. A striking portrait shows his uncle Count O'Connell, the last colonel of the Irish Brigade in the French army of Louis XVI.

**Waterville**, on Ballinskelligs Bay near the end of the peninsula is an old-established resort, with a golf course and good fishing. If you plan to spend two days travelling around the Ring, there's a good choice of bed-and-breakfast accommodation. Standing stones and dolmens in the fields around Waterville show that the area was an important ancient burial site. Although the main road cuts across the peninsula at this point to Cahirciveen, you will miss some of the best scenery if you go that way. If you have the time and your own transport, continue south west along the coast to the tiny harbour of **Ballyskellig** (or Ballinskelligs). A boat trip leaves from here at 10am in summer, weather permitting, for the offshore islands called the Skelligs (see below). A rough and narrow road going on round the coast to **Bolus Head** comes to a dead end high above the sea. You have to retrace your steps to Ballyskellig, but the scenery and seascapes are worth the effort when visibility is good.

At Portmagee you can cross by a bridge to **Valentia Island**, starting point for the first Atlantic cable, and still an important weather station. On the island, just over the bridge, The Skellig Experience (open in summer only) tells of the life and work of the early Irish Christians in monasteries such as Skellig Michael. Other displays deal with lighthouses, seabirds and underwater life. Weather permitting, a modern cruise boat will take you from the quay near the bridge to circle close to the Skelligs, but on this excursion you won't be able to land. Other boats do make the trip, again depending on the weather and sea conditions, and can give you some time ashore on **Skellig Michael** (Great Skellig), 10km (6 miles) off the coast. This forbidding sharp pinnacle of rock rises to a height of 217m (712ft). From the little landing stage steep steps climb to the site of the monastery, which survived here on and off from the 7th to the 12th century – smaller groups of Christian hermits had lived on the rock as early as the 5th century. Rough walls and partly rebuilt chapels and beehive stone huts cling to the rocky slopes. Nearer the coast, the precipitous islet of Little Skellig is a bird sanctuary, one of the largest breeding grounds for gannets in western Europe, and landings are not permitted.

In spite of its remoteness, Valentia Island feels less rural and untamed than the neighbouring mainland, but many visitors come just because it's as far as they can go: next stop North America. The products of the **Slate Quarry** on the cliffs above the north coast went to roof the Paris Opera, the Houses of Parliament and Charing Cross Station in London as well as being used for countless billiard tables. The great cavern (the 'Grotto') left where some of it was extracted has been fitted up as a rather gaudy chapel.

Back on the mainland, the one-street town of **Cahirciveen**, birthplace of Daniel O'Connell, can be choked with traffic, especially on market days. **Rossbeigh Strand** provides the best stretch of sandy beach in the area. The **Kerry Bog Village** rural museum near Glenbeigh recreates the dwellings and workshops of half a dozen craftsmen and their families so you can see how life might have been in the early 1800s. A lot of research has gone into furnishing and equipping the stable and dairy, thatcher's house, blacksmith's house and forge, turf cutter's and labourer's little cottages with original or replica tools and rudimentary furniture.

Killorglin is an ordinary-looking town in the flat country at the north end of the Ring of Kerry. Its Puck Fair in August has become famous, a magnet for backpackers and eccentrics from far and wide. The star of the show is a wild or semi-wild

*Cloud-capped Valentia Island, joined by a bridge to the mainland and an optional extra when you make the circuit of the Ring of Kerry.*

goat, garlanded and tethered on top of a stand in the town centre. As one story goes, the townspeople were warned of the approach of Cromwell's troops by goats running ahead of them through the town, and they have honoured the breed ever since. Other places used to enthrone a goat during festivals, and some are reviving the custom: it may date from pagan times. As so often happens in Ireland, you have a choice of what to believe.

**The Dingle Peninsula**

You're unlikely to have the time to explore all the peninsulas on the complicated map of south-western Ireland. If you are forced to pick only one, this might be the best choice. Having been 'discovered' so much later, it is somewhat less commercialized than the Ring of Kerry and there's

## THE KERRY WAY

Can't stand crowds or the sight of tour buses? There is another Ring of Kerry, which keeps to the footpaths and only drops down to the coast road here and there. With your walking boots, rainwear, maps and the Tourist Board's leaflet 26C you can walk the tracks and green roads of one of Ireland's long-distance paths. The circuit totals about 190km (118 miles) plus a spur joining it to Killarney, but you can of course pick sections that suit your schedule and stamina.

just as much to see, concentrated in a smaller area.

Coming from Killarney, a dead straight road meets the coast at Dingle Bay. A long tongue of sand called **Inch Strand** almost blocks the head of the bay. Windsurfers hit the beach and archaeologists hit the sand-dunes, where early inhabitants of Ireland subsisted on the sort of shellfish diet you will pay a lot of money for in a restaurant.

**Dingle** (*An Daingean*), calls itself the most westerly town in Europe, not counting the Atlantic islands. Ever more popular over the last thirty years, it seems to be able to absorb throngs of holiday visitors while still looking much the same. Plenty of restaurants have sprung up, and you can find some good seafood. Pubs serve some reasonable grub and put on traditional music nights of varying authenticity: you're as likely to hear country and western as anything Irish. Some have rooms to let, there are a couple of old established hotels, and every second house in the vicinity seems to offer bed-and-breakfast accommodation. The streets are lined with terraced houses and shops, painted in a harmonious rainbow of colours. Few buildings stand out and nothing is notably old. In fact the main landmark in the centre is the big, newish Catholic church. Take a look at its attrac-

tive interior, with a fine statue of the *Madonna and Child* by Imogen Stuart. The big harbour, almost land-locked so it's superbly sheltered, plays host to trawlers and other fishing boats from all over western Europe. When their crews and a multinational tourist crowd mix in the streets, you can hear a dozen tongues. The area west of Dingle by contrast is mainly Gaelic-speaking, and many road signs are in that language only.

**Dunbeg** (*Dún Beag*) is an Iron Age promontory fort on the steep cliffs not far from the road. Structures like this cut off part of a projecting cliff edge, reducing the length of wall to be defended to a minimum. An especially strong refuge, Dunbeg is protected by multiple banks and ditches and a complex entrance, with a *souterrain* (underground passage) which may have been part of an escape route. The *clochán*, or 'beehive' stone hut, inside the wall provided some shelter. Radiocarbon dating suggests the site was fortified about 580 BC and was in use on and off, probably during periods of unrest, until the 11th century AD.

Along the road near **Fahan**, many more beehive huts are scattered over the slopes of the conical Mount Eagle, 517m (1,696ft) high and worth a climb. On a clear day, the views are superb. The hundreds of ruined structures on the hillside date from prehistoric times right up to the 19th century. With one, two and three chambers, the beehive huts are mostly open to the sky now. In dry stone construction the roof was the weak point, and in a modern version you can see near the road, the builder cheated by using cement. In this area, the local farmers – and their children – take the opportunity to charge you a small fee for looking at the antiquities on their land.

At **Slea Head** the coastline turns north, and in calm summer weather a little sandy cove entices hardier souls to swim. Offshore, the rugged Blasketts – Great Blaskett and four smaller islands – were inhabited until 40 years ago. You can read what life was like in Maurice O'Sullivan's classic *Twenty Years A-Growing*, which was translated from the Irish and has rarely been out of print since he wrote it in the 1930s.

In summer, boats sail to Great Blaskett from Dingle and also from **Dunquin** (*Dún Chaoin*), the nearest point on the mainland where a visitor centre stands ready to give you the background information before or after your trip.

*H ead for the hills and you're likely to have the scenery to yourself: sunshine and showers on the Conor Pass over the Dingle Peninsula.*

Smerwick Harbour takes a shallow bite out of the north coast of the peninsula. Hidden among reeds on its western side, **Fort del Oro** (*Dún an Oir*) is a promontory fort, reminiscent of prehistoric versions. This one was built by a small Spanish expedition in 1579, here to support one of several Catholic rebellions during the reign of Elizabeth I. The following year, Italian reinforcements came to join them, but the combined force was cut off by the English Navy, and the Spaniards and their Irish allies in the fort were defeated and slaughtered. Little remains to be seen of any building, but a modern stone monument in high relief pays tribute to the victims of the massacre.

In a maze of lanes east of Ballyferriter, signposts will lead you to the little dry stone church called the **Oratory of Gallarus**. Shaped rather like an upturned boat, blunt at both ends, it has a very low doorway but plenty of headroom inside. Perfect in its way, it was formerly thought to date from as early as the 9th century but the latest opinion suggests the 12th century as more likely. Less than 2km (1 mile) to the north, **Kilmalkedar**'s roofless church has a 12th-century Romanesque door and arches, a strange stone inscribed with letters of the alphabet inside and an Ogham stone outside the door.

The great mass of **Mount Brandon**, at 953m (3,127ft) the second highest peak in Ireland, fills the horizon to the east. From Ballybrack, Saint's Road climbs to the summit and the ruins of St Brendan's oratory. The mountain meets the sea so suddenly at the north coast that there is no room for a road, so cars have to return via Dingle town and take the **Conor Pass** road. This climbs to 450m (almost 1,500ft), and it's worth stopping near the top and taking a walk, if the weather's

agreeable, before dropping down to the sea at Brandon Bay and turning east towards Tralee.

## Tralee

Before reaching the town, look out for the Blennerville working **windmill**, restored and back to grinding wheat for flour 200 years after it was built. There's a craft display including weaving and pottery, and at the nearby quay where many departed Ireland for ever, an Emigration Exhibition tells their story. At Blennerville too, a short stretch of the old **Tralee and Dingle Light Railway**, regrettably closed in 1950, has been put back into service with renovated old carriages and staff in period dress. Retired railwaymen and young enthusiasts lovingly tend the 1892 tank engine.

Even the most loyal citizen might admit that **Tralee** (*Trá Li*) is no beauty spot, especially when it has the rest of Kerry to compete with. The name is the prettiest thing about the town, which has nevertheless gone in for some self-promotion with the August 'Rose of Tralee' beauty contest (anyone with a smidgen of Irish blood welcome). It's turned into a TV spectacular and a full week of parades, horse races and a street carnival. At the other end of the cultural spectrum, *Siamsa Tire*, the **National Folklore Theatre**, has an international reputation as a showpiece of Celtic culture in mime, music and dance. In Ashe Hall in the middle of town, **Kerry the Kingdom** is a three-stage exhibition and 'ride', designed to give people something to do indoors if the weather's bad, not to mention trying to turn an honest penny. A video show extols the landscape and culture of the county and 'The Treasures of the Kingdom' displays the jewels and artefacts of the region

## HERO OR TRAITOR?

Roger Casement was born at Dún Laoghaire (then Kingstown) in 1864. As British consul in the Congo, then a personal fief of the king of Belgium, he revealed the horrifying cruelty to which black labourers there were subjected. A report on similarly inhuman conditions in Peru brought him a knighthood. Poor health forced him to retire to Ireland in 1912. Although from an Ulster Protestant family, he favoured the nationalist cause and helped to form the Irish Volunteers (see page 55).

After World War I broke out, Casement travelled to Berlin to seek direct German help for the cause of Irish independence, and hoped to persuade Irish prisoners of war in German hands to fight against Britain. In both respects he was disappointed. Learning of the plans for an insurrection at Easter 1916, Casement was sure that it must fail, and arranged to return to Ireland in a German submarine in order to contact its leaders. He may have been betrayed, because he was quickly picked up. Despite his conviction for treason, many in England thought he should not be hanged in view of his past service, or to avoid creating another Irish martyr. At the same time, his apparently authentic diaries were circulated, revealing his homosexual activities with the obvious intention of blackening his character. Sir Roger Casement was hanged on 3 August 1916. Like Wolfe Tone, he had tried to further Ireland's cause by joining Britain's enemies in time of war. In British eyes it was treason. Irish nationalists saw it as fully justified. After a long campaign, Casement's remains were brought from London in 1965 for reinterment in a place of honour in Glasnevin cemetery, Dublin.

through the ages. Finally, you board a moving car to twist and turn through a film set of the streets of Old Tralee, as it might have been on a market day in 1450, complete with sounds and smells. The era chosen, the 'Geraldine period', was the time of the powerful Fitzgeralds, earls of Desmond.

**Fenit**, at the mouth of Tralee Bay, is a favourite with anglers. There's great fishing from the beach or rocks, the long pier or one of the deep-sea boats available for hire at the little port.

In the flat land north west of Tralee, the long grey ruin of **Ardfert Cathedral** dates from the 13th century, with a fine Romanesque west door. Many other ruins of even older church buildings are scattered around. It stands on the probable site of the early church of St Brendan ('the

Navigator' see page 216). On the beach a mile away, on Good Friday, 1916, a German submarine put the Irish nationalist Sir Roger Casement ashore at Banna Strand. His intention seems to have been not to join the planned Easter Rising but to try to postpone it. In any event, he was arrested within a few hours and taken to London, where he was convicted of treason and executed.

Golfers congregate at two top-rated championship courses up the coast at the old-fashioned seaside resort of **Ballybunion** ('Ballybee' to the locals), where relaxing hot seaweed baths are also on the menu. At **Tarbert**, the main road turns east to Limerick, but if you want to continue up the west coast, a convenient car ferry operates across the Shannon to Killimer, every half-hour during the day.

# Land of Marvels Between the Lazy River and the Wild Atlantic

There's a world of difference between the gentle green pastures of County Limerick and the stony wonderland of the Burren in northern County Clare. Take a trip on the stately Shannon where the west begins and you could be in another country. You can't ignore the historic city of Limerick either, and the region around offers many attractions to persuade visitors who fly in to Shannon Airport to stay for a while. There's much to entice them away as well. Atlantic rollers break on sandy beaches or crash against towering cliffs. Lively and friendly, Galway City is the gateway to the wilds of Connemara and the mystical Aran Islands.

## Limerick City (*Luimneach*)

This is the crossroads of Ireland's west and south west, and close to Shannon Airport, so you are almost bound to pass through Limerick at least once. The Vikings founded their settlement of *Hlymrek* in 922, tempted by a sheltered island site beside the Shannon. The broad river made a perfect highway to the rich pickings to be had at the monasteries inland.

*D*unguaire Castle at Kinvarra on Galway Bay serves medieval banquets with a literary flourish.

The medieval 'English Town' took over the same site, strengthened by the building of a Norman fortress, King John's Castle. The 'Irish Town' grew up to the south, across the Abbey river. The 1760s saw rapid expansion further southwards in a chequerboard pattern of Georgian streets, an area called Newtown Pery. You can get your bearings by relating these three parts of the city to its rivers and bridges.

The walls of King John's Castle reflect in the river next to **Thomond Bridge** across the Shannon – stroll over it for the best view, and to see the Treaty Stone (see below, page 210). South of the castle, Bridge Street crosses the Abbey river to Irish Town: the fine Custom House (1769) is on the right. A block to the east, the stately 18th-century Granary has been

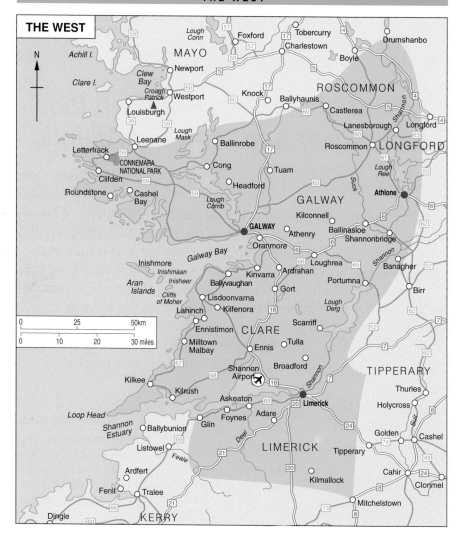

THE WEST

N

Achill I.

Clew Bay

Clare I.

MAYO

Newport

Croagh Patrick

Westport

Louisburgh

Leenane

Lough Mask

Letterfrack

CONNEMARA NATIONAL PARK

Clifden

Roundstone

Cashel Bay

Lough Corrib

Foxford

Charlestown

Knock

Ballyhaunis

Ballinrobe

Cong

Headford

Tuam

GALWAY

Kilconnell

Tobercurry

Drumshanbo

Boyle

ROSCOMMON

Castlerea

Lanesborough

Roscommon

LONGFORD

Longford

Lough Ree

Athlone

GALWAY

Athenry

Oranmore

Ballinasloe

Shannonbridge

Galway Bay

Inishmore

Inishmaan

Inisheer

Aran Islands

Cliffs of Moher

Ballyvaughan

Lisdoonvarna

Lahinch

Kilfenora

Kinvarra

Ardrahan

Gort

Loughrea

Portumna

Lough Derg

Banagher

Birr

Scarriff

0     25     50km
0   10   20   30 miles

Ennistimon

Milltown Malbay

CLARE

Ennis

Tulla

Broadford

Kilkee

Kilrush

Askeaton

Foynes

Shannon Airport

Adare

Limerick

TIPPERARY

Thurles

Holycross

Loop Head

Shannon Estuary

Ballybunion

Glin

Listowel

Ardfert

Fenit

Tralee

Dingle

KERRY

Deel

Feale

LIMERICK

Tipperary

Kilmallock

Golden

Cahir

Mitchelstown

Cashel

Clonmel

restored to serve as the city library. You'll find the tourist information office near the river front at **Arthur's Quay**, opposite a modern shopping centre, with the 19th-century Sarsfield Bridge crossing the river to the south. Behind the shopping centre, Patrick Street continues south west and takes the name of **O'Connell Street**, the central axis of Newtown Pery and Limerick's main thoroughfare. Take a walk along it to find vestiges of Georgian ele-

gance in Mallow Street (which leads to Shannon Bridge) and The Crescent. Some of the terrace houses rival Dublin's best, while others have long since fallen into sad disrepair.

## King John's Castle

Limerick's biggest landmark dates from about the year 1200. Determined to bring both his Norman and Gaelic lords to heel, John ordered the construction of the

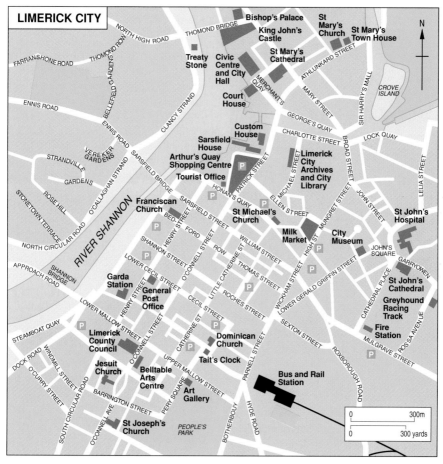

greatest fortress yet seen in the west of Ireland. It was to incorporate the latest techniques learned in the Crusades and his campaigns in France: the massive twin-towered gate was one of the new ideas. English Town and later Irish Town were ringed with walls, but the castle was the fulcrum of the city's defences. Its greatest tests came in four terrible sieges more than four centuries later. In 1642, Irish forces took it with the aid of cannon mounted on the tower of St Mary's Cathedral. After holding out for six months in 1651, it fell to an army commanded by Cromwell's son-in-law Henry Ireton. He

is said to have ordered its bombardment with rotting carcases to induce the outbreak of disease, so it was seen by many as a judgement when he died of the plague himself (at No. 3, Nicholas Street) just 10 days after taking the city.

Following the Battle of the Boyne in 1690, William of Orange's forces surrounded Limerick and waited for munitions and siege equipment to arrive from Dublin. Then in a famous exploit, the Irish second-in-command Patrick Sarsfield led a surprise attack on the supply column at the village of Ballyneety and completely destroyed it. There's scarcely a

*K*ing John's Castle has guarded the Shannon crossing at Limerick since the year 1200.

**A BAD PRESS**

Henry II named his youngest son John Lord of Ireland in 1177, when he was only 10 years old. A first visit when in his teens seems to have been spent partying and annoying local leaders. Then, after John became king of England in 1199, there came a succession of disasters in France during which almost all the rich lands gained in war or by dynastic marriages were lost. He returned to Ireland in 1210, to impose some order on both Norman adventurers and Gaelic chieftains, all of them his supposed subjects. Unlike most of his successors, he didn't favour one lot over the other. He quickly gave Ireland a degree of central administration for the first time. Thanks to him, Dublin Castle was strengthened and enlarged, the first coinage was struck for Ireland, the jury system introduced and sheriffs appointed. Short of stature and temper, derided as 'John Lackland', he was never popular and often unlucky, while his even nastier brother Richard 'the Lionheart' somehow managed to acquire an image to rival Sir Galahad. Contemporary records were mainly written by John's enemies, and later writers haven't been much kinder, but in Ireland credit should be given where it's due.

town in the Republic today without a Sarsfield Street, Square, Bridge or Bar. The respite was short-lived. The following year, with the last Jacobite army in the field beaten, Limerick stood alone and again besieged. After appalling losses, terms were agreed for surrender to avoid further bloodshed. On 3 October 1691, a treaty was signed, giving the defending troops the choice of joining William's army or going abroad. Almost all, Sarsfield included, went to France, the first of the 'Wild Geese' who fought in half the armies of Europe for the next century and more. Also under the terms of the agreement, many Catholic rights were to be restored, but the Protestant parliament in Dublin refused to ratify it. The 'Broken Treaty' has never been forgiven. The

**Treaty Stone**, a battered and grooved block of limestone on which it is said to have been signed, stands on a pedestal by the banks of Shannon, opposite King John's Castle.

A visit to the castle is practically a must. It has been well restored, and a colourful and well-designed exhibition and video show tell the story of the city from Viking times to the present day. Replicas of mighty rock-throwing war machines recall the days before gunpowder. Walkways over the castle's foundations reveal the remains of pre-Norman houses discovered in recent excavations. Traces

*St Mary's Cathedral, Limerick, started in the 13th century and often restored. Irish forces mounted cannon on the tower when they besieged King John's Castle in 1642.*

of a tunnel puzzled the archaeologists until someone remembered a first-hand account of the siege of 1642. Threatened by mines dug under the walls by the besiegers, the defenders bored a countermine of their own. It's still clearly visible.

Construction of **St Mary's Cathedral** began in 1172, even earlier than the neighbouring castle. It has frequently been rebuilt and another renovation is currently in hand. The Romanesque doorway is probably the only relic of the 12th-century design and even here many stones are modern replacements. Inside, the 15th-century choirstalls and carved oak misericords are a rarity in Ireland. St Mary's is the Church of Ireland cathedral: the Catholic **St John's Cathedral** to the east of the city centre is a 19th-century Gothic revival building with an unmissable 85m-(280ft-) spire. The **City Museum** across John's Square has informative sections on ancient history, coins, local history and the struggle for Irish independence. Much more impressively displayed, the **Hunt Collection** is housed at the University of Limerick's campus at Plassey, 5km (3 miles) east of the city off the Dublin road. John Hunt, responsible also for the founding of the Craggaunowen Project (see page. 216), spent 40 years collecting mostly in the fields of Irish art and

**NONSENSE**

Limerick gave its name to a kind of verse with a five-line AABBA rhyming pattern, but it wasn't originally of the 'There was a young lady from Cork...' variety devised by Edward Lear. Rather it seems to have been a spontaneous party piece composed in Irish by local poets in pubs. Indeed, one 18th-century landlord promised free drinks to anyone demonstrating his literary skills in this way. The name later became attached to Lear's nonsense rhymes, which had the same format. They tend to sound feeble to modern ears, since the end of the last line merely repeats the first. Today's limericks at least have a pithy punchline, the prime requirement of the Irish prototype.

archaeology, from Bronze Age jewellery and weapons to early Christian metal and enamel work, Irish and European pottery and silver. (The Collection is open to visitors in summer months only.) The university is also the home of the National Self-Portrait Collection.

### Near Limerick City

Whether you fly in to Shannon or come by road or rail, there's a lot to see in the area and plenty of places to stay. There's no need to base yourself in Limerick itself: you may well find it more pleasant to be in the countryside or one of the smaller towns such as Adare.

As the most westerly airfield in Europe, **Shannon Airport** became important for the transatlantic service in the early days after World War II. The airliners which had taken over from the flying boats based at Foynes (see page 214) had only just enough range and Shannon was perfectly placed for refuelling. When later generations of aircraft could easily fly between New York

*Traditional musical entertainment accompanies the ever-popular 'medieval' banquets at Bunratty Castle.*

and London or Paris non-stop, Shannon devised various temptations to persuade airlines to continue landing, inventing the duty-free shop and offering low cost fuel and barter arrangements. It remains the natural entry point for North American visitors to the west of Ireland.

**Bunratty Castle**, a fine and massive 15th-century rectangular keep, was one of the chief seats of the O'Briens of Thomond. It was heavily restored inside and out in the 1950s and '60s, and the crenellations are modern – old prints show gables and chimneys! The interior is well worth a tour when the crowds are not too great. Great halls taking up most of each floor, and numerous smaller rooms in the towers, are furnished with a fine collection of pieces

212

from the 14th to the 17th centuries. Medieval-style banquets are staged nightly (or even twice nightly when the demand is there), mainly for tour groups. The entertainment is of a highly professional standard, including more or less authentic traditional music and dance routines.

The **Bunratty Folk Park** next to the castle also attracts lots of tourists. Very well conceived and put together, it all began with one old farmhouse standing in the path of a runway extension at Shannon Airport. It was saved and reconstructed here, followed by original and replica buildings from all over the west and south west of Ireland. Cottages in different styles have a lived-in look, warmed by peat fires. Vegetables grow in the gardens, and one outbuilding is home to a sow and piglets. Take a peep inside the schoolroom, a real one brought from County Clare. There's a feeling that the children have just left and the neat rows of double desks might jog the memories of older visitors. The village street looks the way it might have

done in 1900 and McNamara's is a real pub entered from the park or, in the evenings, by an outside entrance.

In summer a *céilí*, or traditional Irish evening in 18th- or 19th-century style, is held nightly (or even twice nightly) in the great barn of the Folk Park. Guests are fed a meal of Irish stew, soda-bread and apple pie while singers and dancers do their stuff to the sound of the fiddle, accordion, pipes and *bodhran* (a goat-skin drum).

## South of the Shannon

The little port of **Foynes** was once the spot where all North Atlantic passenger flights took off or landed, from 1939 until just after the end of World War II.

*S*almon netting on the River Shannon is strictly licensed and controlled.

## IRISH COFFEE

Here's how to make your own, the Foynes way.

Put a generous shot (3 dessert spoons if you're measuring) of Irish whiskey in a stemmed glass, add 2 teaspoons of brown sugar, very hot black coffee, stir quickly and then float a layer of lightly whipped thick cream on the top.

There's no airfield, and there never was. The service was operated by flying boats, their 'runway' the waters of the Shannon estuary. Pan American Airways and BOAC flew Boeing 314 Clippers on the transatlantic run and Short Brothers Sunderlands ferried passengers to and from Poole harbour in southern England as well as operating to Lisbon and west Africa. The flying boats have long gone, but a new hovercraft can take groups on a fast if noisy tour of the estuary.

The old terminal building is now the **Flying Boat Museum**. Historic newsreel film has been edited to make a video presentation, *Atlantic Conquest*, on the history of the flying boat service. And the bar at the museum serves some of the best Irish coffee. It should: the sweet and fortifying brew was invented right here, they say, by Chief Steward Joe Sheridan in 1942. He took pity on some shivering passengers whose flight had been delayed, and put a shot of Irish whiskey in with their coffee, sugar and cream.

**Glin Castle**, an 18th-century country house overlooking the Shannon estuary, belongs to the 29th Knight of Glin whose predecessors have lived here for 700 years. Since he is an art historian and writer on architecture, it's not surprising to find the

*D*isplays in the Flying Boat Museum at Foynes tell the story of the passenger service that flew the Atlantic from here in the Second World War.

## ATLANTIC BRIDGE

A ticket cost a fortune, in real terms about fifty times today's fare. That was if you could buy one, and you probably couldn't: every seat was taken by military top brass, politicians, diplomats and others on wartime business. Refugee scientists headed for the US. Film stars came to Europe to entertain the troops. The crews used to stay in lodgings in Foynes; there was no telephone so a horseman was sent to call them before a flight. The captain enjoyed the greater luxury of the Dunraven Arms in Adare, sharing it, so the story goes, with spies from both sides. Remarkably, in six years of intensive operations in all weathers by the Boeing Clipper fleet, not one life was lost. The museum was opened in 1989 by Irish-born actress Maureen O'Hara. Her husband Captain Charles Blair had piloted the last scheduled flying boat in and out of Foynes in 1945.

house exquisitely restored and decorated, a treasury of furniture and Irish portraits and landscapes. (It is only regularly open for a short period each summer.)

## South of Limerick

Almost too pretty to be true, **Adare** is a picturebook village with its main street lined by thatched cottages. You may think it looks more English than Irish, but thatch was universal hereabouts until landlords started replacing it with slate in the 19th century. About 16km (10 miles) south west of Limerick on the Killarney road, Adare resembled many another collection of poor huts and hovels when the 2nd Earl of Dunraven set about it in the 1820s. It certainly had an above average complement of ruins. Having rehoused the villagers, he restored one abbey as the Catholic church and another to be his

family's mausoleum. The remains of the ruined Desmond castle with two great halls can be seen down by the river, but they are inside the private manor grounds and deemed too unsafe to visit anyway.

The family house, **Adare Manor**, was expanded beyond recognition into a magnificent Elizabethan revival mansion by the 2nd Earl, although he died in 1872 before it was quite completed. A.W.N. Pugin was responsible for some of the neo-Gothic interior features: the minstrels' gallery, great staircase and dining room panelling and ceiling. It is now a luxury hotel in 336ha (840 acres) of grounds, so you may have to make private arrangements to see inside. The vast long gallery with its 17th-century Flemish choirstalls is stunning. Every July, Adare holds a music festival, including performances by international orchestras and soloists. Audiences outgrew any venue the village or even the great house could offer, so the big events are held in a 2,500-seat circus tent. In winter, Adare is a fox-hunting centre. Expert visiting riders are welcome to take part: you can brush up your style with some lessons if necessary, and hire all the appropriate clothing.

## Lough Gur

A small and undramatic lake set in fertile countryside, this was the focus of a succession of past civilizations. Judging by all the treasures found when it was partially drained, or dredged up later, the lake itself seems to have been regarded as sacred. Important excavations in the 1930s revealed Neolithic graves and house foundations dating from 2500 to 2000 BC. Pick up information leaflets and maps at the **Stone Age Centre**, housed in plausible recreations of Neolithic buildings based on evidence from archaeological digs. At popular times, guides may be available to take you on a tour. Otherwise, head off on your own: a circular walking route round the C-shaped lake connecting the main sites is about 8km (5 miles) long. A word of warning: mosquitoes can be virulent here at times, so have some repellent handy. If you feel less energetic, it's possible to drive close to some of the monuments, stopping at several points. The Grange stone circle, 60m (200ft) in diameter and dating from about 2100 BC is one of the biggest and most complete in Ireland, with 113 stones – almost the full complement – still in place.

At **Ballyneety**, on the road back to Limerick, Patrick Sarsfield captured and blew up William of Orange's siege train (see page 209) and the exploit is commemorated in a statue. **Bruree**, 32km (20 miles) south of Limerick, was the childhood home of a modern Irish hero, Éamon De Valéra, who was to dominate Irish politics for 60 years. Born in New York in 1882, he was sent back to Ireland when only two and a half, on the death of his father. The village school he attended is now the **De Valéra Museum**. A leader of the 1916 Rising, founder of the Fianna Fail, several times prime minister and then president, he returned to the village at the age of 90 to open the museum. It contains many relics given by 'Dev' himself, as well as his school desk and books and displays on rural life, local history and archaeology. (It is open from Tuesday to Sunday.)

## North of Limerick

The impressive ruins of **Quin Abbey** look almost ethereal in the misty distance. Close up, there are few details of great interest except to the specialist. Nearby **Knappogue Castle** runs tourist banquets along the lines of Bunratty's. Serving wenches in low-cut dresses bring round the food and drink while story-tellers and singers relate tales of Irish history and legend. The castle itself, built by the MacNamara clan in the 15th century, was just a shell twenty years ago, so all of the exaggeratedly medieval detail has been recreated from scratch.

The **Craggaunowen Project**, on a side road west of Quin, mainly comprises replicas of ancient buildings, set in the grounds of a 16th-century tower house. It was started by the late John Hunt, who also formed the Hunt Collection so beautifully displayed at the University of Limerick (see page 211). The sites, including a Bronze Age hunters' cooking pit, a ring-

---

### ST BRENDAN THE SEAFARER

It all depends on how you interpret the 9th-century manuscript which tells his story. According to one reading the monk from south-western Ireland is credited with reaching America in about the year 565, perhaps by the 'stepping stone' route: The Hebrides, Faroe Islands, Iceland, maybe Greenland, Labrador and Newfoundland. After all, the Vikings went that way a few centuries later. Wanting to show that it was at least possible, the explorer Tim Severin had a vessel built along the lines described in the old tale, which sounded rather like a big version of the leather-covered *currach* still in use today in western Ireland. After some hair-raising adventures almost matching Brendan's own saga, they made it. The leather proved good at resisting the impact of ice floes, something not seen off Ireland, and when it was punctured, the crew were able to sew on a patch.

fort with souterrain and a *crannóg* (lake dwelling) are spread out along woodland paths. A section of a *togher*, or wooden track built across a bog, is not a replica but part of an Iron Age original excavated in County Longford in 1985. A 3,500-year-old dugout canoe is another extraordinary survival. John Hunt also restored Craggaunowen Castle, the tower house which serves as a small museum displaying some medieval religious carvings and furniture. Various ancient crafts – woodcarving, pottery, and weaving – are demonstrated in the summer.

*Could St Brendan have sailed a leather-covered craft like this across the Atlantic in the 6th century? The modern* Brendan *is on show at the Craggaunowen Project.*

A star extra exhibit here, kept under a big glass tent, is the *Brendan*, a hide-covered boat which Tim Severin and his crew sailed across the Atlantic in 1976.

## CRUISING THE SHANNON

Binoculars at the ready for bird-spotting, a novel open but unread in your lap, you'll soon fall into a daydream while the captain does the steering. This is a different way of seeing Ireland: no mountains, no cities and very little traffic. Sometimes you'll be far from shore in the broad expanse of a lough. Then the low green banks of the river close in, from time to time revealing the ruin of an ancient abbey. You can tie up here and there and go ashore to see the sights, go to a pub or spend the night. Only half a dozen locks interrupt the flow, and each of them has a wise old keeper ready to throw a line to any amateur skipper who's having trouble. That's unless you arrive at the lock at lunchtime, when you may have to wait. There's no point in trying to hurry. The boat won't go fast anyway, but you have to run the motor for at least four hours a day to charge the batteries.

If you like the idea, the Irish Tourist Board has details of the cruise companies. The options include four-, six- and eight-berth boats, and you can arrange to pick up and leave them at different points. If you'd prefer to pay someone else to do the work, there's a more expensive way to go. Floating hotel barges take about a dozen passengers at a time, provide all meals, even drinks, airport transfers and onshore excursions and entertainment.

Killaloe, Portumna, Banagher, Athlone and Carrick-on-Shannon are the main bases for the cruise boats. You'll be given a lesson in managing the boat, written instructions and maps. Just like hiring a car, you'll be charged the first part of any bill for damage, unless you pay extra for damage waiver – recommended to novices.

*A haven for pleasure boats, where the Shannon meets the great inland sea of Lough Derg.*

# The Shannon from South to North

Rising on the slopes of Tiltinbane where Counties Cavan and Fermanagh meet, Ireland's longest river soon gathers enough water to form a broad stream. Then it links a succession of lakes all the way to Limerick, its estuary and the Atlantic, a total of about 260km (161 miles). Until the coming of the railways and roads, the Shannon was the chief highway to the heart of Ireland and marked the traditional border of the western kingdom of Connacht. Whether you travel by water or land, there's a wealth of history, scenery and wildlife to be seen.

## Heading Upstream

The southern end of many cruise itineraries, **Killaloe** was an important river crossing point long before its old 13-arch stone bridge was built. Brian Boru had a palace here, and Patrick Sarsfield led his raiders over the river a mile north of the bridge which was held by William of Orange's forces. Inside the restored 12th-century **St Flannan's Cathedral**, the Thorgrim stone is the upright of an early high cross, uniquely marked with both Ogham script and Scandinavian runes. The Romanesque St Flannan's Oratory near the cathedral has the same barrel-vaulted ceiling and very steeply pitched roof as other early Irish oratories.

*St Flannan's Cathedral at Killaloe – a landmark at the beginning and the end of many Shannon River cruises.*

North of Killaloe the banks widen into an inland sea. The 130km$^2$ (50 square miles) of **Lough Derg** make it the biggest of the Shannon lakes and a favourite of bird-watchers and anglers. **Holy Island** (*Inis Cealtra*) in Scarriff Bay is covered with monastic ruins from the 6th to the 17th centuries including high crosses and a capless round tower. At the northern end of Lough Derg, the market town of **Portumna** makes a convenient point to shop for supplies. The Jacobean Portumna Castle is slowly being restored: its huge

*Lough Derg on the River Shannon, great for fishing and sailing, but watch out for changes in the weather.*

grounds have been designated as a forest park and nature reserve. North of here, the Shannon narrows again from broad lough to meandering river.

The one-street town of **Banagher** is a main base for cruise boats. It was the home of Anthony Trollope in 1841 when he was starting out on a career as surveyor for the General Post Office and decided to try writing novels to boost his income. A few miles away by road, **Clonfert** may be only a tiny village, but it's one with a remarkable cathedral! Dedicated to St Brendan, it dates from about 1200. The weird and wonderful Romanesque doorway is one of the sights of Ireland. Six concentric arches stand on inward-sloping columns, their capitals carved into pagan-looking animals' heads, all surmounted by an intricate tall gable. The nearby bishop's palace was last occupied by the one-time British fascist leader, Sir Oswald Mosley, until it was destroyed by a fire.

At **Shannon Harbour**, the **Grand Canal** coming all the way from Dublin meets the great river. It never achieved the commercial importance its builders hoped for, and for years was virtually abandoned. Now the waterway has taken on a new role as a pleasure route: narrowboats can be hired at Tullamore for a cruise to Dublin or down the southern branch to join the River Barrow.

**Shannonbridge** takes its name from a long narrow 16-arch bridge. Look out for the fortified artillery positions built in the Napoleonic Wars. There were real fears that the French would come this far upstream. Although they seem far-fetched now, remember that the river systems were the roads of those days, especially in this land of treacherous bogs. Just a short walk to the east, you can take a ride in one of the comfortable carriages of the grandly named Clonmacnois and West Offaly Railway. Running on an old Peat Board (*Bord na Mona*) track, it carries passengers on an 8km- (5 mile-) trip round the **Blackwater Bog**. Including explanations and stops, the tour takes 45 minutes. The environmental emphasis is partly a public relations exercise for the nearby peat-burning power station, but it does give grounds for some hope that its appetite won't be given free rein to strip the whole of the bog.

## Clonmacnois

Of all the ruins along the banks of the Shannon, this is the star attraction, although more for its atmosphere and tranquil setting than for any distinctive buildings. Founded in about 545 by St Ciaran, it was all too easily accessible by water, and it was sacked at least eight times by the Vikings, then by Irish enemies. Rebuilt in the 12th and 14th centuries it was wrecked almost fatally in 1552 during English campaigns to enforce the Reformation and suppress Irish culture in the west. Even as late as the 17th century, some restoration was attempted, but what you see now are mere vestiges of its glory. Clonmacnois was famous for learning and art, for centuries a city where kings held court as well as one of Ireland's most important monasteries. A new visitor centre dispenses information and a plan of the site.

From the river, the chief landmarks are two round towers named after the chieftains who ordered their construction. **O'Rourke's Tower** near the landing stage is roofless, but **MacCarthy's Tower** by the northern boundary is in fine shape and, unusually, has its entrance at ground level. According to monastic records it dates from 1124, negating the theory that these structures were built in response to the Viking threat, which had long since subsided. The **Cathedral**, near the entrance, is the biggest building though still quite compact. It was started in the 10th century, but the striking north doorway topped by a statue of St Patrick flanked by St Francis and St Dominic dates from a 14th-century reconstruction. The little **Teampull Ciaran**, a tiny 10th-century church where the monastery's founder is said to be buried, stands in the middle of the enclosure, north east of the cathedral.

*O'Rourke's Tower at Clonmacnois has eight lookout slits near the top. It was broken when it was struck by lightning in 1134.*

221

*The Cathedral and high cross at the great monastic site of Clonmacnois, destroyed in the 16th century.*

Opposite the cathedral's west door, the tall **Cross of the Scriptures** is carved with scenes from the life of Christ and the Last Judgement on the west face and the foundation of Clonmacnois by St Ciaran on the east face. A now headless and armless cross of limestone with streaks of dark material in the rock has been heavily eroded, but in its original polished state it must have been extraordinary. Beautifully inscribed and decorated gravestones from the 17th to the 20th centuries are scattered all round the site.

## Athlone

You might expect such a central cross-roads town to be busier and more impressive. It grew up at a ford across the Shannon, the safest for many miles, which the Normans guarded with a castle on the west bank. The medieval bridge and its 19th-century replacement were naturally built below the castle walls. Remodelled in the 16th century and again in the late 18th, even with the lower profile favoured at the time **Athlone Castle** is still the most significant sight in town. As the gateway to Connacht, held by Jacobean forces, it was the object of a massive bombardment by de Ginckel's army in 1691. The destruction all around was enormous, and the centre of gravity of Athlone moved across the river to the east bank, where it has remained to this day. The castle houses a well-designed display on its own and the town's history (open from May to September), a folk museum and a tribute to one of Athlone's most famous sons, the tenor John McCormack (1884-1945). Appropriately, his own gramophone is one of the exhibits and it still works. In the early days of recording, he was an international superstar, crossing every boundary between opera, ballad and popular song. If platinum discs had existed then, he would have been awarded dozens of them. He gave a fortune to help the poor of Ireland and was made a Count of the Papal Court for his work for charity.

Cruise boats can be hired in Athlone, and excursions are run up or down river for those who just want a short trip on the water. Upstream, the Shannon soon opens out into the complexities of **Lough Ree**, famous for its fishing and scattered with islands. Lanesborough is a fishing centre at the north end of the lough, where the waters narrow for the run up to **Carrick-on-Shannon**, the end of the trip for the cruise boats and an important base for their hire.

# County Clare

The soft centre of the county and the lush banks of the Shannon in the south and east give no hint of the drama to come. The majestic Cliffs of Moher on the west coast and the stark grey Burren are among the great sights of Ireland. Clare was too remote and infertile to tempt many Norman or English settlers, so traditional life and language survived here as long as anywhere. The county was in the vanguard of agitation for Irish rights and independence, electing Daniel O'Connell by a two to one majority in 1828 and supporting Parnell and the Land League in the 1880s. Éamon

De Valéra was MP for East Clare for over 40 years. In the last twenty years, tourism and European Community regional and farm policies have generated a degree of prosperity. There has been an astonishing amount of new building – you'll scarcely see an old thatched cottage now.

## The South-west Coast

If you by-pass Limerick and take the ferry across the Shannon, you come first to Clare's handful of seaside resorts. **Kilrush** with its modern marina specializes in yacht rentals and trips to the low, flat **Scattery Island** offshore in the middle of the estuary. (Check at the Scattery information centre near the marina.) Scattery was the site of an important monastery founded in the 6th century by St Senan. The numerous ruins date from later times but the well-preserved round tower is thought to be one of the earliest to be built, perhaps in the 10th century. The last people to live on Scattery left about 20 years ago, and their fields and cottages are being gradually buried beneath weeds and creepers. **Kilkee**'s perfect horseshoe of sheltered sandy beach attracts Irish families to its masses of caravans and holiday homes, and the **Loop Head** peninsula is worth an excursion for the cliff walks and views. Up the coast, Spanish Point takes its name from two Armada shipwrecks: many bodies were washed ashore and even the survivors were hanged or shot. A monument near the beach commemorates them and the visit of the King and Queen of Spain 400 years later, in 1988. Inland, **Miltown Malbay** comes alive every July when the Willie Clancy Summer Music School gets going. Hundreds attend for the classes, but thousands more come for the socializing and the informal sessions in the pubs.

## Ennis

The busy county town is only 40km (25 miles) from Limerick and much closer to Shannon Airport (see page 212: it's in County Clare but described under Limerick). The shell of the 13th-century Franciscan **Friary** is the main landmark, suffering from an ugly restoration of the top of its tower. From here, a stroll down Abbey Street leads to the O'Connell Monument (a column and statue). Ahead along Parnell Street, turn down the narrow 18th-century Chapel Lane to the **Market Place**, packed with stalls and local colour every Saturday. Centrally placed with a surfeit of accommodation and some lively pubs, Ennis can be a base for exploring the area. If you're heading for north Clare and the Burren, it makes more sense to stay somewhere on the scenic coast. The restaurants are better there too.

A few kilometres north of Ennis off the Ballyvaughan road, **Dysart O'Dea** was the site of the historic battle of 1318, when Gaelic forces crushed a Norman army, ending their influence in west Clare. You'll find the ruins of a 12th-century church with a fine Romanesque doorway and broken round tower. In a field behind, a high cross is beautifully decorated with Celtic designs. The nearby O'Dea Castle (a 1480 tower house) is now a museum of clan relics and records, courtesy of an American O'Day.

On the short route from Ennis to the sea, **Ennistymon** is an attractive market town, not much affected by tourism, whereas its neighbour **Lahinch** is entirely dedicated to leisure. Two championship courses bring in the golfers. The wide sandy beach faces towards the south-west wind so the sea often suits surfers more than swimmers.

## The Cliffs of Moher

The Irish coast, so often awe-inspiring, outdoes itself here where a precipice up to 200m (660ft) high drops sheer into the sea. Tens of thousands of seabirds – guillemots, fulmars, puffins, kittiwakes and razorbills – nest in the crevices, and their shrill cries compete with the ceaseless wind and roaring sea. Inevitably the spectacle attracts hundreds, even thousands, of visitors on a summer's day and the atmosphere around the car park and unnecessary visitor cen-

tre can be excessively commercial. If you want to share the views only with the seabirds, come when the sun starts to go down and the crowds have gone. Early mornings are quiet too, but the cliff faces are in shadow. If there is a crowd, just take a walk along the top to the south west to leave them behind. In the opposite direction stands the 19th-century folly called O'Brien's Tower, erected for the eccentric local landlord Cornelius O'Brien in 1835. There is really no need to climb it: the view is no better from the top. Perhaps because a piper entertaining his guests fell over the cliff, 'Old Corny', as he was known, also put up the clifftop fences made of great stone slabs, the local

*F*or those with a head for heights, the edge of the vertiginous Cliffs of Moher on the coast of County Clare.

'Moher flags'. Look closely: some of them are a mass of fossils.

**Lisdoonvarna** is a straggling, unprepossessing place built some way inland. It grew up around sulphurous springs that gave it some pretensions to being a spa, and people still come to immerse themselves in the waters. By long tradition, in September the pubs and hotel bars in the town turn into a kind of marriage bureau for the middle-aged (and more). Unfortunately, any hope of a natural atmosphere in which to find a soulmate has been destroyed by publicity and the resulting rowdy coach tours.

# The Burren

Some find it enchanting, some forbidding. The north-western corner of Clare is a grey, austere plateau of bare limestone, deeply fissured into blocks and sharp ridges by the action of rainwater. The Burren, from *Boireann*, rocky land, is a

perfect example of what geologists call *karst* landscape. The surface is scattered with 'erratics', rocks that don't belong, but were carried here by the moving glaciers of the Ice Age and dumped when the ice sheet melted. Not only a geological textbook, this land is a record of human activity too: hundreds of stone forts, uncounted tombs and spiders' webs of walls. Changes are slow: it is hard to tell if a pile of stones was put there last year or centuries ago.

At first sight it seems as infertile as a desert, but look into the cracks and you'll find a profusion of plant species growing in sheltered pockets of soil. Tiny thorn bushes like bonsai trees hug the rock, folded round its contours by the wind. If you love **wild flowers**, come in May and June to see the brilliant blue gentians, cowslips, creamy mountain avens, little rock roses and 23 varieties of orchids. At any time of the year, the whole area is a natural rock garden, with plants that usually prefer arctic, alpine and Mediterranean climates.

People call the Burren timeless, but modern techniques of pollen analysis show that many trees were growing here after the last Ice Age. So is the bare rocky appearance relatively recent? To build the massive Neolithic tombs and later ringforts would have needed quite a large population. Was there a thin soil covering that was lost as a result of land clearance and farming? The evidence is beginning to point that way.

*You'll find a profusion of plant species growing on the limestone expanses of the Burren.*

At **Kilfenora** on the southern edge of the region, the **Burren Display Centre** features a short audio-visual show and exhibits on the geology, plants, wildlife and archaeology of the region. There's a tearoom with home-made cakes and the well-stocked shop can provide you with detailed maps – essential for exploring the Burren – books and the usual souvenirs. Close by, Kilfenora's small 12th-century cathedral is part roofless ruin, part adapted to serve as the parish church. Five high crosses include a 12th-century example of the crucifixion and bishop type, thought to have been made to promote the influence of the bishops during their power struggle with monastic leaders.

Close to Kilfenora to the north east (ask for directions at the Burren Centre), **Ballykinvarga** (*Cathair Bhaile Cinn Mhargaidh*) is the most impressive of all the rock forts in the area. Like Dún Aengus on Inishmore (see page 236) it's surrounded by a band of *chevaux de Frise*, jagged spikes of limestone calculated to stop any attackers dead

in their tracks. It's hard to date but is probably from the Iron Age, about 200 BC. The Irish name means an important market, so it may have been the site of a Celtic fair.

About 6km (4 miles) east of Kilfenora, near the stark shell of a fine 17th-century fortified house, **Lemaneagh Castle**, the road north towards Ballyvaughan passes through the heart of the eastern Burren. On the left of the road you'll find some of the finest examples of limestone 'pavement', amazingly regular slabs of the rock, as flat as an airfield but slashed by deep chasms. Visible to the west of the road, 11km (7 miles) north of the castle, look out for the big stone ring-fort of Caherconnell (*Cathair Chonail*). Less than 1km (half a mile) further north on the opposite side of the road you'll see the great **Poulnabrone** portal dolmen, topped by a huge flat stone. Recent excavations have dated it to about 3300 BC, the Neolithic period, and they also showed that it needed propping up after all this time; hence the supports. About 1.5km (1 mile) further north, the **Gleninsheen** wedge tomb is one of the best preserved of many on these uplands. A famous gold collar to be seen in the National Museum in Dublin was found here in 1930. It dates from 700 BC, but the tomb is much older. The Burren is scattered with the vestiges of many churches too: some, like Templeline, are positioned on much earlier pagan sites.

### The Burren Coast

North of the Cliffs of Moher, the coast road is missed by many visitors who stick

*T*he little church at Kilfenora, on the edge of the Burren, ranks as a cathedral.

to the main routes inland. A pity, because some of the best of the Burren is to be seen there, especially if you're prepared to walk. Offshore, gannets and terns dive for fish, seals and dolphins play and the low mysterious outlines of the Aran Islands hover like a mirage in the mist.

**Doolin** (Fisherstreet on some maps) is known for its folk music centred on the pubs which are jammed full all summer long. It also has a better than average crafts gallery with innovative jewellery and fabrics. A ferry service operates from the little harbour to the Aran Islands (see page 235) from April to September, though at the times of the lowest tides, the boats cannot approach the jetty, and passengers have to be shuttled out to them in currachs, fitted with outboard motors these days.

You don't see them at first but the hillside is cut by deep ravines and the valley of the River Caher which reaches the coast at **Fanore**. Far from sterile, the Burren supports foxes, badgers and pine martens. With patience and luck, you might glimpse otters along the Caher, the only river in the region to stay mainly on the surface. Between Fanore and **Black Head**, the limestone pavement descends in regular terraces to the sea. The narrow strip of farmland along the shore was built up long ago with seaweed and sand. Stone walls divide it into tiny fields which used to support whole families: now they might provide grazing for a couple of cows. Even on the hill above where at first sight

*D*oolin on the Clare *coast is a centre of traditional music, and one of the points of departure for the Aran Islands.*

all looks grey, the sure-footed local cattle find enough to eat among the rocks.

Several superb walks lead up into the Burren. Although it's possible to pick your way across the 'pavement', you have to spend most of the time looking down to avoid breaking an ankle. So you'll be grateful for the green roads cleared for cattle-droving, through years of unimaginable toil.

**Ballyvaughan** with its two piers is a picturesque fishing village largely devoted to tourism, with several restaurants and plenty of hotel and bed-and-breakfast accommodation.

Dozens of cave systems have been found beneath the Burren. You need local advice and the right equipment before entering most of them but there is one that anyone can visit, 5km (3 miles) south of Ballyvaughan. The commercial **Aillwee Cave** (open from mid-March to October) extends a mile into the mountain. It was an underground river channel until the end of the last Ice Age, so stalactites and stalagmites have had little time to grow and only a few spindly examples are to be seen. More interesting are the hollows scraped out long ago by brown bears who moved in to hibernate. The cave is a

standard stop on many tours but a new tunnel has been blasted through the rock to create a one-way system and relieve the congestion. A big shop and café serve to divert the crowds while they wait.

The tranquil ruins of the 13th-century **Corcomroe Abbey**, nestling under the northern edge of the Burren, have some good stone carving and also the tomb of Conor O'Brien, King of Thomond and recognized by some as the last High King of Ireland (although most historians would say that this was Roderic O'Conor, see page 238).

On a long offshoot of Galway Bay, the picturesque little port of Kinvarra is the home base of a number of hookers, meaning, of course, fishing boats of a special Galway Bay design. **Dunguaire Castle** at the head of Kinvarra inlet holds medieval banquets in the summer months, here with a literary angle to the entertainment: actors read from the giants of Irish letters, concentrating on humorous extracts. There's no shortage of choice – Shaw, Synge, Joyce, O'Casey and more.

# County Galway

Galway packs as many contrasts as any part of Ireland. You'll find Galway City colourful and active, and it's also the gateway to Connemara. When Cromwell confiscated their fertile lands further east and told them to go to 'Hell or Connacht', the Irish trying to scratch a living from these rocks and bogs must have wondered if they would actually be any worse off in the other place. Seen today through the eyes of romantics, walkers or painters, the same landscape is a wilderness paradise. Out in Galway Bay, the Aran Islands are easy to reach these days, but miraculously

---

**WALK THE BURREN WAY**

One of the shorter of Ireland's long-distance footpaths, this one goes from Liscannor near Lahinch, across Hags Head and along the top of the Cliffs of Moher to Doolin. Then it heads inland to join one of the green roads across the high Burren, eventually dropping down to the coast near Ballyvaughan. The total distance is about 42km (26 miles) but you can choose shorter sections. Details are on the Tourist Board leaflet 26L, which suggests suitable maps and detailed guides.

*The mists of legend:
sunrise in Galway Bay.*

preserve some of the atmosphere of their long isolation. We begin in the less dramatic south of the county.

## Southern Galway

Coming from the south or the stony sensations of north Clare, the flat countryside and the plain streets of **Gort** probably won't detain you long, but two of the major stops on any literary circuit are close at hand.

Lady Gregory, playwright and life-long friend of WBYeats, lived at **Coole Park** 3km (2 miles) north of Gort from 1880 until her death in 1932. Yeats was a frequent visitor, first coming here to convalesce in 1898. In his poem *Coole Park,*

*1929,* he not only anticipates the passing of the owner:

*I meditate upon a swallow's flight,
Upon an aged woman and her house,*

but with chilling prescience of the house itself:

*When all these rooms and passages
  are gone,
When nettles wave upon a shapeless
  mound ...*

The house was demolished in 1941, and little remains to show where it was except an avenue of cedars. The gardens are now a popular though neglected public park. The unusual objective of literary pilgrims is a great copper beech initialled by Yeats and his brother Jack, the painter, Shaw with an elaborate monogram GBS, J.M. Synge, Sean O'Casey, John Masefield and many more. A key has thoughtfully been provided to help you decipher them and

230

railings ensure that new sets of initials aren't added.

Back on the main road and a short distance north, signs point to **Thoor Ballylee**, down a lane to the east. This is the 16th-century tower which Yeats bought for £35 in 1916. He was living here when he was elected to the Senate of the new Irish Free State in 1922 and when he was awarded the Nobel Prize for Literature the following year. He continued to spend time here on and off until 1928. A stone tablet in the wall is inscribed with his lines:

*I, the poet William Yeats*
*With old millboards and sea-green*
   *slates*
*And smithy work from the Gort forge*
*Restored this tower for my wife*
   *George*
*And may these characters remain*
*When all is ruin once again.*

Indeed it did fall into ruin again, but was again restored in 1965 as a Yeats museum.

*I declare this tower is my symbol; I*
   *declare*
*This winding, gyring, spiring tread-*
   *mill of a stair*
*is my ancestral stair;*
*That Goldsmith and the Dean, Berke-*
*ley and Burke have travelled there.*

Thus he wrote after moving in, shortly after his marriage to Georgie Hyde Lees in 1917. The first floor was their living room. It now contains a collection of Yeats first editions and a tribute to his friend Robert Gregory, Lady Gregory's son who was killed in action in 1918. The bedroom on the second floor has a fine barrel-vaulted ceiling.

*Upon a moonless night*
*I sat where I could watch*
*her sleeping form ...*

In the third floor room, you can hear recorded readings of some of his most famous and powerful poems. Passing an old jackdaw's nest – sadly the birds have to be excluded now – the narrow winding stair continues up to the roof. The tranquil view over meadows where sheep and lambs graze can hardly have changed, and most of the time the only sound is still that of the river. Back at ground level, there's a good 15-minute audio-visual presentation. The shop has a comprehensive stock of books, not only by or about Yeats and his contemporaries, but almost anything related to Irish writing.

**Kilmacduagh**, 5km (3 miles) west of Gort, was a cradle of Christianity in the area, founded by St Colman in about the year 600. It became a major religious centre, judging by the complex remains dating from that time until the 16th century, when it suffered the usual devastation at the hands of Elizabethan agents of the Reformation. Several of the ruined churches include Romanesque features. The tall round tower has been partly rebuilt.

North of Gort on the Galway road at Ardrahan, **Rathbaun Farm** is a real working sheep and cattle farm, but one which welcomes visitors. It's open from April to October, when there are usually plenty of lambs and frequent demonstrations of sheep-shearing. The ticket includes tea or coffee in the old farmhouse. (Lunch is served too, from noon to 2pm.)

## Galway City

Connacht's capital has seen a lot of benefits from tourism and European Community regional policies, and managed to keep growing when rivals went into recession. A young population boosted by university students keeps things lively and the place is colourful and friendly. There's

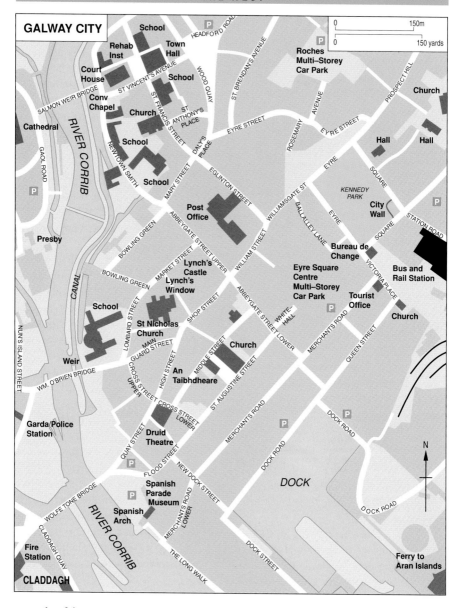

GALWAY CITY

Headford Road — School — Town Hall — Rehab Inst — Court House — Conv Chapel — Cathedral — Church — School — School — School — Presby — Post Office — Lynch's Castle — Lynch's Window — School — St Nicholas Church — Weir — An Taibhdheare — Church — Garda/Police Station — Druid Theatre — Spanish Parade Museum — Spanish Arch — Fire Station — CLADDAGH — RIVER CORRIB — CANAL — Roches Multi–Storey Car Park — Church — Hall — Hall — KENNEDY PARK — City Wall — Bureau de Change — Eyre Square Centre Multi–Storey Car Park — Tourist Office — Bus and Rail Station — Church — DOCK — Ferry to Aran Islands

150m / 150 yards

enough of interest to attract visitors to spend some time here, perhaps on the way to Connemara or the Aran Islands.

The site was a natural choice for a settlement, defended by the Corrib river to the west side and an arm of Galway Bay to the south east. The Norman de Burgo gave it to 14 families from among his supporters to defend and they and their descendants succeeded in holding it, even while Norman power in Connacht declined. (Just for the record, the 14 families were those of Athy, Blake, Bodkin, Browne, D'arcy or Darcy, Deane or Dean,

Font, French, Kirwan or Kirwen, Joyce, Lynch, Morris, Martin and Skerret, with various other spellings. Their descendants are still found in Galway, all over Ireland and wherever the Irish have emigrated.) Massive city walls were built to keep out the fierce Gaelic tribes, principally the O'Flahertys. Thus protected, Galway's merchants, many from the same 14 families, traded with France and Spain.

Having been hammered into submission by a Cromwellian army in 1652, the city judiciously agreed terms the next time a siege was threatened, after the Battle of Aughrim in 1691 (see page 234). Even so, there were confiscations of the property of former Jacobite supporters. Restrictions on Irish trade hit Galway hard, and the famines made matters worse, precipitating decades of depression which only lifted in the 1960s and '70s. Now, the city is as bright and cheerful as you could wish.

The open space of **Eyre Square** and Kennedy Park used to be just outside the massive city walls. The main city gate stood where Willamsgate meets the square at its western corner, and a section of the city wall has been preserved inside the Eyre Square Shopping Centre. It was discovered forming part of a builder's yard, behind centuries of accumulated rubbish. The same shopping centre offers a computerized genealogy service for Irish names: you call up your name on the screen, and pay for a print out of the derivation if you like it. The very active and useful Tourist Information Office is just off the square to the south, in Victoria Place.

Heading along Williamsgate into the heart of the old city, the street changes its name to William Street and then Shop Street. On the corner of Abbeygate Street, **Lynch's Castle** is by far the best pre-served of the townhouses built by prosperous merchant families. (For centuries, the post of Mayor of Galway was rarely held by anyone but a Lynch.) Dating from around 1600, the four-storey house with its elaborate carved stonework now serves as the Allied Irish Bank. There must once have been many fine mansions like it. A visitor in 1614 wrote 'The towne is small, but all is faire and statelie buildings. The fronts of the houses are all of hewed stone, uppe to the top, garnished with faire battlement.'

Just off Shop Street on the same side, the Collegiate **Church of St Nicholas** is the largest medieval church in Ireland, dating from about 1320 although the spire was added much later, in 1683. There's some fine 15th- and 16th-century carving round the west door and on the font inside on the left. In the so-called Lynch Aisle, tombs of members of the family take up much of the wall space. Most striking is 'the' Lynch Tomb with its flame-like stone tracery (an architectural style known as Flamboyant and found on many 15th- and 16th-century tombs in Connacht), and traces of original paintwork.

Back on Shop Street, a left fork down narrow High Street – which soon becomes Quay Street – leads on to Wolfe Tone Bridge. Instead of crossing, turn to the left to find a section of old city wall known as the **Spanish Arch**, perhaps because Spanish ships used to tie up at the quay here, and a blind arch beside it. Through the arch and to the left, you'll see a beautiful section of stone parapet. Next door to the Spanish Arch is a small but interesting local **museum**. Upstairs and out on the roof, you'll get a good view of this part of the city.

Upstream, an old salmon weir gave its name to another bridge over the River

Corrib which leads to the modern Catholic cathedral, built in a controversial version of neoclassical style. From any of the bridges, there's a lot to see, and in a good year plenty of salmon still make their way upstream to Lough Corrib.

The road over Wolfe Tone Bridge leads to **The Claddagh** ('the beach'), formerly a Gaelic-speaking fishing village of thatched huts, older than the city itself, but long since transformed into an unfashionable inner suburb. The Claddagh ring design of hands clasped around a crowned heart, which is now sold by half the jewellers in Ireland originated here. Further west along the shore of the bay, **Salthill** is Galway's rather downmarket local resort.

*T*he 16th-century
*Spanish Arch, part of Galway's city wall close to the old quays, where Spanish ships used to tie up.*

## East of Galway City

Built at the end of the 19th century, the Catholic cathedral at **Loughrea** is notable for its still controversial modern stained glass. The adjoining museum contains a rich collection of earlier ecclesiastical art, including medieval wood carvings, rare survivors of the mass destruction of such images in the 16th and 17th centuries. About 6km (4 miles) north east of the town, in a field beside a farmhouse near Bullaun, stands an extraordinary relic. The egg-shaped, metre-high **Turoe Stone** (*Tuar Ruadh*) dates from the Celtic Iron Age, perhaps 2,200 years ago. By its style, it appears to be a product of the La Tène culture, which originated in central Europe, roughly where Switzerland is today, and was spread to Brittany and then to Ireland by Celtic immigrants. The swirling carved patterns are also found on gold and bronze ornaments of the period. They look almost random but when viewed from above, they are actually perfectly organized into quadrants.

West of Ballinasloe on the road from Loughrea, an exhibition centre marks the battle site of **Aughrim**. Here in 1691, the last Jacobite army in the field, a mainly Irish force commanded by the French General St Ruth, was defeated by a smaller multinational Williamite army under its Dutch commander de Ginckel. At first things went well for the Irish, who held the higher ground while their opponents struggled through a bog towards them. It's said that a causeway was betrayed to de Ginckel's men; then at a critical stage of the battle St Ruth was killed, and confusion set in. Even before his victory at Aughrim, de Ginckel had been bargaining with Irish Catholics, offering toleration in return for their surrender in an attempt to bring the war to an end. Now

Galway accepted the terms. Limerick alone declined to submit. Tradition says that St Ruth was buried amid the impressive remains of **Kilconnell Friary**, a few miles north west of Aughrim. This is notable for a tall and elegant tower typical of Franciscan architecture – look up to see a little carved stone owl in the vaulting of its ceiling. A 15th-century canopied wall-tomb has the same exquisite flame-like tracery as the Lynch tomb in Galway City.

Respectable-looking **Ballinasloe** takes on a different character every October, the time of the sheep and horse fair, an ancient gathering of dealers, gypsies and tinkers from all over Ireland. Its origins are put as far back as the 5th century and perhaps the most famous sale ever made here was that of Napoleon's horse Marengo, after Waterloo. By the 1850s and '60s, up to 4,000 horses and 100,000 sheep were changing hands during the week of the fair. People claimed the roads were so jammed with livestock they had to walk from the station to the town on the sheeps' backs! These days, car dealers as well as horse-dealers can be seen bargaining. Held on Fair Green and overflowing into all the open spaces in town, the fair is more like a big agricultural show with all sorts of peripheral activities.

While in this area, you might want to visit the evocative monastic ruins beside the Shannon at Clonmacnois (see page 221) and the little jewel of a cathedral at Clonfert (see page 220).

# The Aran Islands

Three low limestone outcrops in Galway Bay are actually a geological extension of the Burren (see page 226). Tiny in size

*T he view of the Aran Islands from the mainland is rarely this clear; they're more often hidden in the mist.*

## GETTING TO THE ISLANDS

Competing passenger ferries operate from Galway City to Inishmore (June to September), and from Spiddal (in summer) and Rossaveal (all year) to all three islands, the service being much more frequent in summer. Rossaveal and Spiddal, to the west of Galway along the Connemara coast, are linked to the city by bus. In addition, there's a ferry route from Doolin on the Clare coast in summer to Inishmore (May to August) and Inisheer (April to September). If it looks like being rough and you're a poor sailor, take one of the short routes: from Rossaveal to the islands takes only about 25 minutes, or fly.

Daily flights serve all three islands from the Connemara Airport west of Galway City. In summer there's a continuous shuttle service to Inishmore. You may wish the flight time could be longer – six minutes hardly gives you enough time to appreciate the views.

Few people stay overnight: there is bed-and-breakfast and hostel accommodation but for limited numbers. Some of it is tied to advantageous package deals run by the airline or ferry companies or Irish Rail. In summer you'll need to make reservations.

and population, they have exerted a magnetic influence on the Irish imagination ever since the 19th-century renaissance of Gaelic culture and language. It was recognized that their isolation had preserved ways of life which were vanishing if not already gone from the rest of Ireland. Isolation is a thing of the past now. Flights arrive every day on all three islands, weather permitting, and frequent ferries disgorge daily doses of visitors in the morning and take them away again in the afternoon. And yet, the magic remains. The tourists head off to see the sights and most of the islanders get on with what they're doing, even if it's knitting Aran sweaters or getting ready for the bed-and-breakfast guests.

## Inishmore (*Inis Mór*, 'the Big Island')

The ferries dock at Kilronan (*Cill Rónáin*), home of the island's fishing fleet which lands most of its catch at Rossaveal. Two fleets of bicycles for hire are based at the end of the quay, and in reasonable weather cycling is a great way to get around. Take note that it's about 8km (5 miles) of hilly, winding lanes to Dún Aengus (see below) and you'll need to cover about 40km (25 miles) if you want to see a good part of the island. Walking is a wonderful way to experience all the islands, if you have the time. For those who haven't, or are not so mobile, pony-and-trap drivers and minibus tour operators wait to meet the ferries. The airfield is south of Kilronan harbour.

The narrow island, about 15km (9 miles) long, slopes gently to the sea along its north coast, where you find all the villages and a succession of sandy bays. Lanes meander between a maze of stone walls enclosing little fields of pasture or potatoes. Most of them were once bare rock: the soil was built up from layers of seaweed and sand. At Kilmurvey, 7km (4 miles) west of Kilronan, a track leads to the cliffs which line the south coast of Inishmore and the prehistoric fortress of **Dún Aengus**. If this were in the middle of a flat field, it would still be worth going a long way to see. Perched on a 90m (300ft) vertical cliff, it is heart-stopping. Massive semicircular walls and concentric outer ramparts end only at the very edge of the precipice. A low table of rock has been left standing roughly at the centre, perhaps for ceremonial use. Many questions remain unanswered. Dún Aengus is

*The south coast of Inishmore, Aran Islands, where the Iron Age fortress of Dún Aengus hangs on the edge of a precipice.*

presumed to date from the Iron Age, perhaps 100 BC, but that's a guess. It is tempting to suggest that the fort used to be circular, and half has dropped into the sea in cliff falls. So much erosion along a straight face seems unlikely, and the prodigious defences are perfectly logical the way they are. Make a point of walking outside the outer concentric rampart to inspect the broad band of sharp limestone 'teeth' called **chevaux de Frise** (literally 'Frisian horses', devised by a north German tribe who *had* no horses). Any attacker could scarcely walk through them

– try it. Those with the time can find three other important Iron Age forts on Inishmore. The beautifully preserved circular **Dún Eoghanachta** stands north west of Dún Aengus. The double circle of **Dún Eochla** (or Dún Oghil) on the highest point of the island west of Kilronan has been well restored but with a consequent loss of some of its magic. **Dún Dubh Cathair** is a spectacularly sited promontory fort on the south coast.

The north side of the island is liberally dotted with the ruins of monastic sites and old churches, and a few which have been restored. The 12th-century Teampull Chiaráin (St Ciaran's Church) and ancient well are just off the coast road west of Kilronan. In the overgrown fields near the shore west of Kilmurvy, remains of several *clocháns* include one large and still fully roofed example. In the same area, the so-called Seven Churches amount to scattered ruins and the restored church of St Brecan. The saint's grave is marked by the carved shaft of a broken high cross.

Back at Kilronan, the **Aran Heritage Centre** (*Ionad Arann*) in the old coastguard station examines the history and culture of a long isolated community. Superb photographs and displays make it well worth a visit, perhaps while you're waiting for the ferry.

### Inishmaan (*Inis Meán*)

Less than 5km (3 miles) long, the middle island gets far fewer visitors than Inishmore or even little Inisheer. You get the feeling that life has changed less here. Like the other islands, it's a tight network of stone walls enclosing tiny fields of pasture and potatoes. Men still go fishing, off the shore, from small craft or out on the handful of bigger boats. The main prehistoric sites are the partly rebuilt oval

Dún Conor (*Dún Chonchobáir*) fort on the central ridge and a Bronze Age chamber tomb called, as many in Ireland are, Dermot and Grania's Bed (or Diarmaid and Gráinne's – spellings vary. See page 260). During the revival of interest in all things Celtic at the end of the 19th century, the writer J.M. Synge spent several summers here. Even more than his book, *The Aran Islands*, the photographs he took make a unique record of island life.

### Inisheer (*Inis Oirr*)

The smallest of the three, Inisheer is lower and flatter, apart from a rocky outcrop topped by the irregular Creggankeel ringfort re-used in the 15th century as the outer wall of an O'Brien castle. The daily flight and the ferry from Doolin have started to bring a flow of visitors in summer, though nothing like the traffic to Inishmore, and a few houses offer bed-and-breakfast accommodation.

# North of Galway City

The market town of **Tuam** was once the seat of the kings of Connacht. One of them, Turlough O'Conor, became the most widely recognized High King of Ireland since Brian Boru. Tuam's cathedral was originally built during his reign, in about 1150, but it had fallen into disrepair by the 19th century and the landmark you see today is largely a reconstruction. Inside, though, the old chancel was preserved, with its great semicircular Romanesque arch supported by odd, pagan-looking heads. Also inside the cathedral now after years of standing in Market Square, you'll find the intricately carved but much worn cross of Tuam, dating from the same period.

West of Tuam, near Headford stand the imposing ruins of the Franciscan **Rosserrilly Abbey** (or Ross Abbey), worth a stop to see its remarkably preserved cloisters and domestic buildings. The broad expanses of Lough Corrib, favourite of anglers, are close by to the west. Near the lough's north shore, **Cong Abbey** in County Mayo is conveniently visited from here. In the middle of the little village of Cong the ruin gives few hints of its former importance. It was given a limited restoration in the 19th century, but one which aimed more at the picturesque than the authentic. A painfully ugly modern church has unfortunately been built right next to it. Ashford Castle, now a luxury country house hotel, is an elaborate piece of Victorian romanticism, something out of a pre-Raphaelite painting. It was built for Lord Ardilaun of the Guinness family, who also paid for the work on the abbey.

---

**HIGH KINGS**

The last true High King of Ireland, Turlough's son Roderic O'Conor (Ruaidrí Ua Conchobáir) never gained such wide acceptance as his father. The post was not hereditary but even so, Ireland might in due course have evolved into a unitary kingdom in the same way as Scotland, for example. It was Roderic's ill luck to have to face the Anglo-Norman incursions triggered by the king of Leinster, Dermot MacMorrough, whom he had banished. After the stunning initial successes of the Normans, many lesser kings acknowledged Henry II of England as their overlord. Roderic felt he had no choice but to do the same. Perhaps in regret for his part in the events that led up to the invasion, he spent his declining years as a pilgrim at Cong Abbey, and died there in 1198. He was buried at Clonmacnois near the high altar of the cathedral beside his father.

Between Ballinrobe and Clonber, not far west of Cong, you'll cross the channel of a canal built to connect Lough Mask and Lough Corrib. It seemed such a good idea at the time, in the 1840s, putting people to work and solving an old problem: the river between the lakes went underground for most of its short length. Unfortunately, it did so because the local limestone leaked, so when the 5km (3-mile) canal was finished, complete with bridges and locks, it didn't hold water. Lining it with impervious material was reckoned too expensive, so that was that. The 'Porous Canal' is still there, and still empty though you may see some water in it if there has been recent heavy rain.

**Joyce's Country**, the name given to the mountains, deep valleys and loughs west of Clonber has nothing to do with James Joyce, for a change. This lovely but bleak country was settled by Welsh adventurers of that name after the Norman

*Spiddal on the north coast of Galway Bay: fishing and craft centre and summer ferry port for the Aran Islands.*

invasion and somehow held against all comers including the fierce O'Flahertys and O'Malleys.

## Iar Connacht

West of Galway City, this land of granite outcrops and bogs is crossed by few roads. Follow the coast and you'll come to the fishing village of **Spiddal** (also spelt Spiddle) where there's a ferry service in summer to the Aran Islands, and a notable crafts centre with workshops and a gallery. **Rossaveal**, on its own inlet near the mouth of Galway Bay offers a year-round service to the Aran Islands. The nearby town of Costelloe (*Casla*) is the HQ of a Gaelic language radio station for the Gaeltacht areas of Connacht. You'll find it loud and clear on your car radio and even if you don't follow the talk, you'll get an idea of the local taste in music. At the head of the bay the poet and nationalist Pádraig Pearse, executed for his part in the 1916 Easter Rising, had a summer cottage. It is now a memorial to him, and is open during the summer.

A more direct road (the N59) towards Connemara heads north west from Galway and meets the shores of Lough Corrib at **Aughnanure Castle**. A six-storey 16th-century tower house, it was a stronghold of the O'Flaherty clan, whose name alone was enough to set the citizens of Galway shivering behind their city walls. The sheltered village of **Oughterard** is the place to hire boats for a fishing expedition on the lough, reckoned to be one of the best in Ireland for salmon and trout. Fishing schools here will teach you the finer points of casting.

## Connemara

What now looks so picturesque was once the scene of great suffering, as too many people tried to subsist by growing crops on the poorest of soils. Almost all the land was either mountain or bog. Coming from Galway City, the main road picks a narrow path between the two. On the left is a seemingly endless wild waste of peat, swamp and a thousand little lakes. On the right come the Maumturk mountains rising to 668m (2193ft), then the cluster of peaks known as the **Twelve Bens of Connemara** (often called the Twelve Pins), the highest being Benbuan at 730m (2395ft). Hill walkers will want to explore, and can acquire good maps and route guide booklets from local Irish Tourist Board offices. The weather can be treacherous, and it sometimes seems as if the higher you climb, the boggier the ground becomes. Walking alone is not advisable.

If you have the time, take the long way round by the coast instead of sticking to the main (N59) road westward. The attractive rocky inlet of **Cashel Bay** has a notable hotel and other accommodation. **Roundstone** is a fishing village in a magnificent setting, with the surprising addition of workshops where all kinds of traditional Irish musical instruments are made. On a clear day, take a walk up to the isolated 301m (987ft) summit of Errisbeg for a surreal view north over the Roundstone Bog. The white sand beaches found here and further to the west come as another surprise.

On the northern edge of the great bog, John Alcock and Arthur Whitten Brown crash-landed their converted Vickers Vimy bomber after making the first non-stop transatlantic flight in 1919. They were both knighted for their achievement. Just off the road to Clifden, about 6km (4 miles) south of the town, a wing-shaped stone monument marks the event: the landing site itself is down a side track.

**Clifden** (*Clochán*) is quite small but still the main centre of the area and 'capital of Connemara'. A couple of broad attractive streets are mainly turned over to the holiday business in summer, with several good restaurants where you may find local salmon, lobsters, oysters and mussels. Hotels and bed-and-breakfast places provide plenty of accommodation and in July and August every room is needed, so you should make a reservation. **Letter-**

**frack**, up the coast at the head of the next big inlet, began as a Quaker settlement. (Many landowners all over Ireland invited non-conformist groups to move in, hoping they would be more tractable and hard-

*Mighty machines harvest peat from the bogs of Connemara.*

241

working than the Catholic Irish, whose resentment and despair over past treatment made them resistant to new ideas.) Letterfrack is the north entrance to the **Connemara National Park** and the park Visitor Centre here can tell you about the flora, fauna and local sights. The park was started with a fairly modest 2,000ha (5,000 acres) but more land purchases are planned. It includes the nearby Diamond Hill, supposedly named because it glistens after rain, and some of the most impressive scenery of the Twelve Bens. Kylemore Abbey to the east of Letterfrack is no ancient foundation but an extravagant 1860s Tudor revival stately home, now a convent school. You can visit the grounds at any time, and parts of the house, too, from April to November.

The deep, narrow inlet of **Killary Harbour** is sometimes called Ireland's only real fjord, winding nearly 15km (10 miles) inland between the mountains. The lower slopes are lined with the ridge and furrow patterns of long-abandoned potato fields: shellfish are cultivated now, on hundreds of frames in the sheltered waters of the harbour and salmon are farmed in pens here as in many of the west coast's bays. Near the head of the inlet, the Leenane Cultural Centre on the theme of sheep and wool puts on occasional demonstrations of shearing, spinning or weaving. Sheep, including some old and rare breeds, graze placidly in the field behind, and in season you may be invited to feed a pet lamb.

*T*he deep inlet of Killary Harbour is one of Ireland's longest. Fish farms have become a major industry.

# Epic Scenery to Enchant Poets and Pilgrims

Mayo and north-western Donegal can be as wild and remote as anywhere in Ireland. Huge cliffs alternate with sandy beaches, all endlessly washed by the cleanest waters in Europe. Whether fishing in the sea or the rivers, hill walking or riding on horseback or bicycle, there's no end to the outdoor activities on offer in the varied north west. If the weather is fickle, you'll appreciate the bright days all the more. The traces of history are thick on the ground in this region. Stone Age builders picked spectacular and prominent sites and here they had plenty to choose from.

## County Mayo

The coastline, all inlets and islets, is astonishing. Achill Island, Ireland's biggest offshore island, offers stunning views, vertigo-inducing cliffs and holiday beaches. The streets and quayside of the pretty little town of Westport take on a Mediterranean air every summer. Two places in the county bring a host of pilgrims: the mountain of Croagh Patrick ever since the saint spent one Lent on its stony summit, and Knock after the miraculous apparitions of 1879. Now Knock's international airport has made Mayo's marvels even more accessible.

### The South West and Clew Bay

The main road into Mayo is scenic enough, heading for Westport up the valley of the Erriff. Famous for its runs of salmon, the river pours over Ashleagh Falls and down into Killary Harbour. However, there's an even more beautiful route, just a few miles longer, although the sights on the way might delay you for quite a while. Crossing the river at Ashleagh, it follows the north side of Killary Harbour, then cuts due north through the mountains along the Bundorragha river. Fishing parties stay here at Delphi Lodge, given its name by the 1st Marquess of Sligo who had travelled in Greece with Byron.

*T*he shrine at Knock reproduces the visions reportedly seen in 1879 on the end of the parish church.

After passing Doo Lough, almost walled in by mountains, the road meets the coast again at **Louisburgh**, a planned estate town of neat houses, bars and holiday cottages. (No, the Louisburgh in Nova Scotia is not named after this one. It was the other way round: in 1758, the uncle of the Hellenophile Lord Sligo had been present at the capture of the Canadian fortress from the French in the Seven Years' War.) **Clare Island**, 8km (5 miles) offshore in the mouth of Clew Bay, was the stronghold of the 16th-century firebrand Grace O'Malley (or *Granuaile*), something between a queen and a pirate captain who visited Elizabeth I in London

in 1575, treating her as an equal. You can visit the island by the regular ferryboat from Roonagh Quay west of Louisburgh. Assuming that most people won't have the time, the Granuaile Visitor Centre in Louisburgh tells the story of the female chieftain and the O'Malley clan, and publicizes the attractions of the area.

One of them practically speaks for itself. The peak of **Croagh Patrick**, 765m (2,510ft) looks almost conical from some angles, like a volcano. The mountain is as wreathed in legend as it often is by cloud. St Patrick is said to have spent the 40 days of Lent here in the year 441 praying for Ireland's deliverance from paganism, and

THE NORTH WEST

ordering the mass suicide of the island's snakes. Ever since, it has been a place of Christian pilgrimage. Not so much at Lent, now, but on the last Sunday in July when thousands make their way to mass on the mountaintop, some going barefoot in spite of the sharp stones. It figured in pagan ritual too – the end of July corresponds to a Celtic festival taken over by the early Christians. The climb is a straightforward slog up rough tracks, unfortunately dis-figured in places by litter. If you are fit and walk non-stop you'll take about an hour to reach the top, not a sharp summit but a small plateau and a plain white chapel. With luck, you'll be able to see south to the Twelve Pins and the lakes of Connemara, and north across Clew Bay, dotted with 365 oddly shaped islets left after the last Ice Age. The figure seems suspiciously exact but don't bother to count: the number changes with the tide.

'The most beautiful view I ever saw in the world', wrote William Makepeace Thackeray when he spied Clew Bay from his carriage in 1842. He was on his way to **Westport**, a model town laid out in 1780 with the advice of the eminent

*Magnet for pilgrims, the summit of Croagh Patrick is frequently obscured by cloud.*

architect James Wyatt. The octagonal centre is an original touch, with the later addition of a statue of St Patrick on a tall column. A wide main street with colourful shops and pubs leads down to the Carrowbeg river, which Wyatt tamed into a tree-lined canal crossed by a series of arched bridges. Children fishing seem oblivious of the hypnotic gaze of Major John MacBride, one of the leaders of the 1916 Rising, depicted in a startling bust (see page 205).

The 18th-century **Westport House** (open from May to September), with beautiful plasterwork, furniture, glass and paintings, was an early tourist attraction, and has a children's zoo in the grounds. The cold dungeons under the house are all that remains from an earlier castle on the site. Wide lawns and woods around the great house lead down to **Westport Quay**, once the focus of high hopes for commercial development. They were to be blighted, first by British competition and the restrictions put on Irish trade by Parliament in London, then by famine and depression. Now some of the old warehouses have been given a face-lift and turned into restaurants, bars and shops. Westport is a great centre for fishing, sailing, riding and touring the region. Its musicians have made a name for themselves too. The Chieftains' flute player Matt Molloy owns a pub here, and the town stages festivals in July and September.

*Westport House, County Mayo, built for the Marquess of Sligo in the 18th century. It was one of the first Irish stately homes to get into the tourism business.*

Irish visitors still outnumber the rest, although Westport's international reputation is spreading. Several hotels and dozens of bed-and-breakfast places provide accommodation but you'll need to make reservations in summer.

**Newport**, the village on the north corner of Clew Bay, is dedicated to sea-angling. The Georgian mansion, Newport House, is now a country house hotel, as well known for its cooking as for elegant interiors and plasterwork.

## Achill Island

The golden eagles that gave the island its name are a rare sight now, but Ireland's biggest offshore island is still a natural paradise. People didn't always find it so. Between rocky, heather-covered mountain slopes and sodden bogs, patches of barely cultivable land were never enough to survive on. Thousands emigrated, often sending money to support those who stayed. Recently, a modest degree of tourism has transformed the island. In the handful of villages, many old cottages have been replaced by spacious and modern white houses, and you'll meet locals who have come back after spending years in New York, Toronto or London.

If you are touring in the area, watch for good weather, listen to the forecasts and if there's a hint of a fine spell, take the chance. You won't need even to wait for a ferry: for more than a century, there has been a bridge across the narrow Achill Sound. July and August can bring a rush of Irish visitors with their sailboards and fishing equipment. On the mountains, you'll only have sheep for company.

**Keel** has a long, beautiful beach and a golf course in the dunes. Land-locked Keel Lough gives novice windsurfers a chance to practise before trying their skills in the bay. The lane inland from Keel leads to the lower slopes of **Slievemore**, 670m (2,200ft). Look out for a side turning to a cemetery on the hillside. The abandoned stone huts nearby used to be occupied in summer, and the ridges and furrows in the grass show where potatoes used to be grown. About an hour of steady effort will take you to the top where the views to the north are almost enough to induce vertigo. Like many Irish mountains, there's no real path up it, just the areas grazed by sheep amid rocks and clumps of heather. **Dugort** on the north coast has some places to stay and makes an alternative starting point for climbing Slievemore. Boats can take you to see the Seal Caves in the cliffs. There's a good chance of spotting seals, and further out to sea, basking sharks (the harmless kind).

West of Keel and Dooagh, **Croghaun** nearly matches Slievemore in height, and a 550m (1,800ft) precipice to the north west is even more spectacular, forming Europe's highest sea cliffs. On the moderate eastern slopes, Corrymore House below Corrymore Lake was one of the homes of the hated Captain Boycott (see page 152).

## The Céide Fields

On exposed cliffs above the coast of County Mayo, near Ballycastle, local farmers have sliced down through a peat bog that took thousands of years to form. They started to come across big white stones, and noticed that they lay in patterns. Called to investigate, archaeologists found a maze of stone walls beneath the peat. They proved to be the field boundaries, building foundations and standing stones left by Neolithic farmers over 5,000 years ago. The layers of peat accumulated later as the climate turned nasty and

## EARTH WORKS

Mayo may be littered with ancient monuments already, but today's sculptors wanted to get in on the act. As part of 'Mayo 5000' (the approximate age of the Céide Fields), they held a competition for landscape art projects. The winning designs were built in various spots along the north coast, from Blacksod on the tip of Belmullet peninsula to Ballina. Mostly off the beaten track, these striking earth sculptures can be visited separately or as a trail, about 88km (55 miles) long. You can pick up a map showing the locations at Moy Valley Resources, Cathedral Road, Ballina.

blanket bog claimed the area. There is now a network of paths to let you reach part of the site and see the ancient stones, sparkling white from centuries under the acid peat. Even though experts enthuse about the site ('unparalleled', 'deserves the widest acclaim') non-specialists may find the tumbled stones less than thrilling. Perhaps they will be persuaded by the new interpretative centre, a remarkable pyramid with a glass gallery on top. Whatever will future archaeologists make of *that*? It's prominently sited but well-landscaped amid peat walls. Inside, a film explains the importance of the Céide Fields, and dioramas show Neolithic people dressed in skins building the walls. (Céide, incidentally, is pronounced KAYduh.)

The stone quays and warehouses of **Killala** tell of past trade, but the port is mainly a base for fishing in the bay these days. A bust of the French General Humbert in the town centre recalls one of the heroic failures of Irish history. He landed at the head of a French expedition in August 1798, already too late to coordinate with the United Irishmen's risings of that year. Joined by many Irish volunteers, brave but untrained,

Humbert's force took Ballina and then defeated local militias at Castlebar. After a few more skirmishes, it was surrounded at Ballinamuck in County Longford by regular troops and compelled to surrender. The British viceroy Lord Cornwallis, veteran of the American War of Independence, had taken the field himself, and this time he was on the winning side.

Two rural abbey ruins which you may have all to yourself stand near the shores of the bay south of Killala. A short hike across muddy fields leads to 15th-century **Moyne Abbey**, with a tall square tower. A stream running right through the building must have been handy for washing. To the south, **Rosserk Abbey** in similar style stands by its own small beach. In **Ballina**, the chief town of the area, the main focus of interest is the number of salmon in the River Moy. From spring to late summer, you might glimpse them from the town's twin bridges or see fishermen handhauling a catch ashore in nets: they have been licensed to take salmon this way for centuries.

**Foxford Woollen Mills Centre** is far more remarkable than it may sound. The story began in 1892 when Mother Agnes Morrogh-Bernard of the Irish Sisters of Charity looked for a way to improve the lot of the people of the depressed town. Knowing something about weaving, she decided to start a woollen mill. She overcame lack of money and countless other obstacles by using contacts, charm, and an iron will to persuade bishops and bankers

*A*chill Island off the west coast of County Mayo has become quite a magnet for holiday visitors (following page).

251

and refusing to take no for an answer. Soon Foxford was famous for its blankets and tweeds. It still is, but some of the fine fabrics woven today go to top couturiers. The history of the mill and the area are movingly told in dramatic tableaux using life-size speaking figures. You can then tour the mill itself, more mechanized these days, although its founder would recognize all the processes. She might be amazed by some of the colour combinations now woven; heather purples, bright oranges and vivid greens as well as soft, traditional shades.

*T he modern basilica at the pilgrimage centre of Knock was built in time for the papal visit in 1979. It can hold 20,000 people.*

## Knock (*Cnoc Mhaire*)

Since 1879, when a group of parishioners saw an apparition of the Virgin Mary, St Joseph and St John on the gable of the village church in 1879, Knock has been a place of pilgrimage. Pope John Paul II timed his 1979 visit for the centenary and the world's attention was focused. Hundreds of thousands came to Knock for the papal mass. There was no convenient airport at the time, a matter that the local priest, Fr. Horan, decided should be rectified. Thinking big, he proposed building a runway long enough to take jumbo jets. His scheme was widely mocked, but he persisted and somehow the money was raised. In 1986, Horan International Airport (also called Knock or Connaught regional) opened. Although it's not exactly busy, and the terminal building can be silent for hours at a time, more flights use

Knock airport than the doubters ever expected. It has been a shot in the arm for the region, bringing in weekenders, fishing parties and locals who work in Dublin or England as well as the steady flow of pilgrims.

The little town is not too commercialized, at least by the standards of other famous pilgrimage destinations. The gable end of the old church has been enclosed by an extension, with the effective use of a glass roof and walls, and statues simulate the 1879 vision. A cavernous modern basilica can hold 20,000 people. The museum of folklore nearby is open only in summer.

# County Sligo

Even if you have never read a word of his poetry, you'll soon be made aware that this is 'The Land of Heart's Desire' of WB Yeats and his artist brother Jack. It won't only be their admirers who will want to visit the beauty spots that inspired them (you will find suggested itineraries on page 79). In a gentler landscape than Mayo to the south or Donegal to the north, the massive mountains of Ben Bulben and Knocknarea stand out all the more. No wonder they are woven round with the epic tales of Celtic legend.

### Sligo Town (*Sligeach*)
This busy, prosperous-looking centre for the whole north-west region stands where the Garavogue river links beautiful Lough Gill to a broad, sheltered bay. The town you see today is mainly an Anglo-Irish creation which grew up in the 18th and 19th centuries. Few traces remain from earlier periods. The tourist office in Temple Street sells a booklet to guide you on a walking tour of the local sights.

The Norman lords Fitzgerald and de Burgo established themselves in the area in the 13th century, although their hold was less than entirely secure. The ruined **Dominican Friary** (Sligo Abbey) in Abbey Street, off High Street, was first built at that time and wrecked in 1641 during the Civil War. Some fine monuments and most of the cloisters survive.

Rohan Gillespie's modern **statue** of a laid-back and raffish-looking WB Yeats stands in front of the Ulster Bank in Stephen Street, just north of the river. Nothing if not controversial, it at least acknowledges the many links between the poet and Sligo – both town and county. His parents were married in the Georgian **St John's Church** in John Street (now the Church of Ireland Cathedral: the 19th-century Catholic Cathedral is nearby on the corner of Adelaide and Temple Streets); he spent most of his school holidays here and returned many times in later life; and his wish to be buried at nearby Drumcliff was eventually fulfilled (see below, page 263). The **County Museum** in Stephen Street has a suitably strong Stone Age bias, given the huge numbers of monuments from the period that pepper the region and crown almost every hilltop. Naturally the museum has a Yeats Memorial room, with first editions, complete collections of the poems, photographs and letters and a copy of the poet's Nobel Prize for Literature medal. The adjoining **Library and Municipal Art Gallery** has a large collection of paintings and drawings by Jack B. Yeats, their father John Butler Yeats and Jack's daughter Anne Yeats, all celebrated artists. George Russell (the poet's friend 'AE') is among other Irish painters represented. Across the river by Douglas Hyde Bridge, the **Yeats Memorial Building** has another Yeats collection and puts on an audio-visual pro-gramme about the writer. It is also the base for the Yeats Summer School held every August.

## Near Sligo Town

Along the bay close to Sligo's small airport, the open sandy beach at Strandhill can be wild and windswept, conditions which sometime produce the kind of rollers that appeal to surfers. Rising steeply behind Strandhill, there is no missing

**Knocknarea**, a flat-topped mountain 329m (1,078ft) high, crowned by a huge cairn, or pile of rock, visible from afar. One legend says it's the grave of Queen Maeve (or *Meadhbh*, one of several Irish spellings: Mab is an old English version). A fire-eating, and man-eating, queen of Connacht in the Amazonian mould, she probably lived in the 1st century AD. The giant cairn is very much older: it is presumed to be a Bronze Age passage tomb from about 3000 BC, on the lines of Newgrange and Knowth

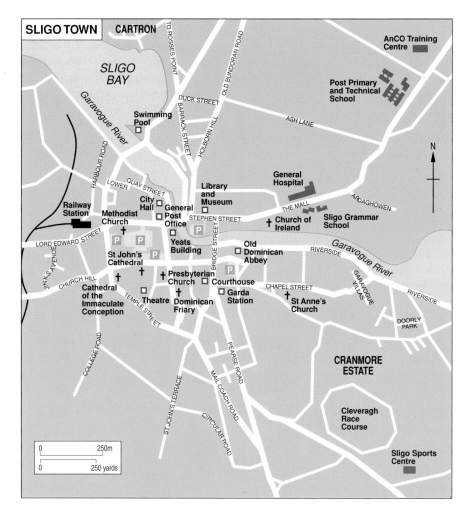

in the Boyne Valley (see page 136). The best route up is from the south, involving 30-40 minutes of vigorous walking and well worth the effort for the views alone. (The north side is too thickly wooded, the west too precipitous.)

Once on top you appreciate the scale of the mound, a truncated cone 200m (650ft) round the base, 90m (300ft) round the top and 10m (33ft) high. A simple calculation estimates the mass of stone in it to be about 40,000 tonnes! Any idea of a modern archaeological excavation is daunting in the extreme, considering the inaccessible site and the need to shift such vast quantities of broken rock while observing present-day standards of care. Even in the past, only very limited digging at the surface ever seems to have been undertaken.

*C*oney Island in Sligo *Bay probably gave its name to the New York version. There the similarity ends.*

*One of many dolmens in the vast Stone Age cemetery of Carrowmore, County Sligo.*

## Carrowmore

A vast Stone Age cemetery lies 5km (3 miles) south west of Sligo town in a maze of lanes, but fortunately well-signposted. Dolmens, small passage tombs and stone circles, about 60 in all, are scattered over a wide area, forming one of the most remarkable collections in Europe. According to legend the mythical King Nuad was killed in battle here, and these are held to be the graves of the slain. In fact they appear to have been built over a long period, between 3000 and 2000 BC, and no doubt the site was chosen with an eye to the view of the colossal cairn on Knocknarea (see above), clearly visible to the west. The small interpretative centre gives the archaeological details with the aid of a video presentation. A walk across green pastureland takes you to some of the sites, but the best are to be found on the opposite side of the road.

## Lough Gill

The lovely lake just south east of Sligo would have become a favourite excursion anyway, but as the setting of Yeats's *The Lake Isle of Innisfree* it is assured of an extra measure of fame. To be honest, apart from the literary reference, there is no special reason to visit the islet in the lough, but the waterbus which makes trips on the lake sometimes stops there. If you're touring by land, the road on the north side gives the best views. Near Sligo, take the signs for Hazelwood and Half Moon Bay, where there's a sculpture trail along the shore, a forest walk punctuated by the works of Irish and international artists. Close to the water at the north-east corner of the lake, **Parke's Castle** (or Newtown Castle) is a restored fortified manor of the Plantation period in the early 17th century.

It houses an interpretative centre publicizing the attractions of the region.

To the south, 22km (14 miles) from Sligo, **Ballymote** is a market town known for its coarse fishing, traditional music and the massive ruins of a Norman castle built by the powerful Richard de Burgo. At Temple House, on the site of a Knights Templar foundation, you can experience life in a fine, rambling Georgian mansion. A few of its hundred-odd rooms are set aside for guests, and there's fishing and shooting on the vast estate. To the west, Tobercurry is another centre for angling and noted for its traditional music: this is where the internationally famous Chieftains first made their name.

*A*ll that rain keeps the rivers flowing fast into Lough Gill near Sligo Town, favourite haunt of WB Yeats.

## North of Sligo Town

With its big sandy beaches, golf course and a backdrop of purple mountains **Rosses Point** is Sligo's seaside resort on the north side of the bay, to match Strandhill on the south. The low flat shape of Coney Island, stretching across the mouth of the bay, can be reached by causeway at low tide. This is a busy feeding ground for ducks, geese and wading birds. They claim here that New York's Coney Island was given the same name by a Sligo captain who saw quantities of rabbits there that reminded him of the Irish original.

Due north of Sligo town, the outline of **Ben Bulben**, 527m (1,730ft), rears up like the prow of a mighty ship. Great Irish landmarks have usually been the scene of dramatic events, whether historical, mythical or even something in between, and this majestic mountain is no exception.

# The Tale of Diarmaid and Gráinne

Long ago, say the story-tellers, there lived a beautiful princess, the daughter of the High King of Ireland, Cormac MacAirt. Her name was Gráinne and her home was in the Royal Palace of Tara. At this time none other than Finn MacCumhail was leader of the fabled army of warriors, the Fianna. But by now he was growing old. Not only his son Oisin was in the Fianna, but so was Oscar, son of Oisin. Nevertheless, Finn was looking for another wife, and he asked Cormac MacAirt for the hand of Gráinne. Finn and the Fianna were essential to the peace of his kingdom, so if Cormac had any doubts, he kept them to himself, and agreed. The young princess would be betrothed to the old hero.

From childhood, Gráinne had been taught to obey her father in all things, and always to put her duty above all else. So if the forthcoming marriage was not the one she had dreamed of, she gave no sign. A great feast was held at Tara to celebrate the engagement, all the kings and queens of Ireland were invited and Finn MacCumhail brought the members of the Fianna. To be accepted into this legendary army, a man had to be a supreme athlete, a fearless warrior and a poet too. Among these mighty men, Gráinne spotted the handsomest of them all, Diarmaid O'Duibhne, and fell in love with him at first sight. She began to search for a means to escape from the marriage to Finn and somehow she found an opportunity to whisper to Diarmaid of her love. The attraction was mutual, although he could see no way to take her from under the nose of his leader without the direst consequences. But

Gráinne was determined to have him. She extracted his solemn pledge that if she could arrange the chance, he would elope with her.

Gráinne now obtained a powerful sleeping draught and put it in the drinks to be served to all at the feast, except her beloved and four of his closest comrades, one of whom was Finn's own son, Oisin. Soon the High King, all the kings and queens and the men of the Fianna fell into a deep slumber. With the help of Diarmaid's friends, the lovers fled the palace to begin a journey that was to last for seven years. Safe for the moment across the River Shannon, Dairmaid built them a hut and bed out of boulders, the first of many. To this day, you can see dozens of the beds of Diarmaid and Gráinne, massive piles of stone, rocky ledges and caves in every part of Ireland.

When Finn awoke to find his bride missing, his anger was beyond imagining. He sent for his most skilful trackers, ordering them to bring the fugitives back, but they lost the scent at the bank of the Shannon. Finn in his rage threatened to kill them all if they could not find the track again. Eventually, the lovers were traced to a forest and seemed to be cornered. Now, Diarmaid as a child had been raised by the magician Aengus who had often saved him from harm. Sensing the danger he was in, Aengus flew to the hiding place to spirit him away under his cloak. Diarmaid would not leave that way but sent Gráinne, and made his own escape by a way the old magician had told him was unguarded.

Before he left them, Aengus gave the lovers strict instructions: 'Enter no tree which has only one trunk; enter no cave which has only one mouth; visit no island with only one landing; cook your food in one place but eat it in another and sleep in a third; and where you sleep tonight, do not sleep tomorrow. Only thus will you evade Finn's anger.' The two promised to do as he had said. And so they lived for seven years, every night in a different bed which Diarmaid had made. They became accustomed to their new life, and were intensely happy. As the years went by, the never-ending flight became more and more difficult as first one son, then a second, a third and a fourth and then a daughter came along. Diarmaid's guardian Aengus urged him and Finn Mac-Cumhail to make peace, and although Finn's fury had not abated, he was weary of the chase and agreed. The lovers and their children settled at last

*The unmistakable outline of Ben Bulben, north of Sligo Town. It's the setting for many Irish myths and legends.*

in a beautiful place called Rath Gráinne, not so far from Ben Bulben.

One day, Diarmaid heard hunting dogs barking in the distance. Although Gráinne sensed danger and tried to prevent him, he strode off to find out what was happening. The sound led him to the slopes of Ben Bulben, where he found Finn hunting, just as in their old days together. 'The great boar of Ben Bulben has killed fifty of the Fianna,' Finn told him. 'I'll hunt him myself,' said Diarmaid. Then Finn revealed a secret he had never spoken of before. It seems that Diarmaid's father had been acting as guardian to the son of a friend, and the boy had died in an accident. The friend had read a spell over his son's body, restoring him to life but changing him into a wild boar. As it ran off, the father had called after it: 'You will live just as long as Diarmaid: no more, no less.'

As Finn spoke, the wild boar of Ben Bulben charged towards them. Diarmaid drew his sword and struck at the beast, but the blade broke in two. He vaulted on to the boar's back, and the boar charged down the mountain in a frenzy, trying to shake him off. Up to the summit and down again he charged, but Diarmaid clung on. Up to the peak once more he ran, and Diarmaid took another blade and drove it into the boar's skull. But as the boar rolled over and died, his tusk stabbed into Diarmaid's side, and the hunter lay bleeding. As Finn approached, the dying hero said to him: 'Only you have the power to save my life now.' 'How so?' asked Finn, although he knew the answer. 'Carry fresh spring water in your cupped hands to refresh me,' said Diarmaid. 'There is no spring on the mountain,' said Finn, although he knew this was a lie. 'There is one just behind you,' said Oisin, Finn's son and Diar-

maid's friend. Finn went to the spring and filled his cupped hands, but as he walked towards Diarmaid, he remembered how the young man had stolen his bride, and allowed the water to leak away. Blood was pouring from Diarmaid's wound and he was close to death but he reminded Finn of the services he had performed for the Fianna in the past. Again Finn went to the spring and filled his hands. Again he walked slowly towards Diarmaid. And again he thought of the disgrace he had suffered from the elopement. He pretended to trip over a stone, and spilled the water. Now Oisin, his own son, told Finn that if he would not save Diarmaid, he as Diarmaid's friend would challenge him to a fight to the death. Finn returned to the spring for a third time, filled his cupped hands and carried the water to Diarmaid. But as he approached, the young hunter breathed his last and the spirit left him.

Gráinne stood outside her home awaiting his return, but when his favourite hunting dog came back without him, she knew the worst. She sent for her family to bring the body of Diarmaid to her, and all then escorted it to the burial place of kings beside the River Boyne. Her family and that of Diarmaid gathered at Tara for a great feast and she addressed the assembled company: 'Be wary and be patient. The time will come to avenge the dead.'

(Footnote: There is scarcely a noteworthy scenic feature or ancient monument in Ireland that isn't associated in legend with the flight of Diarmaid and Gráinne. You will find many parallels between the Irish epics and the tales of King Arthur as well as Germanic mythology. Presumably they have common origins in an era before any of the tales were written down, although how far back it is impossible to say.)

**Drumcliff** clusters around the remains of a monastery said to have been founded by St Colmcille (Columba), with the stump of a round tower near the entrance and a fine high cross, both dating from the 11th century. The details of the carving on the cross are so worn it is hard to decipher, although it looks clearer if you stand further away.

In the churchyard, usually loud with the cawing of rooks in the trees, the grave of WB Yeats stands near the church door, just as he specified in a poem. And he wrote the epitaph inscribed on the austerely plain headstone:

*Cast a cold eye*
*on life, on death*
*Horseman, pass by!*

Yeats died on 28 January 1939 in the south of France, and was temporarily buried at Roquebrune. War interrupted arrangements for his body to be brought home and he was not buried here until September 1948.

**Lissadell House**, west of the main road north of Drumcliff, open from June to September, has a plain enough classical exterior. Even its soaring high halls and 30m- (100ft-) long columned gallery wouldn't single it out among many such Irish mansions. The fame of the place derives from the extraordinary family who lived here: Sir Robert Gore-Booth, who went into debt to feed the hungry during the famines, Henry Gore-Booth, the arctic explorer, his daughter Eva, the poet and

*Constance Gore-Booth grew up in the great house of Lissadell, County Sligo. As Countess Markievicz, she fought in the 1916 Easter Rising in Dublin.*

CONSTANCE
MARKIEVICZ

MAJOR
IRISH CITIZEN ARMY
1916

**ONE A GAZELLE ...**

Constance Markievicz (1884-1927) fought in the 1916 Easter Rising, as second in command of the Citizens' Army at St Stephen's Green. After the crushing of the Rising, she was condemned to death with the rest of its leaders, but reprieved: the authorities were fearful of the outcry that the execution of a woman would produce. Released soon afterwards, she stood in the general election of 1918 as a Sinn Féin candidate and won – the first woman ever to be elected to the House of Commons in London. Like all the other successful candidates from the party, she declined to attend the Westminster parliament, taking her seat instead in the Dáil Eireann, the newly formed and as yet extra-constitutional Irish Parliament. She was named as the Free State's first Minister of Labour but soon fell out with the leadership and died at the early age of 43.

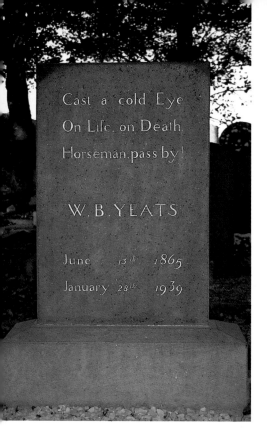

*Y*eats was buried at last where he had wanted, in Drumcliff churchyard 'under Ben Bulben'.

her younger sister Constance (Countess Markievicz), fiery revolutionary and independence fighter. WB Yeats was a frequent visitor, so Lissadell is a magnet for literary pilgrims. Years later he wrote *In Memory of Eva Gore-Booth and Con Markievicz*, recalling the days of their youth together

> *The light of evening, Lissadell,*
> *Great windows, open to the south,*
> *Two girls in silk kimonos, both*
> *Beautiful, one a gazelle ...*

On the dining-room walls, the full-length portraits of members of the family and (an egalitarian touch) servants are by Count Casimir Markievicz, Constance's husband.

**Streedagh Strand** is a vast stretch of sandy beach, with the finger of Streedagh Point at its northern end. Three ships of the Spanish Armada were wrecked here: in recent years divers have begun to survey the site and recover some relics. Close to the roadside, **the Creevykeel** court tomb, the finest example of its type in Ireland, is thought to date from about 3000 BC. Passage graves seem to have been added later, and an iron smelter in the court area dates from the early Christian era. At the crossroads near the tomb a lane towards the sea leads out along a spit of land to **Mullaghmore**. The pretty resort is shielded from Atlantic gales by the headland and its harbour is doubly protected behind walls paid for by the Victorian statesman Lord Palmerston. The strange, pinnacled Classiebawn Castle perched on top of the peninsula was built for him too. It was eventually inherited by Countess Mountbatten and became a favourite holiday retreat of her husband Earl Mountbatten, who chose to ignore warnings about lack of security. In 1979, he was killed when his boat was blown up by the IRA.

You'll probably have noticed the little isle of **Inishmurray**, 6km (4 miles) offshore from Streedagh Strand or Grange. It's deserted now, but boats will take you there from Mullaghmore. The trip takes over an hour so if you tend to suffer from motion sickness, be prepared. On the island's south coast, the best-preserved early monastic enclosure in Ireland is dense with ruins of *clocháns* (beehive houses), tombs, wells and altars. It was probably

founded in the 6th century, and was one of the sites sacked by the Vikings on their first raid along this coast in 795.

## County Donegal

A long and rugged coastline of wild peninsulas faces the North Atlantic, culminating in the most northerly point of Ireland at Malin Head. The Normans scarcely penetrated here and the English fared no better. Now it's almost cut off from the rest of the Republic, and life seems to have changed less than anywhere else in Ireland: there's a substantial Gaelic-speaking minority. Inland, the mountains are strangely streaked white with quartz, and deer roam the Glenveagh National Park, where bleak moorland gives way to beautiful sheltered glens.

*T raditional cottages are fast disappearing, replaced by comfortable modern houses, but many still survive in County Donegal.*

### Bottleneck

Boundaries perform strange tricks hereabouts, interposing a few kilometres of seashore belonging to County Leitrim between Sligo and Donegal. Then County Fermanagh, part of Northern Ireland, comes so near to the west coast that the Republic narrows to a neck of land that is only 5km (3 miles) wide. **Ballyshannon** stands near the mouth of the River Erne, which a dam has turned into a lake stretching 8km (5 miles) and almost to Belleek and the border with Northern Ireland. You can make a convenient diversion here to the Lakes of Fermanagh, Enniskillen or Omagh (see page 299). Near the northern shore of the Erne estuary near Ballyshannon, not much is left of 12th-century Assaroe Abbey apart from some vestiges of wall and a graveyard. A little way downstream, a restored working watermill and craft centre is worth a visit.

### Donegal Town

Donegal was the principal base of the O'Donnell clan, led by the Earl of Tyrconnell. After the Flight of the Earls in 1607 (see page 50), their estates were seized and awarded to English and Scottish colonists. Donegal town and large tracts of land went to Sir Basil Brooke, who transformed the 16th-century O'Don-

nell tower house by putting in big mullioned windows and adding a Jacobean gabled wing. You can only view the impressive shell of the building from the outside while a major restoration project is in progress. Inland up the Eske (Fish) River, the pretty lake of Lough Eske is famous for its fishing, especially for salmon and arctic char.

### The South-west Peninsula

West of Donegal town, the fishing port of **Killybegs** has undergone rapid expansion

*Donegal Town's central market square, typical of many 17th-century plantation settlements, is known as The Diamond.*

in recent years. The smell of its fishmeal factory pervades the town, and a colourful, storm-battered international fleet packs the harbour. The road round the peninsula is frequently rough and narrow, but the views and sights make the extra distance worth while if you have the time. It's a surprisingly densely populated area, by the standards of western Ireland at any rate, with little villages merging one into another. Even in some of the lonelier parts you'll come across peat cutters at work in the hills. The main road is forced away from the coast for much of the way, most notably by the vertigo-inducing sea cliffs of **Slieve League**, dropping almost directly from the 601m (1,972ft) summit to the ocean below. A side road through Teelin comes to a dead end south east of the mountain at Bunglass, where you get a superb view of the cliffs. This is also a starting point for a climb to the summit up well-marked tracks. This is classed as a hill walk rather than a climb, but it shouldn't be undertaken alone, in a high wind or when the mountain is obscured by mist. You'll need a good head for heights and the right boots and rainproof gear.

The northern slopes of Slieve League are a lot less precipitous although they are bleak and boggy, so the fertile green beauty of **Glencolumbkille** with its brightly painted houses is the more wel-

*T*he County Donegal harbour of Killybegs has become one of Europe's major fishing ports, home to an international fleet.

come. The Glen of St Colmcille (or Columba) was a favourite with the saint who was born not far away at Lough Gartan (see below). It has been a focus of pilgrimage ever since, although some of today's secular pilgrims come in tour buses and spend more time in craft shops than holy places. The valley seems also to have been important in pagan times, judging by the number of tombs from various eras. Some of the early monuments appear to have been adapted to Christian purposes: small standing stones and dolmens have been marked with crosses. The information office in the village will provide you with a map to follow the route round the sites they have thoughtfully numbered. On the saint's day, 9 June, hundreds of pilgrims take a similar path, perhaps following in his footsteps. There's a choice of superb walks in the area: take advice at the information centre.

**Ardara** stands at the head of the bay to the north of the peninsula. The approach to it over Glengesh Pass gives some glorious views down the valley. The chief town in the area, Ardara is noted for knitted woollens and homespun tweed cloth, much of it still made in people's homes. Displays in a visitor centre explain the processes and the history.

## North-west Donegal

Unless you have the luxury of time, you'll have to choose between routes. You might follow every twist and turn of the coast road through tiny Gaelic-speaking fishing villages, or head for Mount Errigal and the Glenveagh National Park.

**Dungloe** (or Dunglow) is a cheerful little port and fishing centre and a point where you can take the inland option.

At the Lakeside Centre at **Dunlewy** in an old weaver's house, you can see the carding, dyeing, spinning and weaving of local wool to produce the famous Donegal tweed. Young farm animals and a playground keep the children amused and boats are available for a trip on the lake. When the mists clear away, the shimmering cone of Mount Errigal, 752m (2,466ft), dominates the view to the north. The white areas aren't snow (usually), but quartzite. The walk to the top from Dunlewy is hard work – you often have to pick your way across broken stone – but worth the effort on a clear day. **Glenveagh National Park**, almost 10,000ha (25,000

*Q uartzite deposits on Mount Errigal, highest point in County Donegal, can look just like snow – when the sun shines.*

## COPYRIGHT LAW

According to legend, Colmcille secretly copied a gospel that belonged to one of his tutors, Finnian. When this was discovered, Finnian claimed the copy. The dispute went to the King Diarmid at Tara, whose judgment: 'To every cow belongeth her calf, so to every book belongeth its copy' may represent the first decision on copyright. So far the story may well have a basis in fact. Then, it's said – with no good historical evidence – the furious Colmcille raised an army of his kinsfolk and defeated Diarmid. The Battle of the Book cost 3,000 lives and in remorse, Colmcille sought advice on what penance he should do for causing bloodshed. St Molaise of Devenish Island told him to leave Ireland and never look on it again. Colmcille complied, and went to found the monastery of Iona, off the west coast of Scotland. Legend has it that he did return, once, but remained blindfolded for his whole visit to his homeland.

*T*he little oratory at Lough Gartan, County Donegal, where Colmcille (St Columba) is said to have preached. He was born close by.

acres) embraces the peaks of Errigal and Slieve Snaght south of Dunlewy as well as several loughs. **Glenveagh Castle**, a Victorian Gothic mansion on Lough Veagh (or Beagh) is reached from the road northeast from Dunlewy (the R251). The castle and its fine gardens are open from April to October. The more exciting attraction is the red deer forest reserve to the south west, although you're quite likely to see deer almost anywhere in this area. (The shooting season is from September to February, when except at weekends you have to keep to the roads and main tracks of the park.) In summer **Lough Gartan** to the south east can be reached by a mountain track from Glenveagh: otherwise return to the R251. The Colmcille (St Columba) Heritage Centre at **Church Hill** overlooking the lough honours the energetic saint with an exhibition on the transition from paganism to Christianity which he helped to bring about. It tries to separate the facts from the myths, and includes a display on the production of manuscripts. You can get directions to walk to the place, marked by a giant cross, where the saint was born into a chieftain's family in 522, and other sites connected with his life.

A fine art collection amid the rural beauty of Lough Gartan is an unexpected bonus. West of Church Hill village, a former Georgian rectory overlooks the lake and its outbuildings house **Glebe Gallery**, formed by the artist and collector Derek Hill and then given to the Irish nation in 1981. Apart from his own paintings, you can see works by Degas, Renoir, Picasso and Kokoschka among other famous names. Most unusually, there are striking examples by the naive school of artists which he discovered (and in effect founded) on Tory Island off the County Donegal coast.

The coast north of here breaks up into a ragged pattern of sea loughs and peninsulas, with a handful of historic sites and some small resorts favoured by Northern Ireland people for their holidays. **Rathmelton** (pronounced and often written Ramelton) is a pretty Georgian port and town, fashionable enough to attract a cosmopolitan crowd to settle as well as come for the salmon fishing and the July carnival. Any time of year, there can be some well-known musicians performing in the town's pubs.

**Rathmullan** may be just a small village of pastel-coloured cottages and an ivy-covered ruined abbey, but it has its place in history. For this was where the Earls of Tyrone and Tyrconnell and their supporters sailed for Spain in 1607, leading to the confiscation of their lands and the Plantation of Ulster. The Battery near the little harbour was built against the

threat, not of their return, but of invasion 200 years later in the Napoleonic Wars. Now it houses an exhibition, Flight of the Earls, which tells the story of the events that led up to their departure.

This coast is a mecca for seabirds and waders: you'll see terns diving and oystercatchers searching for mussels, and the beaches are strewn with seashells.

*Little Rathmullan on Lough Swilly, where the Gaelic Earls and their supporters embarked on a voyage into exile in 1607.*

All roads seem to lead through **Letterkenny** at the head of Lough Swilly, the chief commercial centre and county town of Donegal. The 19th-century Catholic cathedral is the chief landmark, and in August the Folk Festival brings in both performers and fans of traditional music and dance.

On a 244m (800ft) summit between Lough Swilly and Derry, just inside County Donegal, stands the ancient stone fort known as the **Grianán of Aileach**. A road climbs almost all the way; then a short walk takes you to the hilltop site. It dates from some time in the Iron Age, perhaps 500 to 200 BC, although there is evidence of earlier ramparts. Claudius Ptolemy showed it on his famous map of Ireland of the 2nd century AD, drawn on the basis of reports he was given by traders. It became an important stronghold of the local kings in the early Christian era, and St Patrick, who seems to have had the entrée to all the royal residences, came to preach. The Grianán was destroyed in about the year 1100 when, the story goes, an invading king of Thomond ordered each of his soldiers to carry away a stone from the walls. How much impact they made is not recorded, but the fort was certainly in poor repair by the 19th century, when it was restored. Like the Staigue Fort in County Kerry (see page 198), this one has chambers in the walls and double staircases up to the gallery which runs right round the inside of the 5m- (16ft-)

*O*n the sheltered shores of Lough Foyle, the biggest natural harbour on Ireland's north coast.

high walls. The rebuilding deprives it of much of its magic, but the views in every direction can be superb. The border with Northern Ireland is only few kilometres away to the east, as the crow flies.

## The Inishowen Peninsula

Not quite the island (*inis*) that its name suggests, the peninsula between Lough Swilly and Lough Foyle is the northernmost tip of Ireland. Yet it's not in Northern Ireland, except for a small 'bite' near Derry. **Buncrana** is a sheltered loughside resort favoured by summer holidaymakers from Derry. At **Cardonagh**, standing by the wall of the old church below the village, you'll find a 7th-century cross decorated with Celtic knot designs and guard stones on either side with primitive carved figures. Malin is a planned village of the plantation period, now known for crab fishing. A few more kilometres north west, **Malin Head** is well known to anyone who listens to weather forecasts for sailors. At this point, you have come as far north as the Irish mainland goes, though from the cliffs you can see the little island of Inishtrahull, deserted since the last inhabitants were taken off in 1930. Several ships of the Spanish Armada came to grief on this coast in 1588. One wreck, that of the *Trinidad Valencera*, was found offshore to the east: you can see some of the objects recovered on display in the Ulster Museum in Belfast.

No road goes right round the eastern tip of the peninsula, **Inishowen Head**, but you can reach it from Greencastle and return by a slightly different route along the shores of Lough Foyle. The same road continues through the little resort of Moville and on to the Northern Ireland border a few miles short of Derry (Londonderry to the Northern Irish).

# Rural Tranquillity and Cities in the News

It isn't part of the Republic, but there's no doubt or dispute that this is part of Ireland. No picture of the country could be complete without a visit to 'the North'. On the Antrim coast, the Giant's Causeway is a geological wonder of the world, but it's only one of many spectacular sights. Belfast is sprucing itself up as heavy industry declines; its Ulster Museum is a world-class treasure house. In County Down, the compact Mountains of Mourne stand out from gently rolling countryside. Armagh is the ecclesiastical capital of all Ireland and further west, the Lakes of Fermanagh attract anglers from all over Europe.

To link up logically with the order of the rest of the book, we start our travels in this part of the island in the north west, moving generally clockwise round the coast to Belfast and into County Down. Then we head inland for historic Armagh, seat of St Patrick; County Fermanagh in the south west; Omagh's superb History and Folk parks; and some of the finest stately homes in Ireland. You could also visit any of these on short forays across the border.

*It's almost easier to believe the legends that are told about the Giant's Causeway than to accept that it is an entirely natural feature.*

Speaking of the border, at many crossing points you'll probably find little evidence of one at all. As often as not you won't even have to stop. The advent of the European single market means there is practically no role for customs to play, so their buildings stand deserted. A few major points, such as the main road to Londonderry from the west, are heavily armoured and guarded. You'll probably be asked your name and where you are going, and may have to show your driving licence or some other identification. Otherwise, security forces prefer to make spot checks or set up roadblocks elsewhere. Even so, it is possible to drive all day, especially in rural areas of Northern Ireland, and not see a single soldier or policeman. The exception is the border villages of South Armagh, where tension often runs high.

# Londonderry/Derry

When you cross the border from County Donegal into Northern Ireland, you soon reach the city officially called Londonderry. Road signs in the Republic point to Derry, and that's what most people actually call it. The 'London' bit was attached when some of the Companies of the City of London were persuaded to invest in the place after the Flight of the Earls in 1607 (see page 50) and the confiscations of land that followed.

Derry (*Daire*, the Irish name, means a grove of oak trees) had been an important monastic site, possibly founded by St Colmcille (Columba), but frequent sackings and burnings had left little more than two old churches and a fortified tower

### STROKE CITY

A few years ago, a disc jockey on Radio Ulster didn't want to offend either community so he began calling their home 'Derry stroke Londonderry'. It caught on. The short form Stroke City neatly allows the locals to say where they come from without revealing their religious or political persuasions.

house. With the arrival of Protestant settlers, a new town was built on the site, west of the River Foyle. Like those going up in the New World at the time, it was laid out on a grid pattern. The strong defensive walls were the last of their kind to be built in Ireland and the best preserved to this day. Growth was slow: by the 1680s, the population had barely reached

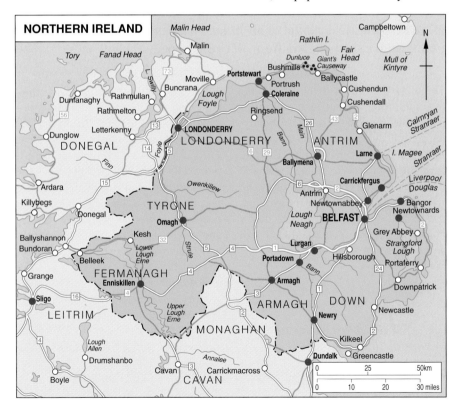

2,000, although that made it the largest town in Ulster. When James II landed in Ireland to launch an attempt to recapture his English throne from William of Orange, a new garrison came to take over Derry. Seeing them as Jacobites and Catholics, young apprentices slammed the gates against them, an event commemorated annually in the Apprentice Boys March. James himself arrived with his army in April 1689 and was refused entry. He returned to Dublin but left a force to besiege the city. As many as 30,000 people were crowded inside the walls and over the next 105 days they suffered bombardment, disease and starvation. Finally at the end of July, ships of a relief force broke through a boom which the besiegers had put across the River Foyle. The supplies and reinforcements they brought turned the tide, and the siege was lifted.

The Protestant community celebrates these events with parades and speeches every 12 August. Not surprisingly, the Catholics, who are the majority in areas such as the Bogside housing estates north west of the city centre, don't join in the jubilation.

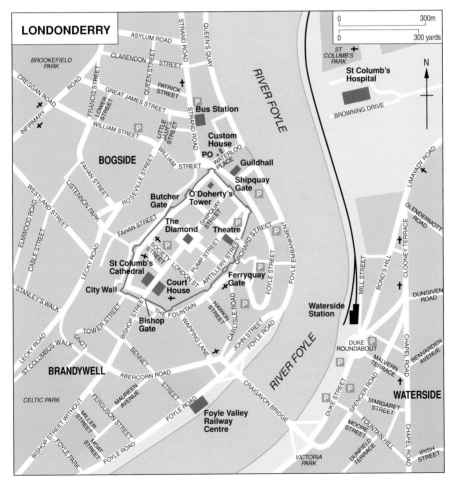

---

**NAMES AND NUMBERS**

It's easy to make mistakes, but people have heard them all so often that they probably won't be offended. Northern Ireland, comprising the six counties of Antrim, Londonderry (Derry), Down, Fermanagh, Armagh and Tyrone, is part of the 'UK', the United Kingdom of Great Britain and Northern Ireland. Especially in Northern Ireland itself, people may call it Ulster, although that's the name of the old province of Ireland with nine counties. Some say 'the province', risking the same confusion, or 'The North', although on the basis of geography the most northerly point of Ireland is in 'The South'! Anyone calling Northern Ireland 'the Six Counties' probably favours an end to the division, by one means or another. 'Ireland' can mean the whole island, or just the Republic.

In Northern parlance 'Union' does *not* mean joining up with the Republic, but the existing link with Britain, which Unionists are determined to preserve. They point with suspicion at clauses in the Republic's constitution which imply a right to govern the whole island. 'Loyalists' are of the same persuasion as Unionists, often more likely to emphasize their opinions with actions rather than words.

Both sides in Northern Ireland have their extremist wings, illegal armed organizations (the 'paramilitaries') which assume the right to defend their communities and attack their perceived enemies. The Provisional IRA is the main Nationalist underground force, claiming descent from the fighters for Irish independence in the past, notably in 1916 and 1919-23, although few in the Republic would agree. It has been responsible for numerous bomb attacks against military and civilian targets throughout the UK and beyond. The illegal loyalist groups include the Ulster Defence Association (UDA) and the linked UFF (Ulster Freedom Fighters), using assassination as their main weapon against the Nationalists.

---

As Derry industrialized, it became a magnet for many people from Donegal, then one of the poorest parts of Ireland. Mainly Catholic suburbs grew up until there was actually an overall Catholic majority but the electoral system kept them under-represented in city government. Civil rights marchers clashed with police in 1968 and 1969, and British troops fired on demonstrators on 31 January 1972, killing 13, on what became known as Bloody Sunday. In more recent times, Derry has led the way in developing a working relationship between former irreconcilables, and a generally happier atmosphere.

You probably won't stay in Derry, but its place in history makes a visit worth while. Parking is difficult inside the walls, so if you are driving, leave the car in one of the large car parks, for example off William Street, and walk. The focus of the compact walled city is the attractive central square, called the **Diamond**. Just off it, in Bishop Street, you'll find a helpful information office. (The main Tourist Office is in Foyle Street, down by the river.)

You can climb up on the **city walls** at several points and even walk a section of them, but security installations and restoration work mean that you can't make a complete circuit. Many cannon used by the defenders during the siege of 1689 are still in position but the famous 'Roaring Meg' is out of sight now that the impressive Double Bastion in the southwest corner has been turned into an army observation post.

Behind the classical Georgian Court House in Bishop Street, **St Columb's**

**Cathedral** was built like many an English parish church, although the style is known in Ulster as 'Planters' Gothic'. (This is of course the Protestant cathedral: St Eugene's Catholic cathedral overlooks the Bogside suburbs.) There are some good Georgian houses in the side streets below the cathedral. Down near Shipquay Gate, still inside the walls, you might think you are looking at a 16th-century tower house, but no building older than the 17th-century walls themselves survives in Derry. **O'Docherty's Tower** is a clever pastiche. The Tower Museum tells the story of the city: you pass through a labyrinth of audio-visual wizardry from prehistory to the present day. Below the gate, the quaysides along the river saw tens of thousands of 19th-century emigrants leave Ireland for ever in successive waves, driven by depression in Ulster and famine in the west.

Near the double-decker **Craigavon Bridge**, the Foyle Valley Railway Museum preserves some entertaining photos and documents and a small collection of rolling stock.

*Craigavon Bridge across the River Foyle and the historic city of Londonderry (Derry).*

# The North Coast

Once a centre of the linen industry, **Coleraine** is now the major campus of the University of Ulster. Its modern look would hardly lead you to think so, but the earliest known human settlements in Ireland were right in this area. Around Mount Sandel Fort, only 1.6km (1 mile) south east of town, flint blades and other tools were found, with burnt bone fragments which gave radio-carbon dates of about 7000 BC. (See page 135 for a note on dating.)

Perched on the clifftop 10km (6 miles) west of Coleraine, the round, classical **Mussenden Temple** (1785) is in the care of the National Trust. It was built as a library and summerhouse as well as a memorial to his sister by the fabled eccentric Frederick Hervey, who was not only Bishop of Derry from 1768 to 1803 but also succeeded to the title of Earl of Bristol. A great traveller in the era of the Grand Tour, he was known for demanding the highest standards of lodging. So when the world's first luxury hotels were created in his wake, many took the name of Hotel Bristol.

The coastal resorts here, **Portstewart** and **Portrush**, have had to survive on mainly local visitors, missing out on the booms and busts of international tourist fashion. They are reminiscent of seaside holidays in Britain in the fifties: rows of Victorian guesthouses, bracing breezes, buckets and spades, ice-cream parlours and a funfair.

*D*unluce Castle on *the north coast was abandoned after parts of it began to slip into the sea.*

Portrush occupies the north-pointing Ramore Head so it enjoys both east- and west-facing seafronts, with sandy beaches and a famous golf links nearby. Accepting the unpredictable weather and cold sea, Waterworld provides a sheltered environment and heated pools.

The romantic ruins of **Dunluce Castle** stand atop a rocky promontory, almost cut off by a deep gorge that is crossed by a bridge where the drawbridge used to be. The waves have eaten away at the cliffs below the castle, taking parts of the buildings as well. It was once a stronghold of the MacDonnells, but they abandoned it in the 17th century: perhaps they were put off when the kitchens and several servants fell into the sea. If you visit in the spring or early summer, look for the fulmars which nest on the cliff ledges.

Little **Portballintrae** to the east is a quieter resort than Portrush, with a fine long beach. Not far inland, the handsome buildings of **Old Bushmills Distillery** house what claims to be the oldest licensed distillery in the world: Sir Thomas Phillips was granted a permit to make whiskey here in 1608. That was merely making legal what had been going on for centuries. The process has hardly changed, except in scale, and the water still comes from the same stream. Old malt kilns where the sprouted barley used to be dried over peat and coke have been converted into a museum and the Potstill Bar, where you can sample the product after a tour. The Visitor Centre opens during normal working hours on weekdays (and on Saturdays from July to September).

The River Bush, flowing through the village, is one of Ireland's great salmon streams.

# Irish – Whiskey with an 'E'

The monks had something to do with it. They often led the way in developing alcoholic drinks – brewing, winemaking, distilling and preparing liqueurs. This is understandable: for centuries the monasteries had a near-monopoly of education and science in western Europe. And think how a glass or two must have have brightened up an austere life!

Distillation was probably developed in the Middle East to make perfumes. The technique was brought to Ireland by about the 6th century, but not to make beautiful smells. The monks had another idea: to distil fermenting brews into strong drink. By the 12th century when the Normans and their English and Welsh soldiers arrived, there must have been quite a bit of it about. They are on record as praising the local *uisce beatha* (water of life) which they called *fuisce*, not far from today's pronunciation of whiskey.

By the 16th century there was some commercial production. Queen Elizabeth I is said to have enjoyed a drop, and legend says that Sir Walter Raleigh picked up some casks of whiskey on his way to South America. Tsar Peter the Great of Russia, a famous imbiber, gave it his seal of approval: 'Irish is best'.

## Rules and Regulations

Seeing a promising source of revenue, the government decided that commercial producers must have a licence. In 1608, the very first was granted to the Old Bushmills Distillery in County Antrim, near the Giant's Causeway, which had been running since 1276. Mere licence fees didn't generate much income, so in 1661, a duty was slapped on spirits. Attempting to bring the business under control and force out the countless home distillers, an Act of Parliament in 1758 specified a minimum size for stills.

In 1780, John Jameson established his distillery in Bow Street, Dublin, north of the River Liffey. From the start, he encouraged local farmers to grow the best barley for the purpose: even today, only Irish barley is used to make Irish whiskey. Jameson's Three Star was to become known around the world ('Not a Drop is Sold 'Til It's 7 Years Old') and today, Jameson's is still the best-selling brand of Irish.

James Power set up his operation south of the Liffey in 1791. As John Power and Son's 'Three Swallow' (!) it became a Dublin favourite and the first to appear in miniature bottles. In 1825, the big Midleton distillery began production. 1829 saw the birth of Tullamore Dew ('Give Every Man His Dew') and in 1867, several small distillers amalgamated as the Cork Distillers Company to produce the celebrated Paddy brand. It's supposed to be named after a particular salesman: the buyers had got into the habit of asking for 'Paddy's' whiskey.

## Setbacks and Recovery

By 1900, over 400 brands were being exported to the United States alone. Growth looked unstoppable until a succession of blows hit the industry. In the aftermath of World War I, the US introduced prohibition. Exports of Irish whiskey to neighbouring countries mysteriously increased, but not enough to make up the lost trade. Worse still, in the long run, was the sale of illegal and inferior 'hooch' labelled Irish, giving the real product a bad name. The independence and civil wars in Ireland from 1919 to 1923 hurt the home market too,

*Old Bushmills in County Antrim claims to be the oldest licensed distillery in the world. The permit was granted in 1608.*

and the great depression which struck in 1929 was the last straw for many producers. Even the repeal of prohibition couldn't save them, and hundreds were forced to close.

The road back was a long one. World War II impeded trade, and US service personnel sent to Europe acquired a taste for Scotch. By 1966 only five big brands were left: Jameson, Power's, Paddy, Tullamore Dew and Old Bushmills. The first four combined to form Irish Distillers' Group and Bushmills joined them in 1972. Apart from Old Bushmills which continues at its historic home in the north, all production was concentrated at a new distillery at Midleton near Cork, next to the old Cork Distillers' buildings which have been magnificently renovated as the Jameson Heritage Centre. The position is much the same today although (don't shout it from the rooftops) Irish Distillers are owned now by the French drinks giant, Pernod Ricard. They no longer have a total monopoly, however. Cooley Distillery of Louth, the first independent for decades, has matured enough whiskeys to launch them on the market, reviving old brand names such as Tyrconnell. Some of their stocks are held at the 1757 Locke's Distillery, not currently operating but run as a museum in Kilbeggan, County Westmeath.

## What's the Difference?

Some of the barley is malted: that means soaked in water and left for 2–3 days to sprout before being dried in a kiln, or 'killun' as it sounds in an Irish brogue. In Scotland the smoke of a peat fire penetrates the sprouted barley, but in the Irish process the heating is indirect, keeping smoky tastes out of the final product.

283

*The great water wheel at Midleton powered the machinery for over a hundred years until pensioned off in 1975.*

*Comparing the tastes at the Jameson Heritage Centre, Midleton.*

Dried malted and unmalted barley are mixed; the more malted, the stronger the flavour of the whiskey. (In the five standard brands, 30–50 percent malted barley is used, and a higher proportion in Bushmills' Black Bush. Bushmills Single Malt speaks for itself.) The barleys are ground, mixed with water and yeast and left to ferment for about 70 hours, time for the starches to turn to sugars and then to alcohol.

Alcohol has a lower boiling point than water, so heating in a still for 12 hours turns most of the alcohol (and some water) to vapours. Cooling converts these to a colourless liquid, much stronger than whiskey. This is then distilled again, for greater purity. Then – and this is another thing that makes Irish whiskey special – the resulting product is given a third distillation.

It still isn't anything like whiskey, although with the addition of some water it might resemble *poteen*, the illegal firewater which somebody's uncle's friend's brother might be able to get from a farm over the next horizon. Some water is added, to reduce the alcohol content to about 78 percent, and the precious liquid is stored in second-hand oak barrels, previously used for sherry, port or American whiskeys, for example. They aren't trying to save money: it's just that new oak would put too much tannin into the product. And there's a bonus in all the subtle flavours and golden colour to be gained from the old barrels. Now at least seven years are allowed to go by (more than for the average Scotch) before blending to get the desired taste, and bottling. If different ages are blended, the age given is that of the youngest.

## Whiskey Wonders
● The IDG distillery at Midleton produces 6.5 million litres of whiskey a year. The old distillery – now the Jameson Heritage Centre – could produce 1.5 million litres.
● The biggest pot still in the world, built of copper in 1825 in the old distillery, can hold 144,500 litres.
● Whiskey barrels vary from 200 to 500 litres. They're weighed empty and full to check how much they contain. Even the smallest (about 42 gallons of whisky) would carry a tax of £3,600!
●The giant waterwheel at Midleton ran the machinery from 1852 until 1975. The back-up steam engine, for when the river was low, dates from 1834. It also worked beautifully until 1975.

## The Giant's Causeway

Thinking they were looking at a castle, the crew of a ship of the Spanish Armada fired their cannons at it. And legend says the Causeway was built by the giant Finn MacCool (or Mac Cumhail) so he could walk to Scotland. People have always found it difficult to accept that a structure so exact could be entirely natural, and equally hard to see how anyone could have made something so massive. Even knowing the geological explanation, you may have the same feeling.

Thousands of columns of basalt stand in terraces descending to the sea. Most are hexagonal in section, although few are as perfectly regular as they first appear, and a high percentage are pentagons, or have seven or even more sides. In the most spectacular part of the Causeway, a procession of pillars seems to march down into the waves. Apparently they were formed during volcanic activity some 60,000,000 years ago when molten rock flowed out in a layer on the earth's surface. Cooling very slowly over many years, it contracted and crystallized into this remarkable structure (seen also at Fingal's Cave on Staffa off Scotland). The columns also split into lengths as they contracted, forming a convex and a concave surface at the break, like a ball and socket joint.

The car park is at the top of the nearby cliffs. The National Trust, custodians of the site and a long stretch of adjoining Antrim coast, have a shop and information centre here. Look for their excellent booklet and map of walks in the area. There's an easy path down to the Causeway (and a shuttle bus for those who prefer or need one), but the rocks themselves can be slippery when wet. Watch your step or you'll be taking an unplanned dip.

Try to allow plenty of time for a visit, not only at the main promontory to look at some of the special formations, but to take a walk along the coastal path to the east. Go as far as you have time for: this section of path is 15km (9 miles) long. The wild flowers and bird life are remarkable: look for fulmars, guillemots, cormorants and shags, razorbills, oystercatchers and perhaps gannets fishing.

Less than a kilometre (half a mile) from the main part of the Causeway, the path rounds a headland into **Port na Spaniagh** (Spanish Inlet), so named after a galleass of the Spanish Armada was wrecked here in 1588, with the loss of all on board. It so happened that this ship, the *Girona*, had picked up the officers and precious possessions from two galleons disabled earlier, so she was carrying a particularly rich cargo. Some of the treasures recovered from the wreck by a team of Belgian divers in the 1960s are now in the Ulster Museum in Belfast.

## Suspense

Between the Giant's Causeway and Ballycastle, about 8km (5 miles) from either, watch for signs to the 'Rope Bridge' at **Carrick-a-Rede**. After a 15-minute walk along a clifftop path and down a flight of steps, you'll be looking across at a pinnacle of rock, cut off from the mainland by a deep vertical chasm. From May to September, a suspension bridge (reassuringly supported by wire cables, not rope) is thrown across the gap. It is not primarily designed as a test of nerve for

*The suspension bridge at Carrick-a-Rede sways alarmingly, but it's safer than it may look.*

visitors, despite the two narrow planks that form the bridge's walkway and its tendency to sway, the reason no more than two people should be on it at a time. The real purpose is to allow fishermen to cross and catch salmon as they migrate along the coast. The island (its name means 'rock in the way') serves to divert them into the nets fixed to it. In spring, kittiwakes come ashore to nest on the cliffs, and even when the bridge is not in position, the scenery makes the walk worth while.

Out to sea, the view is dominated by rugged **Rathlin Island**, where Robert the Bruce sheltered (and one of several claimants to be the place where the persistent spider inspired him to 'try, try, try again'). It's a bird sanctuary now, but there is some limited accommodation. In good weather, motor launches make the 45-minute trip from **Ballycastle**, a holiday centre with a golf course.

At **Fair Head**, a great cliff rearing up to 194m (636ft) marks the point where this dramatic coastline begins to turn south. If the weather's favourable, the vigorous walk to the top pays off with superb views over Rathlin Island and north east to Scotland – the Mull of Kintyre is only 21km (13 miles) away. Peering giddily over the edge, you might see wild goats picking their way on the slopes far below. In Lough na Cranagh behind Fair Head you'll see a genuine *crannóg*, or site of a former lake dwelling, to compare with the dozens of modern models in the history parks.

The main route south east through forest and moorland is less exciting than the tortuous minor road along the rugged coast. **Cushendun** is a picture-book village in the care of the National Trust, with a beach and harbour. The matching houses, all with slate roofs, whitewashed walls and black paint, were designed by Clough Williams-Ellis (architect of Portmeirion in Wales) and built about 1920 for Lord Cushendun and his wife. She was Cornish and wanted to be reminded of her home.

## The Glens of Antrim

After the coastal spectacle to the north, turn inland for some gentler excursions. Pretty valleys, nine in all, cut down from the moorland of the Antrim Mountains through wooded hills to the sea. They became a favourite with Victorian travellers after the building of the coast road made them accessible for the first time.

Glenaan, one of the smallest, runs down to the sea at the little port of **Cushendall**. A short distance into the valley, and up a track to the south, a sign directs you to 'Ossian's Grave'. This is not really connected with the semi-mythical warrior poet of perhaps AD 300, but is a much older court tomb, sadly not well preserved. The pretty waterfalls of **Glenariff** are reached by a short walk through a forest park by the side of the road through the glen. Back on the Antrim coast road, **Waterfoot** comes alive in July when the *Feis na nGleann* Gaelic games and folk festival is held. To the south round rugged Garron Point, Carnlough is handsomely built of the limestone from local quarries. Another quarry disfigures the view at the village of **Glenarm**, where the castle, much altered over the centuries, was the historic seat of the MacDonnells, Earls of Antrim after they moved from Dunluce on the north coast. The industrial port of **Larne** is the terminal for ferries to Stranraer and Cairnryan in Scotland. If you don't have to catch one, you may as well bypass it. For the next 13km (8 miles), what looks like an island, and is called one ('Island Magee') fills the view to the east.

288

*The* he east coast of County
Antrim is punctuated by a dozen
fast-flowing streams like this one
at Glenoe waterfall.

In fact this is a peninsula reached by road
from Ballycarry or Whitehead, or boat
from Larne. On the east, basalt cliffs
called the Gobbins drop sharply to the sea.
From the little harbour of Portmuck, you
can visit the bird sanctuary on little Muck
Island.

**Carrickfergus**
A small town on the north shore of Belfast
Lough, this was once the most important
port on this coast. Now the harbour is used
only by pleasure craft and a few fishing
boats. It's dominated by one of the most
massive Norman castles in Ireland, begun
by John de Courcy in the 12th century.
Housing an army garrison right up to the
20th century, it was kept in good repair
while others fell into ruin.

Carrickfergus has seen its share of historical limelight. Edward Bruce, brother of
King Robert the Bruce of Scotland, was
crowned King of Ireland here in 1316. His

supporters no doubt hoped that the English rout at the hands of the Scots at Bannockburn in 1314 could be repeated in Ireland. It was not to be. Despite several successes and nearly two years in which he controlled much of Ireland outside the Pale, Edward's army was defeated in 1318 at Dundalk and he was killed.

William of Orange landed at Carrickfergus in 1690 on his way to the Battle of the Boyne. A French force seized it in 1760 in a daring but pointless raid, and in 1778, the American naval hero John Paul Jones surprised and defeated the British ship *Drake* just offshore. On the coast just north of the town, the ancestors of US president Andrew Jackson (1767-1845) once lived in a cottage in the little street now bearing the odd name of Boneybefore. The cottage has long gone: the Jackson Homestead visitor centre here is a reconstruction.

*Carrickfergus, with its early Norman castle, was once a more important port than Belfast. William of Orange landed here in 1690.*

# Belfast

Capital of the North, Ireland's second city always surprises visitors, one way or another. Some expect riot and destruction and find it oddly quiet: unfinished schemes of urban renewal have left far more damage than any bombs, including Hitler's. It is hard to find traces of the Georgian town which grew prosperous on trade and linen. During the 19th century the population grew from 20,000 to 300,000, and earlier buildings were replaced in self-confident Victorian style. The city became a world leader in ship-building, tobacco manufacture and textiles, competing with industrial dynamos of the likes of Manchester and Glasgow. The Partition of Ireland in 1921 made Belfast the capital of Northern Ireland, but gradually reduced its markets in the new Free State, and the depression of the 1930s hit it hard. World War II bomb damage

*B*elfast's Donegall *Place and the imposing dome of City Hall, which was completed in 1906.*

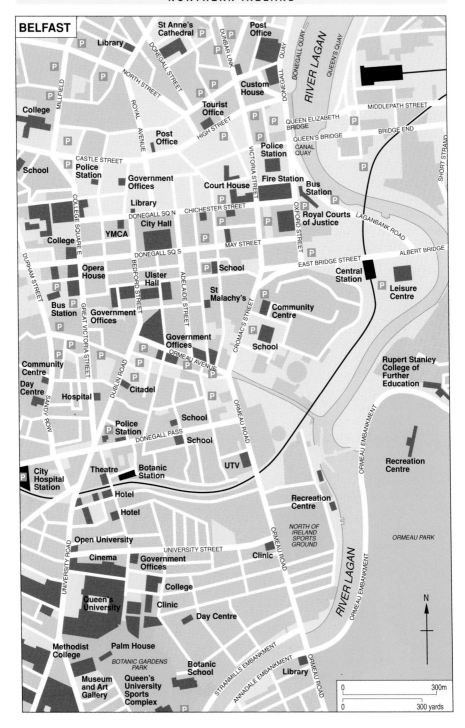

was balanced by increased industrial activity as the Short Brothers aircraft factory and the Harland and Wolff shipyard worked at full stretch – they had been the main targets of the air-raids.

Civil rights marches by the large Catholic community in 1968 quickly led to violence. British troops were brought in, to attempt to break the cycle of reprisal and counter-reprisal, but soon became targets themselves. The poorer housing estates, already largely segregated along sectarian lines, had to be separated physically by high fences. The city centre was ringed by checkpoints and many streets became pedestrian-only.

These days, security measures are less obvious: on a day visit you might not see a patrol at all. Belfast tries to live an ordinary life, with restaurants, pubs, theatres and cinemas functioning normally. The people are as friendly and helpful as everywhere else in Ireland.

The copper dome of the **City Hall** on Donegall (here spelt with two ls) Square is a central landmark. Modelled on London's St Paul's Cathedral, the 1906 building trumpets the civic confidence of its time. Outside by green lawns stand memorials to war dead and the victims of the sinking of the Belfast-built *Titanic*. You can join a tour of the interior to see the marble halls and carved oak council chamber, scene of many a fractious debate between the representatives of communities which have been at loggerheads for decades. The streets to the north of City Hall are a mainly pedestrianized area: Royal Avenue and the connecting streets have most of the big shops. The tourist information office is at 48 High Street, on the way to the Albert Memorial clock tower and the River Lagan quayside. North along Donegall Street, **St Anne's**

**Cathedral** (Church of Ireland) is a solid example of Romanesque revival.

Again starting from Donegall Square, Bedford Street leads south to the **Ulster Hall**, venue of symphony, rock and pop concerts. A couple of blocks to the east, the **St Malachy's** Catholic Church in Alfred Street has a fine Victorian Gothic interior with delicate lacy fan-vaulting in Tudor style.

Ambitious plans are afoot to restore the rundown waterfront all along the River Lagan, creating new leisure, office and residential space. Across the river in East Belfast, the **Transport Gallery** in Witham Street off the Newtownards Road caters for nostalgia, with its great steam locomotives and old Belfast trams. It's part of the Ulster Folk and Transport Museum whose main site is near Holywood (see page 295) and some exhibits are exchanged between the two locations.

If you're curious to see the places which figured for years in the news of the troubles, enterprising drivers are ready to take you on a trip round Protestant or Catholic West Belfast – but not both on the same tour. Ask at the Northern Ireland Tourist Office in High Street where to find the taxi ranks which serve each area. The Catholic estates of Divis Street, Falls and Ballymurphy and, slightly further north, Protestant Shankill Road and Crumlin Road are about equal in grimness, relieved by colourful murals and pavement painting that leave you in no doubt of local allegiances.

## South from the Centre

The most agreeable aspects of Belfast are to be found along the north–south strip of Great Victoria Street (not to be confused with Victoria Street), Shaftesbury Square, University Road and Stranmillis Road.

The city's promotional literature does exaggerate its attractions in labelling it the 'Golden Mile', but this is certainly the best area to look for somewhere to eat. And especially around Queens University, you'll find a choice of places to stay if you want to be conveniently near the centre and yet not right in it.

Two gems of Victoriana have been restored in Great Victoria Street – but since sadly damaged more than once during repeated bombings of the nearby Europa Hotel. The 1890s **Grand Opera House** with its richly gilded interior may still be undergoing repairs. Across the street, the **Crown Liquor Saloon** is a symphony of fine woodwork and brass, engraved glass and tiles, with private boxes ('snugs') as well as a long bar where, on a good day, you can enjoy some local oysters and a Guinness.

South down Great Victoria Street, past Shaftesbury Square, you'll come to the impressive 1849 main buildings of **Queen's University**, designed in the style of a palace for the first Queen Elizabeth – or an Oxford college. Adjoining them are two of Belfast's biggest attractions. The **Botanic Gardens** are a popular public park with lush green shrubs and brilliant flower displays. The highlight is the curvaceous **Palm House** of cast iron and hundreds of glass panels, many of them in complex shapes. Older than the one at Kew Gardens or London's vanished Crystal Palace, it has been beautifully restored to pristine splendour.

*C*olourful springtime azaleas in Belfast's Botanic Gardens.

### The Ulster Museum

Inside the gates of the Botanic Gardens, several different and magnificent collections have been brought together in one modern museum building – it houses the city's main art gallery too – so you will need plenty of time to do it justice. The paintings, watercolours and drawings are on the top floor, so if they are your chief objective, take the lift up and start there. You can then work your way down and pick out other highlights later.

The **art collection** is international, but Irish landscapes and portraits of figures from Irish history remind you where you are. Irish artists have pride of place: Roderic O'Conor who was inspired by

Van Gogh, Belfast-born Sir John Lavery, Jack B. Yeats (*A Soft Day*, 1908), Anne Yeats and Gerard Dillon. The water-colours and drawings – British and Irish – are exceptional. Look out for the work of Edward Lear, who would rather have been remembered for his art than his nonsense, Samuel Palmer, Paul Sandby, Rowlandson and Fuseli.

Glass, silver, ceramics and textiles are also on the upper floors. The whole world of **natural history** comes next: geology, flora and fauna, fossils and dinosaur skel-etons. Archaeological finds include Ne-olithic flint tools, Bronze Age gold jewellery and relics from the early Chris-tian era.

Most visitors will want to see the trea-sures recovered by divers in the 1960s from the Spanish Armada ship *Girona* which was wrecked near the Giant's Causeway in 1588. Those on show include gold jewellery set with precious stones, as well as some of the weapons and countless domestic objects. The lower floors cover local history, celebrating Belfast's leading role in the industrial revolution.

## South and East of Belfast

By road or rail along the south shore of Belfast Lough, the **Ulster Folk and Transport Museum** is about 13km (8 miles) from the city. In the grounds of Cultra Manor near Holywood, original historic buildings and traditional houses have been brought from all over the province: cottages and houses, a weaver's workshop, a mill, a forge, a school and a church. A whole Ulster village has been assembled, beautifully set in the land-scape. Peat fires burn in the houses, which are furnished and equipped as they might have been over a century ago. Do ask questions – talking to the staff is half the

fun – and don't miss the **Folk Gallery**, where exhibitions of early photographs, prints and drawings are mounted.

The **Transport Museum**'s galleries are bright and modern, with the carriages, cars, horsedrawn vehicles and railway rolling stock that you expect, but here put into an Irish context. The collections are outstanding: particularly unusual are the primitive rural panniers, sleds and carts, and the range of bicycles and motorcycles. Among the shiny veteran cars are the Belfast-built 1906 Chambers and the ill-starred De Lorean of 1982. The section on Belfast's shipbuilding industry recalls the days when it led the world. There's a range of models of the aircraft produced by the pioneer Short Brothers, especially their famous flying boats, plus the actual 'Flying Bedstead' which tested the verti-cal take-off techniques that were used later in the Harrier.

A short diversion south will take you to **Stormont**, just off the Belfast to New-townards road. Built to impress, this coolly classical palace was built for the Northern Ireland parliament. It dates from 1928, when it was felt that the Partition of 1921 would endure, if not for ever, then at least indefinitely. The Protestant Union-ist majority in the province led to what was effectively a one-party state, until the events of 1968 and after impelled the United Kingdom government in London to suspend Northern Ireland's parliament in 1972. **Bangor** has been Belfast's sea-side resort since the first railway made it accessible. The same rail link and good roads now carry commuters to the city.

**The Ards Peninsula**, a long finger of land to the south, is a traditional retreat for Belfast people. If the weekend weather is fine, crowds head for the sandy beaches on the east coast. The sheltered waters of the almost landlocked **Strangford Lough** to the west are good for fishing, windsurfing and birdwatching (the foreshore is a nature reserve). **Mount Stewart**, with extensive grounds facing the lough, was the birthplace and home of the statesman Viscount Castlereagh, one of the architects of the treaties that ended the Napoleonic Wars. The Georgian house, of a dark stone, looks slightly more modest than many stately homes built in Ireland in that era, but the neoclassical interior is impressive. The entrance hall recalls a Roman villa, and the staircase is dominated by a huge dramatic 1799 painting by Stubbs of the racehorse *Hambletonian.* Various Castlereagh memorabilia and portraits are found throughout the house, but it bears the more recent stamp of the Marchioness of Londonderry, wife of the 7th Marquess. It was she who also designed the marvellous **gardens** in the 1920s. A paradise of parterres and vistas, terraces, borders, surprises and secret corners, dotted with statuary including every mythical animal imaginable, they are one of the National Trust's greatest treasures. The elegant **Temple of the Winds**, a banqueting hall dating from 1785 and based on the ancient Greek original in Athens, can be reached by a separate entrance further along the loughside road.

The village of Greyabbey takes its name from the ruined Cistercian monastery of **Grey Abbey**, founded in the 12th century and showing some of the earliest influence of the Gothic style. The ruins stand in wooded parkland south east of the village. If you are heading south, there's no need to retrace your journey back up the Ards Peninsula. A passenger and car ferry runs every half-hour from Portaferry to Strangford across the narrow mouth of Strangford Lough.

## The Lecale Peninsula – St Patrick's Country

The bulge of land south of Strangford Lough has countless monuments from all periods of Irish history and many connections with the patron saint. He is believed to have landed west of Strangford at the mouth of the Slaney river and set up his first church in a barn at **Saul** – the village's name is derived from the Irish *Sabhall* which means 'barn'. The modern replica of an early church with a round tower was built in 1932 to commemorate the 1,500th anniversary of St Patrick's landing. He returned many times to Saul, and died here in about 461. A 10m (33ft) statue of the saint, also built in 1932, stands at **Slieve Patrick** near Saul. The hilltop site is reached by a zig-zag path past the stations of the cross.

Just out of the little village of Strangford, **Castle Ward** has something for everyone. The 18th-century house was built with a Classical west front and a fanciful 'Gothick' east front, in accordance with the tastes of the Lord and Lady Bangor who thereby agreed to differ. The 280ha (700-acre) estate, run by the National Trust, includes formal gardens, woods, lakeshore and seashore: many species of ducks, geese and wading birds make their home here. There's an adventure playground and Victorian children's games centre, an information centre on Strangford Lough and the old castle and a working cornmill to see as well as the eccentric two-in-one house itself.

Down the coast from Strangford, **Kilclief Castle**, in excellent repair, is one of the earliest tower houses in this part of Ireland, dating from about 1420. It may well have served as a model for hundreds of similar towers built during the next two hundred years, reflecting the uncertainties of the times. **Ardglass**, a lively fishing port, has a number of these fortified houses including Jordan's Castle near the harbour, and several later merchants' mansions. A mile or two inland, in tranquil pasture land at Ballynoe near Killough, the Neolithic **Laggamaddy stone circle** is one of the most complete in Ireland. In effect it's a double ring, though the elliptical inner ring is incomplete. The long burial mound inside may be from a somewhat earlier period, but both date from before 2000 BC.

**Downpatrick**, the quiet county town of County Down, was a local chief's stronghold when the Norman lord John de Courcy marched up from Dublin with his 300 fellow adventurers and seized it. Earlier, St Patrick is said to have founded a monastery, perhaps on the steep hill where the Church of Ireland **Down Cathedral** now stands. There has long been a belief that he is buried here: de Courcy seems to have thought so, for he brought the supposed remains of St Colmcille and St Bridget to be reinterred, as he announced, beside the patron saint. But Armagh has contested the claim, and there is no evidence to back up the position of the stone now to be seen in the graveyard. The largely modern cathedral itself retains the now rare box pews which were common in the late 18th and early 19th centuries. Near the main door, an old font contains a smaller and even more ancient, perhaps pre-Norman font, discovered in a local farmyard. Steam train enthusiasts can ride a short section of relaid track in carriages of the old Belfast and County Down Railway, towed by the 1919 locomotive *Guinness*. The station is just below the cathedral hill off Market Street.

The **Mountains of Mourne**, says the old song, 'sweep down to the sea', but more to the point, they rise quite suddenly and steeply out of gentle countryside to provide a great hill-walking and climbing region. The highest peak is **Slieve Donard**, 852m (2,796ft), on the very outskirts of **Newcastle**, an old-established seaside resort with a sandy beach. If the water's too cold for you, or the weather uncooperative, the town has heated indoor pools as well.

The track from the town to the summit of Slieve Donard starts in Donard Park. It's a vigorous walk rather than a climb,

*E*asily reached from *Belfast or Dublin, the Mountains of Mourne in County Down make beautiful walking country.*

and the view from the cairn and hermit's cell on the summit can be superb. Go equipped for rain, but on a clear day you can see, if not for ever, then at least to the Isle of Man, Scotland and the Antrim Mountains as well as the dramatic landscapes of the rest of the Mourne range.

# South West from Belfast

Worth a short diversion from the motorway, **Hillsborough** is an attractive model village of the Protestant Plantation. The fine 17-18th-century house, later the governor's residence, was the site of the signing of the controversial 1985 Anglo-Irish Agreement (see page 57). The commercial and industrial centres of Lurgan, Craigavon and Portadown need not detain you: the road bypasses them.

## Armagh

This compact little city has been the religious capital of all Ireland since St Patrick himself established his bishopric here in the middle of the 5th century. Not surprisingly, it has two cathedrals, both dedicated to the patron saint. The circular street pattern follows the lines of ancient fortifications, and since it stands on a hilltop at the centre of the circle, the Church of Ireland (Protestant) **St Patrick's Cathedral** probably occupies the site of the saint's own church. The present building owes most of its appearance to 18th-century rebuilding and 19th-century restoration. Brian Boru and his son are said to have been brought here for burial after the victory of Clontarf in 1014 which cost them their lives.

The Perpendicular-style Catholic **St Patrick's Cathedral** on a hillside to the north west was finished in 1873. The striking interior is airy and spacious and shines all over with brilliantly coloured mosaics. Some good public buildings and townhouses survive from the 18th century, particularly around the long green **Mall**, formerly a racecourse but now surrounded by fine houses. The **Observatory** on the hill overlooking the Mall is two centuries old: now the neighbouring **Planetarium** (a rarity in Ireland) and exhibition on astronomy and space exploration have been added. In the Georgian outbuildings of the former archbishop's palace south of the centre, the **Palace Stables** Heritage Centre sets out to recreate the daily life of the archbishop and his household in the 18th century.

## Navan Fort (*Emain Macha*)

West of Armagh City just across the River Callan rises a grass-covered mound like an upturned saucer, ringed by earthwork ramparts roughly 230m (750ft) across. There is little doubt that this was the prehistoric capital of Ulster, Emain Macha, between the 4th century BC and the 4th century AD. The intriguing evidence of excavations shows that in 94 BC a huge wooden temple 45m (148ft) across was built on the mound. It consisted of 275 timber columns and when completed, it was filled with stone to make a cairn. Then, within the year, the wooden structure was set on fire and burnt out, presumably deliberately, leaving holes where the posts had been. Earth was piled on top to make a great barrow. What could have been the purpose of all this? The certainty about the year (from tree-ring dating) contrasts with the general mystery. Could it have been a huge funeral pyre? None can say for sure, but Celtic epics speak of palaces full of feasting warriors being set alight as a ritual sacrifice. Perhaps this was a substitute which didn't involve wasting valuable fighting men.

In the Loughnashade lake near the mound, 200 years ago, a farmer discovered four 2,000-year-old bronze trumpets and several human skulls. (One of the trumpets can be seen in the National Gallery in Dublin: the rest have been lost.) A swampy area called the 'King's Stables' that seems to have been an artificial pool was excavated and found to contain the bones of dog, deer, cow and pig and the sheared-off front of another human skull. The 26ha (65-acre) site has been designated as an archaeological park to protect it from the quarrying that had reached its very edge, and a visitor centre was opened in 1993 to provide some background information and high-tech displays. Some remarkable discoveries of jewellery, weapons and tools are on show.

---

### EPIC TALES

From his palace at Emain Macha, King Conchobáir (Conor) ruled Ulster with the Red Branch Knights, Ireland's order of chivalry. So goes the legend, based no doubt on some original truth. Their exploits are told in the poems of the Ulster Cycle, the Celtic world's equivalent of the Greek *Iliad* or *Odyssey*, probably dating from more than 2,000 years ago but only written down after the 7th century AD. Oddly, in one of the highpoints of the cycle the knights scarcely appear. Under a spell, they lie sick and helpless in the palace while Queen Maeve and her army from Connacht prepare to invade. The queen covets the great brown bull of Cooley, the mountainous peninsula east of Dundalk, and will stop at nothing to get it. Only the hero Cúchulainn, called 'the Hound of Ulster', can save the kingdom. He sallies forth from his *dún* at Dundalk and holds off the invaders single-handed at the Gap of the North. Ulster is saved. Leaders throughout Irish history from St Patrick to the 1916 Rising have invoked the spirit of Cúchulainn, and the old Celtic tales inspired Yeats, Synge and their contemporaries. As for Emain Macha, the traditional date of its fall is AD 332 (but may have been up to a hundred years later) when the Collas brothers took and destroyed it and moved the capital to where Armagh now stands.

## County Fermanagh

**Enniskillen** grew up on an island site where Upper and Lower Lough Erne meet. Its mostly modern buildings include an excellent information centre in Shaw Road. The old **castle** was given a Scottish look in the early years of the Plantation. Now it houses local and military museums. The Doric column which stands above the town is a monument to Sir Lowry Cole, one of Wellington's generals, who was born here. In summer, you can climb its 108 steps to the top for a view of the town and lakes. On the south-eastern outskirts, **Castlecoole** is a magnificent neoclassical mansion built in the 1790s by Wyatt for the Earl of Belmore. Now owned by the National Trust, it is filled with fine furniture, books and pictures.

Stately **Florence Court** (also National Trust) is a mid-18th-century house 13km (8 miles) south west of Enniskillen. It was built for the Cole family, later Earls of Enniskillen and descendants of William Cole who was awarded the town in the Plantation. It contains notable collections of Irish furniture and Meissen porcelain and the gardens have an original ice house and water-powered sawmill.

A few miles west of Florence Court in Claddagh Glen, **Marble Arch Caves** are some of the most spectacular in Ireland. You are taken on a 75-minute tour, including a boat trip on an underground river through brilliantly lit caverns. If you are heading for County Donegal in the Republic, the border town of **Belleek** is noted for a curious kind of china made to look like basketware which you will see in shops all over Ireland. The pottery welcomes visitors to its museum and restaurant.

## The Lakes of Fermanagh

First the geography. They are 80km (50 miles) long, taken together. Lower Lough Erne is further north (and west) and is studded with islands. Upper Lough Erne is a maze of waterways, inlets and reed beds whose southerly end straddles the border. The excellent fishing, from boats or piers, draws visitors from as far as Italy and Germany. Short cruises on Lower Lough Erne start from Enniskillen, stopping at Devenish Island (see below).

*Stately Castlecoole near Enniskillen was built in the 1790s. It's one of several great houses in Northern Ireland owned by the National Trust.*

The Palladian mansion of **Castle Archdale** was allowed to decay into a dangerous condition and had to be demolished. The huge stable block remains, set in a forest park and housing a youth hostel and rural life and natural history museum. The now tranquil waters of Lough Erne once echoed to the roar of flying boat engines as Sunderland and Catalina flying boats of the RAF flew round-the-clock patrols of the North Atlantic during World War II. Part of the museum tells their story.

**BATTLE OF THE ATLANTIC**

In the early part of World War II 'Black Gap' in the North Atlantic where convoys were unprotected by airborne anti-submarine patrols. Looking at the map of Ireland you'll see that it was imperative to obtain the permission of the Irish government to overfly the narrow strip of neutral territory on the way to the Atlantic. It was secretly granted, on condition that the agreement be kept secret. If the patrols had been denied that approval, the advantages of the base would have been lost. Those who saw 50 or 60 flying boats operating from the lake are surely right when they say there will never be such a sight again.

Boats can be hired by the day or week from Enniskillen, Castle Archdale, Kesh and Belleek to go fishing or just cruising around and relaxing. Be sure to get full instructions and charts from the hiring company. Bear in mind that the weather can be treacherous: mists and storms can blow in with very little warning. You can rent holiday chalets built like log cabins on Lusty Beg island – motor boats to enable you to get there and a lesson on using them are included.

**White Island**

Strange carvings from the pagan and Christian eras have been found on many of the islands in Lower Lough Erne. On White Island, seven intriguing stone figures and a later head are now set in a row in the walls of a ruined church. Reaching only waist high, with a primitive look and round, staring eyes they probably date from the 6th to 8th centuries. They are presumably Christian, the largest and most conventional certainly is, with a crozier and bell. The oddest, on the left of the line, appears to be a *sheila na gig*, a female fertility symbol probably adapted from pre-Christian cults to serve as a warning against the sin of lust. There is no basis for a fanciful identification of the figures with the seven deadly sins: only the numbers match.

Just north of Enniskillen, a track leads down to a fishing pier. Just offshore on **Devenish Island** lie the extensive ruins of a monastery said to have been founded by St Molaise in the 6th century. The tall round tower (12th century) is one of the best preserved in Ireland, unusual for its decorated frieze and four heads facing the compass points. A boat service runs to the island in summer.

**Omagh** may be the county town of Tyrone, but most visitors arrive here only to leave it, heading for the scenic attractions of the Fermanagh Lakes to the south west, or one (or both) of the two excellent 'Parks' a few kilometres north of town. Take the A5 road out of Omagh to reach the **Ulster American Folk Park**, which highlights the connections betwen this part of Ireland and North America. In the 18th and early 19th centuries, a quarter of a million people left Ulster to make new homes across the Atlantic. No fewer than 11 US presidents including Andrew Jackson and Woodrow Wilson traced their ancestry to Ulster, whereas only Presidents Kennedy, Reagan and perhaps Bush had forebears who came from the rest of Ireland. The exhibition hall at the entrance houses frequently changing displays. Armed with a plan of the park, it's best to follow the numerical sequence, starting with typical buildings of early 19th-century Ulster. Some are replicas, some have been brought from other places and reassembled, like the little schoolhouse which seems as if the pupils have only just left. They are all furnished and looked after by staff dressed in the clothes of the period.

The nucleus of the park was the Mellon homestead, on its original site, where the ancestors of the financier Andrew Mellon lived before emigrating to the United States in 1818. The philanthropist Paul Mellon has been a main contributor to the establishment of the park. You make your way past the shops of an Ulster street to the 'dockside' to board the sailing ship *Union*, bound for Baltimore, and – in a great piece of theatre – disembark to emerge in an American street! Buildings on this side of the street include a log farmhouse like the one the Mellons built soon after they arrived in Pennsylvania, complete with outbuildings housing live pigs, hens and turkeys.

The UAFP (as it's often known) stages festivals and concerts of American folk music and dance, and marks American holidays such as the 4th of July and Hallowe'en just the way they do at home in the USA. Anyone in search of their Ulster roots may be able to get some clues from the Emigration Database of ships' passenger lists, letters and details of births, deaths and marriages on both sides of the Atlantic.

The **Ulster History Park** (on the B48 road north from Omagh) is the best and most ambitious project of its kind in Ireland. With meticulous scholarship, attention to detail and superb landscaping, they have built full-scale models of neolithic houses, a stone circle and tombs, a

*An early 19th century Irish street scene, re-created at the Irish American Folk Park, near Omagh in County Tyrone.*

*crannóg*, a ring-fort with souterrain, an early monastic settlement with church and round tower, a Norman motte-and-bailey castle, an impressive working watermill and typical 'Plantation' houses of the 17th century. Still more are under construction. Not only is it all of a very high standard, it's tremendous fun (just see the reactions of children). Don't rush through the reception building. Its historical displays are brilliantly done, with models, photographs and hilarious cartoons. A full-size replica of an early high cross will have you reeling in amazement – it's in full, garish colour! Is there any evidence for thinking this was the way they used to be? Not directly – no traces of paint survive on old examples – but tastes in religious art at the time invariably tended towards bright colours. The interiors of churches, now so austere, were once brilliantly painted. The arguments are convincing, but we are so used to bare stone crosses that anything else is a shock.

303

# Adjust to the Pace, Relax and Enjoy Yourself

You will not want to spend all your time rushing about: Ireland isn't that sort of place. There's a lot going on and you will be welcome to join in. For the major events and festivals of all kinds from opera to oyster tasting, check the Tourist Boards' lists. For just as much fun, find out about local happenings. You only have to ask in the pub, the post office or the village store and you'll be deluged with advice, some conflicting, and so much you won't be able to take all of it in. Someone will certainly know the time and place of the next Gaelic football match or horse race, and the best pubs for traditional music.

## Sport

Some visitors to Ireland don't travel around, they just go to one place, sometimes year after year. They ignore the castles or abbeys, stay away from the cities and museums. They're here for one reason: the **fishing**. Wild Atlantic salmon, sea-trout and brown trout seasons are longer, stocks are better and costs are as low or lower than anywhere else in Europe. Coarse fishing on lakes and rivers

*Golfers can choose from some great courses including seaside links like Lahinch in County Clare, modelled on St Andrews.*

can be excellent too. Sea anglers can fish from piers, rocks and the sea shore, and many small ports all round the coast have fully-equipped deep sea boats for hire.

The Tourist Boards publish leaflets every year with details of licences required and the costs. They also list fishing schools catering for beginners or advanced anglers who want to brush up their skills. There are plenty of places to stay where your hosts are used to anglers' ways: they'll dry your clothes and feed you at odd times and even smoke your catch ready to take home.

All those lakes and rivers are an invitation to get on to the water somehow. You can take a **cruising** holiday on the Shannon (see page 217) and the canals, or on Lough Erne in Northern Ireland. For the more energetic, **canoeing** trips or

whole canoeing holidays are offered. Like everywhere else, **windsurfing** has boomed. From placid sheltered shallows to mighty Atlantic rollers, conditions can suit any level of experience, but you'll need your wet suit.

*S̲ee a different aspect of Ireland from one of the Shannon cruisers. For beginners, lessons are part of the package.*

---

**IN PRAISE OF IRELAND (1858)**

The leading purpose of the Authors is to induce VISITS TO IRELAND. Those who require relaxation from labour, or may be advised to seek health under the influence of a mild climate, or search for sources of novel and rational amusement, or draw from change of scene a stimulus to wholesome excitement, or covet acquaintance with the charms of nature, or wish to study a people full of original character – cannot project an excursion to any part of Europe that will afford a more ample recompense.

From the 1858 guidebook *A Week at Killarney* by Mr & Mrs SC Hall

---

The white sandy beaches, pristine and uncrowded, would be perfect for **swimming** if the weather could be relied on – and the water were a bit warmer. Even so, you'll see plenty of hardy souls taking a dip.

Whether you're just out to enjoy the scenery or heading for a particular objective, **walking** is the ideal way to appreciate the subtleties of the Irish landscape. Use canal towpaths, cliff paths, green roads made for driving cattle to market and the tracks that country people used to get to church, but remember to close farm gates behind you. Equip yourself with good rainwear and strong shoes and take local advice before heading into the mountains. Paths are few and tempting tracts of open hillside can conceal impenetrable bogs. Several long distance 'Ways' have been designated and marked (see LEISURE ROUTES, page 75) and various guided walks and walking holidays are offered by tour companies.

Uncrowded roads and short distances make **cycling** a good option. Bikes are available for hire by the day or week at many holiday centres. Most weekends,

*T*he rocks and bogs of Connemara, with some of the Twelve Bens (or Pins) in the distance.

you'll see dedicated locals out training, some hoping to emulate Sean Kelly and Stephen Roche, the Irish superstars who won the Tour de France.

Lonely coasts and islands, so much open country and so few people make for one of the best environments left in the whole of western Europe for wildlife and especially **birdwatching** (see LEISURE ROUTES, page 69).

Ireland has some of the world's most beautiful and challenging **golf** courses: Portmarnock near Dublin, Mount Juliet in County Kilkenny, Ballybunion and Lahinch among many on the west coast, and Royal Portrush in the north. (See also LEISURE ROUTES, page 84). More good news for golfers: green fees are comparatively low.

The Irish love their horses, and every sort of **equestrian sport** is popular. You can go **trail-riding** with a group and a guide, for a day or even a week if you like. Residential and other riding schools offer classes at all levels. In winter, experienced riders are welcome to join one of the many hunts.

## Spectator Sports

To most of the locals, following the horses means having a bet. Actually going to the races is a bonus, and wonderful entertainment for visitors. **Race meetings** are held all over the country, often in beautiful settings. The Curragh near Kildare is the site of the Irish classics, Leopardstown south of Dublin has regular meetings and two dozen more courses figure in the calendar. Flat racing runs from March to November. Steeplechasing – they claim to have invented it here – is just as popular and the season lasts all year, if that's not an Irish contradiction. The Irish Grand National is run at Fairyhouse, County Meath; Killarney has a meeting in July and Tralee in August. The atmosphere at the races is utterly informal and you'll see more characters concentrated in one place than you thought possible. Summer polo matches take place in Phoenix Park and the Dublin Horse Show is the pinnacle of the show-jumping and social year.

Two fast and furious forms of sport are purely Irish. Grab any chance you have to see either one. **Gaelic football** has some elements of rugby, but it's even more like Australian Rules Football, and sometimes looks like open warfare. Played all over Ireland, it's almost a religion in Donegal, the south and the west. **Hurling** may be one of the most ancient team games in the world, with elements of hockey and lacrosse but a lot faster and more

dangerous than either. They are mad about it in Kerry and the south but it's played everywhere. All-Ireland finals take place in Dublin in September. A real Irish oddity is **bowling**. Not the sanitized indoor ten-pin game, nor genteel lawn bowls, but a test of strength, propelling an iron cannonball along a country lane to see how few throws you need to cover a two- or three-mile course. It's most popular in rural Cork and Armagh in the North.

**Soccer** has a broad appeal – both the Republic and Northern Ireland teams do well. The **rugby football** field is one arena in which Ireland is united: the international team is drawn from the whole island and famous for its hell-for-leather, do-or-die approach. Tickets for a Five Nations championship match at Dublin's Lansdowne Road are hard to come by, but you can join the crowds watching on TV in the pubs.

# Entertainment

If you start in the pubs, that may well be as far as you get. So although they are undoubtedly the focus of Ireland's social and musical life, we'll review some other possibilities first.

Dublin can offer some of the world's best English-speaking **theatre**. Both the Abbey and its smaller neighbour the Peacock put on Irish classics and important new plays. The Gate, the Project Arts Centre and the Tivoli are more experimental. The Gaiety plays host occasionally to visiting opera and ballet companies. Otherwise it and the Olympia are more in the music hall and variety tradition. For the programme details of these and more, check the *Events Guide* and *In Dublin* as well as the daily press.

*S*haw's Dublin birthplace has taken its place on the literary
trail, although he left the city when young and rarely returned.

# Irish Music

There's music in the air. Street performers, radio stations and a fair fraction of all the pubs in the country on a Friday or Saturday night see to that. Authentic? Traditional? That's another matter entirely. A lot of it is country and western, maybe with a local accent, or multinational rock. Other groups come and go but the home-grown U2 seem to be fixed in the firmament and they've got plenty of would-be emulators. But you won't go far in Ireland without hearing music that couldn't have come from anywhere else. Audiences know what they like and pack the places where they can hear it. In sentimental ballads and rousing rebel songs, they'll join with ever-increasing fervour as closing time approaches.

Traditional music harks back to something older, and the Irish folk music scene is claimed to be Europe's richest and most active. Why should it be so alive in Ireland, but mainly the preserve of academics and over-serious artists in Britain? Indeed, a lot of Scottish and English folk songs were taken to Ireland and kept going there when they'd been lost in their homeland. The Irish naturally put some of the blame on Cromwell, of course: the Puritans did ban singing and dancing, but the rule was more easily enforced in England, and the Irish took no notice anyway. Surely a mere ten years' prohibition in the 17th century can't have made that much difference. Doesn't it really come out of the more sociable, less introverted, Irish character? 'We played, we sang, we drank. If there's music in you, you've got to play', say the old characters in the bars who kept the torch burning until a new generation could take it over and run with it. In modern times, travellers and tinkers have been another force for preserving the musical and performing tradition: they didn't have electricity in their caravans, so no TV, records or radio!

Possibly the purest musical inheritance is the unaccompanied voice, *port an bheal*, weaving a spell with endless subtle variations of a basic verse. Some songs sound almost North African. Perhaps Celtic and Berber music came from a common root: that seems more likely than a direct transfer from one to another.

Dozens of ancient instruments have been found preserved in bogs, some of them from pre-Celtic times, over three thousand years ago. Bronze horns up to 1.5m (5ft) long from the Celtic Iron Age were discovered in beautiful condition, with a U-shaped bell, flute section and mouthpiece.

*The solo flute can carry an Irish air or wistful lament like no other instrument.*

Two sorts of percussion instrument probably dating from the Bronze Age are mainstays at many a session today. The small, single-sided goat-skin drum called a *bodhran* is tapped with the hand or a double-ended stick. Bones, usually two ribs from a sheep or goat, are held in one hand rather like chopsticks and used to point up the rhythm.

A few examples of the ancient Irish harp (*clairseach*) survive in museums, like the 14th-century example in Trinity College Library, Dublin, the so-called harp of Brian Boru. They had a massive soundbox carved out of a block of wood and a gracefully curved neck and forepillar. The frame had to be strong, with about 40 brass strings tightly stretched across it. They were plucked

*National symbols: the warm smile that says 'A Thousand Welcomes' and the traditional Irish harp.*

with the fingernails to make a bell-like sound. Deprived of their power and their lands, the Gaelic lords couldn't support court musicians. The harpists died out, and with them much ancient musical lore was lost. In the 19th-century revival of interest in traditional music, a lighter, more portable harp was made possible by the lower loading of gut strings. Fortunately many of the tunes composed or preserved by the 18th-century master harpist Turlough O'Carolan were written down and are back in the repertoire today.

The Irish 'union' pipes (the word is a corruption of the Gaelic *uilleann*) differ from Scottish bagpipes in that they're pumped by bellows, squeezed between the player's right elbow and hip. The flute-like chanter can be stopped on the player's knee to jump to a higher octave or to break up the sound into a staccato effect.

Violins, usually called fiddles, are just like you'd find in a symphony orchestra but Irish virtuosi are at their best playing solo, in a clean strong style, almost like unaccompanied singers. They may join with other instruments at times but the massed fiddles of Scottish dance bands are anathema here.

The wistful sound of the flute, usually a wooden one, carries many an Irish lament. A variety of whistles – no children's toys but requiring great skill – and old-fashioned concertinas complete the line up.

A session (*seisiúin*) has a special meaning, a more or less impromptu evening of music and song, usually in a pub. Someone turns up with a fiddle, another with a *bodhrán*, a third with a tin whistle. There's a bit of discussion and tuning up; it's all deceptively casual. Then they're off, quietly and low key at first. Later they may have the whole room singing and clapping and urging them on. Interchanges with the

*Traditional musical entertainment accompanies the ever-popular 'medieval' banquets at Bunratty Castle.*

audience play a big part in deciding what gets played. It's in late night sessions that fresh tunes are forged and old ones renewed. Excitement and the creative impulse make it hard for even the most austere traditionalist to remain aloof. It's in this living tradition that bands such as the Chieftains have renewed and popularized Irish music around the world, appearing everywhere from the US Capitol to the Great Wall of China. They don't try to preserve the exact sound of the past, but the spirit, as flute player Matt Molloy builds up a reel, each subtly varying repetition multiplying the excitement, or

Seán Keane's flashing bow cuts out a tune with the precision of a surgeon.

There's a musical turn of phrase that can only be Irish, and it pervades all sorts of non-traditional compositions. The modern classical works of Mihael O'Sulabhainh are unmistakably folk-inspired. On a popular level, Donegal's Enya creates an ethereal 'electronic-Irish' sound all by herself in the studio, sometimes adding up to thirty layers of her own voice. Heard on the soundtrack of major films and countless TV commercials, her success has spawned a thousand imitators far from Ireland. What could be more different than the abrasive style of Van Morrison, the grim-visaged Belfast man who packs in the fans? Or Sinead O'Connor, feminist icon and crusader for social causes, familiar on TV screens across the world. All are unmistakably Irish.

Cork has its Opera House, which is the venue for plays by Irish greats such as J.M. Synge and Samuel Beckett, and the modern writers Brian Friel and Frank McGuinness, as well as occasional performances of opera. In Galway City, the Druid Theatre puts on the classics, while *An Taibhdhearc* presents traditional music and folkloric performances. So, in Tralee, does the celebrated *Siamsa* Theatre Group. Belfast is shorter on theatre than Dublin, but the Arts Theatre in the Queen's University area and the Lyric

*T he nautical theme of a Galway pub celebrates the city's centuries-old rôle as a trading and fishing port.*

further south both offer varied programmes which are well worth investigating.

Dublin's National Concert Hall in Earlsfort Terrace is the venue for **concerts** by local and visiting orchestras and soloists as well as the major pop and rock events. In Belfast the Ulster Hall covers the concert spectrum. International releases reach the **cinemas** quickly, and there's some creative home-grown film making going on. The stringent censorship of the past has vanished.

Hotel **cabaret nights** are an institution: some of them have been running for decades. Visitors will miss half the jokes and won't recognize any of the performers. The show band is another favourite, designed to give locals a good evening out at a hotel. The nearest equivalent for the tourists would be one of the **banquets** which are laid on at restored castles in the Shannon region. These come complete with high quality entertainment – folk song and dance or storytelling. The Shannon Céilí in the Bunratty Folk Park is a cheerfully commercial enterprise, but you should ask about other more natural versions wherever you are, especially in the west.

Most of Ireland sleeps early. Only Dublin caters much for night-owls, with clubs and **discos** in the basements of Leeson Street, south of St Stephen's Green, and a few in the entertainment zone of Temple Bar. On Fridays and Saturdays when the play's finished at the Olympia Theatre, they put on midnight musicians and there's dancing in the aisles.

From big city to village, the **pub** can act as a club, home from home, debating society, dating agency, dealing room, dance hall or theatre. Pubs (or bars, the

# EVENTS AND FESTIVALS

**February–March**: International Rugby, Lansdowne Road, Dublin.

**March**: Dublin Film Festival; Arklow Music Festival; Dublin Feis Ceoil, Music Festival; St Patrick's Day (17 March); St Patrick's Week parades; Kilkenny Irish Week.

**April**: Sligo Feis Ceoil, Music Festival; International Pan Celtic Festival, Galway City; Cork International Choral Festival; Circuit of Ireland Motor Rally; Punchestown Festival: Races and National Hunt Sale.

**May**: International Motor Rally of the Lakes, Killarney.

**May–June**: Dundalk International Maytime Festival; Kenmare Walking Festival, walking and climbing in Kerry; Fishing Festival, Fermanagh Lakes; Ballyclare Horse Fair, Co. Antrim.

**June**: Music in Great Irish Houses, concerts in stately homes; An Tostal Drumbshanbo, traditional music and dance; Irish Derby at The Curragh; Glencolumbkille Seafood Festival, Co. Donegal; 'Bloomsday' (16 June) in Dublin.

**July**: Dún Laoghaire Festival, arts, crafts, concerts and sports; Jazz and Blues Festival, Holywood, Co. Down; Proms Concerts, Belfast; Longford Festival of arts, music and sports; Willie Clancy Summer Music School, Miltown Malbay, Co. Clare; Adare Music Festival; James Joyce Summer School, Dublin; Glencolumbkille Walking Festival, Co. Donegal; Pilgrimage up Croagh Patrick, Co. Mayo.

**July–August**: Siamsa, Galway Folk Theatre, performances of drama, music and dance; Ballyshannon Folk and Traditional Music Festival; Ulster Air Show, Newtownards.

**August**: Gorey Summer Fair, Gorey, Co. Wexford; Puck Fair, Killorglin, traditional music, gathering of travellers; Rose of Tralee International Festival, Tralee, election of Rose of Tralee; Kilkenny Arts Week, recitals, exhibitions, literary events; Dublin Horse Show, social event of the season; Kinsale Regatta and Festival; Enniskillen, Street Entertainers' and Buskers' Championships.

**September**: Match Making Festival, Lisdoonvarna, traditional place to search for a mate; Clarenbridge, Co. Galway, Oyster Festival, oyster tasting, music and dance; Galway Oyster Festival; Sligo Arts Festival; Gaelic football and hurling finals, Dublin.

**September–October**: Waterford International Festival of Light Opera.

**October**: Clifden, Co. Galway, Arts Week; Ballinasloe Great Fair and Festival, horse fair and entertainment; Cork Film Festival; Dublin Theatre Festival; Wexford Opera Festival; Sligo Choral Festival; Cork and Kinsale Jazz Festivals.

**November**: Dublin Indoor International Horse Show; Belfast Festival at Queens, arts, music, theatre.

terms are interchangeable) were traditionally given the owner's name: 'Mulligan's Bar', 'O'Sullivan's Bar' although there's a fashion now to give them a fancier title. There are so many it seems impossible they can all be making a living. Don't be surprised to find some cold, empty and inhospitable, where you won't be tempted to linger. In most you'll find at least handful of people in conversation, still a lively art, and you'll probably be welcome – even expected – to join in. Open the door to another pub and you may have to fight your way through the crowd to get to the bar. A third might have a rapt audience listening to a traditional singer; another could be on pain threshold with hard rock. Country and western packs them in too, with everyone singing along. Its popularity may seem strange but after all, it developed partly from Irish music taken to America.

A purer form of Irish tradition is found at the headquarters of *Comhaltas Ceoltoiri Éireann* in Monkstown near Dublin. They stage nightly performances from June to September and a céilí every Friday night.

Half the fun is searching out the kind of place with the atmosphere and the music that suits you. Don't hesitate to ask where you can find it: you're bound to come across fellow enthusiasts. If you need to justify a Dublin pub crawl, try taking in the places with historical or literary connections (see LEISURE ROUTES, page 78). And if you fancy doing it in the company of a group of actors, sign up (and pay the fee) at the Tourist Board's office in O'Connell Street.

*F*ashion fabrics roll off the looms at the historic Foxford Woollen Mills in County Mayo.

# GLOSSARY

A selection of some of the words you may encounter on your travels around Ireland are listed below. For more familiar phrases, perhaps some you did not even realize were Gaelic, see also page 26.

| | |
|---|---|
| **ard** | *high place* |
| **ath** | *ford* |
| **baile, bally** | *settlement, town* |
| **bawn** | *walled enclosure attached to a tower house or castle* |
| **ben** | *mountain, peak* |
| **bodhrán** | *goatskin drum* |
| **caher, cahir** | *stone fortress or castle* |
| **cairn** | *heap of stones, often over a grave* |
| **cashel** | *stone fort* |
| **clochán** | *stone hut, 'beehive' hut* |
| **crannóg** | *lake dwelling, artificial island* |
| **cromlech** | see *dolmen* |
| **currach, curragh** | *grassy plain, also tarred leather boat* |
| **daire, doire, derry** | *oak tree grove* |
| **dolmen** | *Stone Age tomb of supporting stones and capstone* |
| **dún** | *fortress, stronghold* |
| **fulacht fia** | *ancient cooking place, often a pit where water would be boiled using hot stones* |
| **inis, ennis** | *island* |
| **glen** | *valley* |
| **kill** | *early church* |
| **knock, cnoc** | *hill* |
| **lis** | *area inside a fort or fence* |
| **lough** | *lake, or coastal inlet* |
| **mór, more** | *big* |
| **ogham** | *early script with letters represented by sets of lines* |
| **rath** | *circular earthwork or fort* |
| **sliabh, slieve** | *mountain* |
| **souterrain** | *underground passages and chambers for defence, refuge and storage* |
| **strand** | *beach* |
| **teampull, temple** | *church* |
| **togher** | *roadway across a bog* |
| **torc** | *twisted metal armlet, collar or belt* |
| **uilleann** | *Irish bagpipes* |

# Shopping

Any country with a flourishing tourist trade will have no shortage of tacky trinkets, and Ireland has its share of plastic leprechauns and silly signs. A bit more appealing are the accurate wooden replicas of a full glass of stout complete with creamy head, or a candle that looks just like an Irish coffee in a glass.

Souvenir shops all over the country tend to have similar selections: **dolls** in traditional dress, reproductions of **old crosses**, semi-precious stones and coloured marbles from Connemara, enamelwork and **jewellery**, often in Celtic motifs. The Claddagh ring, a clasped-hands-and-heart design originally from Galway is sold by jewellers everywhere now. Curiosities include ornaments carved out of **bog oak** preserved for thousands of years in acid peat, and others made from a compressed form of the peat itself.

All these are produced in quantity but they can be well made and attractive. There's a flourishing creative **craft** tradition too, and you'll find plenty of good original designs in glass, pottery and various fabrics. Look in the Cork and Kilkenny Design Centres, the Dublin branch of the latter and the Tower Design Centre in Pearse Street, but be prepared for high prices. The Powerscourt Centre (S. William Street) and St Stephen's Green Centre also include craft shops among their many small outlets.

Among traditional crafts, **rushwork** and **basket making** have been revived and turned to artistic effect. Hand-knitted **Aran sweaters** in natural wool are still a favourite, on sale almost everywhere. There aren't enough knitters on the islands themselves to keep up with demand, but mainland workers are able to fill the gap and match the quality. The same can't be said for machine versions from the mainland and even from outside Ireland. There's a wide choice of other knitwear too. **Lace** used to be widely made by hand in Carrickmacross, Youghal and Limerick, for example, but only a few nuns and amateur enthusiasts produce it these days. What you see for sale now will probably be machine-made and some of it imported, except for a few expensive antique pieces.

Flax is still grown in Northern Ireland and woven into **linen**. If you've never slept between pure linen sheets, you've missed something special. Prices are likely to be lower in Belfast, if it's on your itinerary, than they are in Dublin or anywhere else in the Republic.

**Tweed**, handwoven in the old way by cottagers in Donegal, no longer has to be heavy and chunky. Lighter and finer tweeds are high fashion fabrics these days, and you'll find rack upon rack of made-up clothing in tweed – plain or plaid. Cashmere, lambswool and mohair blends add to the range: soft mohair shawls make a lightweight present.

Woven **woollen blankets** and **dress fabrics** roll from the modern looms of mills from Dublin to Sligo. Some are in traditional colours of heather and moss but many more are in shades that change with every season according to the demands of Paris designers.

Waterford may be the best-known name in **glass**, whether crystal (cut glass) or blown, but several other factories and smaller workshops have entered the field and you may find you prefer their designs. Pottery too is a matter of taste: the Belleek factory in County Fermanagh produces pale, basket-like designs which are widely available.

*Y*ou can witness the weird and wonderful things they do with Waterford crystal.

## TAX-FREE EXPORTS

If you have come from *outside* the European Community, obtain proper receipts and take the goods home or have them shipped, you can avoid paying VAT (equivalent of sales tax) or have it refunded. Ask, when making major purchases, how this works.

In the Republic, the rate is from 12.5 percent to 21 percent or more on some luxuries. In Northern Ireland, it's 17.5 percent on most purchases.

Well-educated Ireland has a big appetite for **books** and the excellent shops, new and secondhand, are worth looking over. It's fun looking through the **antique shops**, and the bric à brac and plain junk shops too, though you are very unlikely to find any great bargains these days. Dealers are all too aware of world prices. In the record shops, look for **cassette tapes** and **CDs** of the Irish music you may have discovered. Anglers often find some item of **fishing gear** to add their armoury.

For general shopping, only the two capitals have a full range of department stores, chain stores and international names. In Dublin, they're concentrated in the Grafton Street area and to a lesser degree O'Connell Street. In Belfast they're in and around Royal Avenue and Donegall Place. If you're going to both, you'll find prices are lower in Northern Ireland.

Some Irish **foods** are packed ready to take home, notably smoked salmon and other delicatessen specialities. Inevitably, if you wait until you're at the departure airport, you will pay much more for such things. Not of course for Irish whiskey, other spirits (liquor) and perfumes which will be quite a bit cheaper at the **duty-free shops**. Shannon in particular, where the concept was practically invented, has large and well-stocked shops.

*You'll enjoy rummaging among the relics of bygone eras, though the boundaries between antiques, bric-à-brac and junk are sometimes hard to define.*

319

# The Right Place at the Right Price

Irish hotels come in all shapes and sizes but they're almost invariably comfortable, run by the friendliest of people and good value for money. We have chosen a selection right across the spectrum, ranging from luxury hotels in country houses and castles to modest guesthouses. We have not included any of the countless Bed and Breakfast places which typically cost from £12 to £18 per person.

The choice of good restaurants in Ireland is still limited, but improving year by year, especially in fashionable holiday retreats. Some in the country house hotels are excellent: those in town hotels can be dull although quantities are generous. Prices in general are high by the standards of the rest of Europe.

**Hotels**: the figures quoted are the price per person sharing in a double room, with breakfast, including service and tax.
I    under £30;
II   £30 to £60;
III  over £60.

**Restaurants**: the figures quoted are the price per person for a three course dinner, without drinks, including tax and service.
I    under £12;
II   £12 to £20;
III  over £20.
Hotels are coded **H**, restaurants are coded **R**, and hotel/restaurant are marked **HR** in the following listings.

## Dublin City

All Dublin and Dublin area phone numbers with only 6 figures are in the gradual process of becoming 7 figures, generally by addition of a prefix.

**Ariel House**          H    I
52 Lansdowne Road, Dublin 4
Tel. (01) 668 5512; fax. (01) 668 5845
*28 rooms. Pleasant and friendly guesthouse, like a country house in town.*

**Bad Ass Café**         R    I
9/11 Crown Alley, Dublin 2
Tel. (01) 671 2596
*Pizzas and burgers in a big barn.*

**Berkeley Court**       HR   III
Lansdowne Road, Dublin 4
Tel. (01) 660 1711;
fax.(01) 661 7238
*195 rooms. Modern block, but with an elegant interior. Indoor swimming pool, tennis.*

**Bewley's Oriental Café**  R    I
Grafton Street , Dublin 2
Tel. (01) 677 6761
*A famous Dublin institution, for coffee, snacks or meals, open lunch and early evening.*

**Bloom's**              HR   II
Anglesea Street
Dublin 2
Tel. (01) 671 5622;
fax. (01) 671 5997
*86 rooms. Modern, central and informal. Closed Christmas.*

**Burdock's**            R    I
2 Werbaugh Street
Dublin 2
Tel. (01) 540306
*Fish and chips the old-fashioned way, take-away and sit down. Evenings only, closed Sunday, Tuesday.*

**Burlington**           HR   II
Upper Leeson Street
Dublin 4
Tel. (01) 660 5222; fax. (01) 660 8496
*451 rooms. Modern block. Friendly efficient service, tailored to groups.*

**Capers**               R    I
4 Nassau Street
Dublin 2
Tel. (01) 668 4626
*Upstairs, vegetarian food in the evenings.*

**Chapter One**          R    II
The Writers Museum
18/19 Parnell Square
Dublin 1
Tel. (01) 873 1388
*In the vaulted basements below the Writers Museum, Irish and international food. Lunch Monday–Friday, dinner Thursday–Saturday. Closed public holidays.*

**Clarence**             HR   II
6-8 Wellington Quay
Dublin 2
Tel. (01) 677 6178;
fax. (01) 677 7487
*67 rooms. Friendly, central and lively; owned by rock group U2.*

**Conrad**               HR   III
Earlsfort Terrace
Dublin 2
Tel. (01) 676 5555;
fax. (01) 676 5424
*190 rooms. Central, near St Stephen's Green. A modern, elegant hotel, part of US Hilton chain.*

**Elephant and Castle**  R    II
18 Temple Bar
Dublin 2
Tel. (01) 679 3121
*Casual atmosphere. Creative cooking with some south-east Asian flavours. Good salads.*

**Gresham** HR ‖
23 Upper O'Connell Street
Dublin 1
Tel. (01) 874 6881;
fax. (01) 878 7175
*200 rooms. Historic hotel in a*
*Georgian building, partly*
*modernized. Nightclub.*

**Harcourt** HR ‖
60 Harcourt Street
Dublin 2
Tel. (01) 478 3677
*32 rooms. Central. Jazz*
*on Sundays.*

**Hibernian** HR ‖‖‖
Eastmoreland Place
Ballsbridge
Dublin 4
Tel. (01) 676 3286;
fax. (01) 676 3287
*30 rooms. Imaginative recent*
*conversion of Victorian buildings*
*into luxury hotel.*

**Jury's Hotel and Towers** HR ‖‖‖
Pembroke Road
Ballsbridge
Dublin 4
Co. Dublin
Tel. (01) 660 5000;
fax. (01) 668 5772
*384 rooms. The newer Towers has*
*larger rooms and extra services.*
*Indoor swimming pool. Irish cabaret*
*entertainment (except Monday).*

**Kilkenny Kitchen** R ‖
1st Floor
6 Nassau Street
Dublin 2
Tel. (01) 677 7066
*At the Kilkenny craft gallery.*
*Self-service of Irish traditional*
*dishes, quiches, salads and snacks.*
*Closed Sunday, public holidays.*

**Lane Gallery** R ‖‖‖
55 Pembroke Lane
Ballsbridge
Dublin 4
Tel. (01) 661 1829
*Elegant, French-inspired cooking.*
*Closed Saturday and Sunday lunch,*
*Sunday and Monday dinner.*

**Lansdowne** HR ‖
27 Pembroke Road
Ballsbridge
Dublin 4
Tel. (01) 668 2522;
fax. (01) 668 5585
*28 rooms. Compact, friendly*
*business hotel in pleasant area.*

**Le Coq Hardi** R ‖‖‖
35 Pembroke Road
Ballsbridge
Dublin 4
Tel. (01) 668 9070
*Creative French cuisine. Elegant*
*restaurant with a fine wine list.*
*Closed Saturday lunch, Sunday,*
*public holidays.*

**Les Frères Jacques** R ‖‖‖
74 Dame Street
Dublin 2
Tel. (01) 679 4555
*Creative and traditional French*
*cooking and service, bistro-style.*
*Closed Sunday, public holidays.*

**Locks** R ‖‖‖
1 Windsor Terrace
Portobello
Dublin 8
Tel. (01) 538352
*Beside the Grand Canal. Fresh*
*modern French cuisine. Closed*
*Saturday lunch, Sunday.*

**Longfield's** HR ‖
10 Fitzwilliam Street Lower
Dublin 2
Tel. (01) 676 1367;
fax. (01) 676 1542
*26 rooms. Elegant Georgian*
*townhouse hotel. Central.*

**Lord Edward** R ‖
23 Christchurch Place
Dublin 8
Tel. (01) 542240
*Noted for fresh fish. Closed*
*Saturday lunch, Sunday.*

**Mont Clare** HR ‖
Merrion Square
Dublin 2
Tel. (01) 661 6799; fax. (01) 661 5663
*74 rooms. Modernized, well-*
*equipped, central and comfortable*
*hotel.*

**Nico's** R ‖
53 Dame Street
Dublin 2
Tel. (01) 677 3062
*Informal Italian. Good fresh pasta*
*and fish a speciality. Closed*
*Sunday, public holidays.*

**Oisins** R ‖
31 Upper Camden Street
Dublin
Tel. (01) 475 3433
*Irish traditional and modern dishes.*
*Dinner only. Closed Sunday,*
*Monday.*

**Orchid Szechuan** R ‖
120 Pembroke Road
Ballsbridge
Dublin 4
Tel. (01) 660 0629
*Attractive basement setting for spicy*
*Szechuan and other Chinese dishes.*

**The Oyster Shell** R ‖
Powerscourt Townhouse Centre
50 South William Street
Dublin 2
Tel. (01) 679 1517
*Oysters, fish and pasta. Closed*
*Sunday, Monday.*

**Pasta Fresca** R ‖
3/4 Chatham Street
Dublin 2
Tel. (01) 679 2402
*Delicatessen and wine bar. Italian*
*cooking, not only pasta. Closed*
*public holidays.*

**Patrick Guilbaud** R ‖‖‖
46 James Place
Lower Baggot Street
Dublin 2
Tel. (01) 676 4192
*Rather formal restaurant with fine*
*French cooking. Closed Sunday,*
*Monday.*

**Polo One** R ‖
Molesworth Lane
Dublin 2
Tel. (01) 676 3362
*Imaginative Mediterranean cuisine.*
*Good seafood. Closed Sunday.*

**Recess House** H ‖
55 Eglinton Road
Donnybrook
Dublin 4
Tel. (01) 269 3199;
fax. (01) 283 7991
*8 rooms. Comfortable guesthouse in*
*southern suburb.*

**Shelbourne** HR ‖‖‖
27 St Stephen's Green
Dublin 2
Tel. (01) 676 6471;
fax. (01) 661 6006
*164 rooms. Historic landmark facing*
*the park. Grand traditional luxury*
*and a noted restaurant. Central.*

**101 Talbot** R ‖
101 Talbot Street
Dublin 1
Tel. (01) 874 5011
*Informal and friendly bistro, home*
*cooking. Closed Monday evening,*
*Sunday.*

# Excursions From Dublin

**Ayumi-Ya**  R  ‖
Newpark Centre
Newtownpark Avenue
Blackrock
Co. Dublin
Tel. (01) 283 1767
*Authentic Japanese restaurant
with full range of traditional
dishes. Dinner only, except
Sunday lunch.*

**Tulfarris House**  HR ‖‖‖
**Country Club**
Blessington
Co. Wicklow
Tel. (045) 64574;
fax. (045) 64423
*21 rooms. Elegant Georgian house.
Notable restaurant and bistro.
Golf, fishing, indoor swimming
pool.*

**Royal Hotel**  HR ‖
Main Street
Bray
Co. Wicklow
Tel. (01) 286 2935;
fax. (01) 286 7373
*72 rooms. Central. Traditional
hotel in seaside town.*

**Tree of Idleness**  R  ‖‖‖
Seafront
Bray
Co. Wicklow
Tel. (01) 286 3498
*On the seafront. Creative
Mediterranean/Greek cooking.
Closed Monday, early-
September.*

**Doyle's School**  R  ‖
**House Inn**
Main Street
Castledermot
Co. Kildare
Tel. (0503) 44282
*Fine country cooking, with game a
speciality. Closed Monday. Dinner
only except Sunday lunch.*

**Kilkea Castle**  HR ‖‖‖
Castledermot
Near Athy
Co. Kildare
Tel. (0503) 45156;
fax. (0503) 45187
*45 rooms. Magnificent battlemented
tower now a luxury hotel. Indoor
swimming pool, fishing, tennis and
other sports.*

**Il Ristorante**  R  ‖‖‖
108 Coliemore Road
Dalkey
Co. Dublin
Tel. (01) 284 0800
*Innovative Italian cuisine, upstairs
at the Club Bar. Dinner only.
Closed Monday.*

**Casa Pasta**  R  ‖
12 Harbour Road
Howth
Co. Dublin
Tel. (01) 393823
*Informal bistro-style restaurant
overlooking harbour. Evening only
(plus Sunday lunch).*

**Deer Park**  HR ‖
Howth
Co. Dublin
Tel. (01) 322624;
fax. (01) 392405
*48 rooms. Four golf courses.
Overlooking Dublin Bay. Closed
Christmas.*

**St Lawrence**  HR ‖
Harbour Road
Howth
Co. Dublin
Tel. (01) 322643;
fax. (01) 390346
*12 rooms. Friendly small hotel
facing the attractive harbour.*

**King Sitric**  R  ‖‖‖
East Pier
Howth
Co. Dublin
Tel. (01) 325235
*Long-established restaurant by
the harbour, well-known for
fresh fish and especially
shellfish. Closed Sunday, public
holidays.*

**Killiney Fitzpatrick's**  HR ‖
**Castle**
Killiney
Co. Dublin
Tel. (01) 284 0700;
fax. (01) 285 0207
*91 rooms. Hilltop castle with
modern extensions. Indoor
swimming pool, tennis, squash,
nightclub.*

**Station House**  HR ‖
Kilmessan
Co. Meath
Tel. (046) 25239;
fax. (046) 25588
*10 rooms. Family run guest-house
and notable restaurant.*

**Breakers**  R  ‖
1 New Street
Malahide
Co. Dublin
Tel. (01) 845 2584
*Informal. For steaks, salmon and
Italian dishes. Sunday lunch,
otherwise evenings only.*

**Mr Hung's**  R  ‖
5a The Crescent
Monkstown
Co. Dublin
Tel. (01) 284 3982
*Cantonese food in an informal
setting.*

**Red House**  R  ‖‖‖
Newbridge
Co. Kildare
Tel. (045) 31516
*Traditional country inn, using
fresh local produce. Dinner
Monday–Saturday, lunch
Sunday.*

**Conyngham Arms**  HR ‖
Slane
Co. Meath
Tel. (041) 24155;
fax. (041) 24205
*16 rooms. Traditional hotel in pretty
village in the Boyne valley. Closed
Christmas.*

**Kildare Hotel and**  HR ‖‖‖
**Country Club**
Straffan
Co. Kildare
Tel. (01) 627 3333;
fax. (01) 627 3312
*45 rooms. Luxury hotel in 19th-
century mansion. Golf, fishing,
swimming pool, tennis, squash,
sauna. Extensive grounds.*

**Sutton Castle**  HR ‖
Red Rock
Sutton
Co. Dublin
Tel. (01) 322688;
fax. (01) 324476
*19 rooms. Country house in
gardens overlooking Dublin Bay.
Closed Christmas–mid-
January.*

**Old School House**  R  ‖
Coolbanagher
Swords
Co. Dublin
Tel. (01) 840 2846
*Traditional Irish cooking. Informal,
attractive setting. Closed Saturday
lunch, Sunday.*

322

# The South East

**Cliff House**          HR  II
Ardmore
Co. Waterford
Tel. (024) 94106; fax. (024) 94496
*20 rooms. Family-run hotel with
fine view over Ardmore Bay. Closed
October–mid-April.*

**Lawless's**          HR  I
Aughrim
Arklow
Co. Wicklow
Tel. (0402) 36146;
fax. (0402) 36384
*10 rooms. Family-run hotel in the
hills, on the Aughrim river. Fishing.
Closed Christmas.*

**Kilcoran Lodge**          HR  II
Cahir
Co. Tipperary
Tel. (052) 41288; fax. (052) 41994
*24 rooms. Extended former hunting
lodge in a garden setting. Swimming
pool, sauna.*

**Cedar Lodge**          HR  II
Carrigbyrne
Newbawn
Co. Waterford
Tel. (051) 28386; fax. (051) 28222
*18 rooms. Modern country hotel
between Wexford and Waterford.
Closed Christmas.*

**Cashel Palace**          HR  III
Main Street
Cashel
Co. Tipperary
Tel. (062) 61411; fax. (062) 61521
*20 rooms. The former bishop's
palace dates from the 18th century.
Beautifully transformed to a luxury
hotel, a step away from the Rock of
Cashel.*

**Chez Hans**          R  III
Cashel
Co. Tipperary
Tel. (062) 61177
*Long-established restaurant near
the historic Rock. Classic French-
Irish cuisine in an old chapel.
Evening only. Closed Sunday,
Monday.*

**Dundrum House**          HR  II
Dundrum
Cashel
Co. Tipperary
Tel. (062) 71116; fax. (062) 71366
*55 rooms. Georgian mansion with
its own golf course, fishing, tennis.*

**Knocklofty House**          HR  III
Clonmel
Co. Tipperary
Tel. (052) 38222; fax. (052) 38289
*13 rooms. Country house hotel in
large grounds. Squash, tennis,
indoor swimming pool, sauna,
fishing. Fine restaurant.*

**Rathsallagh House**          HR  III
Dunlavin
Co. Wicklow
Tel. (45) 53112; fax. (045) 53343
*12 rooms. Guesthouse and restaurant
(closed Sunday evening, Monday).
Tennis, indoor swimming pool, shoot-
ing. Closed Christmas–New Year.*

**Candlelight Inn**          HR  I
Dunmore East
Co. Waterford
Tel. (051) 83215
*11 rooms. Friendly family-run
guesthouse in pretty seaside village.
Good pub food.*

**Haven**          HR  II
Dunmore East
Co. Waterford
Tel. (051) 83150; fax. (051) 83488
*25 rooms. Comfortable hotel in a
garden setting, overlooking the bay.*

**Ship**          R  II
Dunmore East
Co. Waterford
Tel. (051) 83141
*Attractive restaurant. Imaginative
use of fresh local produce. Dinner
only, closed October–April and
Sunday, Monday.*

**Horetown House**          HR  I
Foulksmills
Co. Wexford
Tel. (051) 63633; fax. (051) 63633
*12 rooms. Guesthouse and noted
Cellars restaurant. Equestrian centre.*

**Glendalough**          HR  II
Glendalough
Co. Wicklow
Tel. (0404) 45135;
fax. (0404) 45142
*17 rooms. Dated but convenient old
hotel close to the picturesque
monastic ruins. Tennis.*

**Marlfield House**          HR  III
Gorey
Co. Wexford
Tel. (055) 21124; fax. (055) 21572
*19 rooms. 18th-century mansion.
Gardens, tennis, sauna. Closed
December–January.*

**Butler House**          H  II
Patrick Street
Kilkenny
Co. Kilkenny
Tel. (056) 22828; fax. (056) 65707
*13 rooms. Comfortable guesthouse
in a Georgian mansion near the
castle.*

**Club House**          HR  II
Patrick Street
Kilkenny
Co. Kilkenny
Tel. (056) 21994; fax. (056) 21994
*23 rooms. Central. Traditional
town hotel.*

**Kytelers**          R  I
St Kieran Street
Kilkenny
Co. Kilkenny
Tel. (056) 21064
*Traditional pub in quaint
street, serving good food, fine
fish. Disco.*

**Lacken House**          HR  II
Dublin Road
Kilkenny
Co. Kilkenny
Tel. (056) 61085; fax. (056) 62435
*8 rooms. Friendly family-run
guesthouse. Notable restaurant
(III) for dinner only, closed
Sunday, Monday.*

**Newpark**          HR  II
Castlecomer Road
Kilkenny
Co. Kilkenny
Tel. (056) 22122; fax. (056) 61111
*60 rooms. Out of town centre,
modern rooms. Indoor swimming
pool, tennis. Favoured by business
people.*

**Kelly's Strand**          HR  II
Rosslare
Co. Wexford
Tel. (053) 32114; fax. (053) 32222
*99 rooms. Holiday and sports
complex. Tennis, squash,
swimming pools, sauna, and
many other leisure facilities.
Closed December–February.*

**Rosslare**          HR  II
Rosslare Harbour
Co. Wexford
Tel. (053) 33110; fax. (053) 33386
*25 rooms. Long-established but
modernized hotel situated near
the ferryport. Squash, sauna.
Good restaurant and prize-winning
pub food.*

**Mount Juliet**  HR ||||
Thomastown
Co. Kilkenny
Tel. (056) 24455; fax. (056) 24522
*32 rooms. Elegant and luxurious
country house hotel. Fine restaurant.
Championship golf course, vast
grounds, shooting, fishing, indoor
swimming pool, sauna.*

**Brown Trout**  R |
Abbey Street
Tipperary
Co. Tipperary
Tel. (062) 51912
*Informal. Generous portions. Bed
and Breakfast rooms available.*

**Dwyers of Mary Street**  R ||
Mary Street
Waterford
Co. Waterford
Tel. (051) 77478
*Good French and Irish cooking in
an attractive old building. Dinner
only, closed Sundays in winter.*

**Prendiville's**  HR ||
Cork Road
Waterford
Co. Waterford
Tel. (051) 78851
*9 rooms in converted lodge. Notable
restaurant (closed Sunday).*

**The Tower**  HR ||||
The Mall
Waterford
Co. Waterford
Tel. (051) 32111; fax. (051) 70129
*125 rooms. Central. Swimming
pool, sauna. Closed Christmas.*

**Bohemian Girl**  R ||
North Main Street
Wexford
Co. Wexford
Tel. (053) 24419
*Bar lunches. Upstairs restaurant in
evening.*

**Ferrycarrig**  HR ||
Ferrycarrig Bridge
Wexford
Co. Wexford
Tel. (053) 22999; fax. (053) 41982
*40 rooms. Modern hotel, out of
town. Good restaurant. Tennis.*

**Talbot**  HR ||
Trinity Street
Wexford
Co. Wexford
Tel. (053) 22566; fax. (053) 23377
*100 rooms. Central. Squash, sauna.
Good restaurant.*

**White's**  HR ||
George Street
Wexford
Co. Wexford
Tel. (053) 22311; fax. (053) 45000
*82 rooms. Central. Historic former
coaching inn. Closed Christmas.*

**Old Rectory**  HR ||
Wicklow
Co. Wicklow
Tel. (0404) 67048;
fax. (0404) 69181
*6 rooms. Fine old country house
and notable restaurant (dinner
only). Closed November–Easter.*

# The South West

**Gougane Barra Hotel**  HR ||||
Gougane Barra
Ballingeary
Co. Cork
Tel. (026) 47069;
fax. (026) 47226
*28 rooms. Lakeside setting near
Kenmare. Fishing. Closed mid-
October–mid-April.*

**Annie's**  R ||
Ballydehob
Mizen Head Peninsula
Co. Cork
Tel. (028) 37292
*Fresh home cooking. Closed Sun-
day, Monday.*

**Ballylickey Manor House**  HR ||
Ballylickey
Near Bantry
Co. Cork
Tel. (027) 50071; fax. (027) 50124
*11 rooms. Country house and
garden cottages. Fine French-style
restaurant. Heated outdoor
swimming pool.*

**Sea View House**  HR ||
Ballylickey
Near Bantry
Co. Cork
Tel. (027) 50073; fax. (027) 51555
*18 rooms. Country house hotel in
garden setting next to Bantry Bay.
Fishing. Closed mid-November–
mid-March.*

**Courtmacsherry Hotel**  HR ||
Courtmacsherry
Near Bandon
Co. Cork
Tel. (023) 46198; fax. (023) 46137
*15 rooms. Family-run seaside hotel
in garden setting. Tennis, horse-
riding. Closed October–March.*

**Bantry House**  HR ||
Bantry
Co. Cork
Tel. (027) 50047; fax. (027) 50795
*10 modern rooms in palatial
Georgian mansion overlooking
the bay. Run by the family.*

**O'Connor's Seafood**  R |
The Square
Bantry
Tel. (027) 50221
*Shellfish a speciality, but meats can
be had too. An old-established
favourite.*

**Crutch's Country House**  HR ||
**Hotel**
Fermoyle Beach
Castlegregory
Co. Kerry
Tel. (066) 38118;
fax. (066) 38159
*19 rooms. On the Conor Pass
Road, Dingle Peninsula, near
Brandon Bay. Closed January–
February.*

**O'Sullivan's**  HR |
Cahirdaniel
Co. Kerry
Tel. (066) 75124
*6 rooms. Friendly family-run
guesthouse on the hill above the
village; home cooking.*

**Arbutus Lodge**  HR ||
Middle Glanmire Road
Cork City
Co. Cork
Tel. (021) 501237;
fax. (021) 502893
*20 rooms. Garden, tennis.
Notable restaurant (|||), innovative
cuisine (closed Sunday). Fine wine
list.*

**Clifford's**  R ||||
18 Dyke Parade
Cork City
Co. Cork
Tel. (021) 275333
*Innovative Irish-continental food.
Closed Saturday lunch, Sunday,
Monday.*

**Jury's**  HR ||||
Western Road
Cork City
Co. Cork
Tel. (021) 276622;
fax. (021) 274477
*185 rooms. Modern hotel.
Swimming pools, sauna,
squash, tennis. Closed
Christmas.*

**Oyster Tavern** R II
Market Lane
off Patrick Street
Cork City
Co. Cork
Tel. (021) 272716
*Historic club-like bar and*
*restaurant. Traditional*
*menu. Closed Sunday, public*
*holidays.*

**Rochestown Park Hotel** HR II
Rochestown Road
Cork City
Co. Cork
Tel. (021) 892233;
fax. (021) 892178
*39 rooms. Extended mansion in*
*garden setting.*

**Armada** R I
Strand Street
Dingle
Co. Kerry
Tel. (066) 51505
*Informal restaurant for fish,*
*meats and vegetarian dishes.*
*Closed November–February.*

**Beginish** R II
Green Street
Dingle
Co. Kerry
Tel. (066) 51588
*French bistro-style restaurant.*
*Good wine list. Closed Monday*
*and winter.*

**Benner's Hotel** HR II
Main Street
Dingle
Co. Kerry
Tel. (066) 51638;
fax. (066) 51412
*25 rooms. Old-established friendly*
*hotel, former coaching inn.*

**Doyle's Seafood Bar &** HR II
**Town House**
John Street
Dingle
Co. Kerry
Tel. (066) 51174; fax. (066) 51816
*8 rooms. Celebrated seafood*
*restaurant. Closed Sunday and*
*mid-November–March.*

**Fenton's** R II
Green Street
Dingle
Co. Kerry
Tel. (066) 51209
*Fresh local seafood and other*
*produce, well presented. Closed*
*December–February.*

**Skellig** HR II
Conor Pass Road
Dingle
Co. Kerry
Tel. (066) 5114; fax. (066) 51501
*115 rooms. Modern hotel on the*
*outskirts. Swimming pool, tennis,*
*sauna. Closed mid-November–mid-*
*March.*

**Towers** HR I
Glenbeigh
Co. Kerry
Tel. (066) 682121; fax. (066) 68260
*28 rooms. On the Ring of Kerry,*
*overlooking the sea. Fishing.*
*Hotel with traditional pub and*
*entertainment. Closed mid-January–*
*mid-March.*

**Barleycove Beach** HR II
Goleen
Co. Cork
Tel. (028) 35234;
fax. (028) 35100
*11 rooms. Family-run hotel near*
*beach and southernmost tip of*
*Ireland. Tennis. Closed 2 January*
*to mid-March.*

**Lime Tree** R II
Shelbourne Street
Kenmare
Co. Kerry
Tel. (064) 41225
*Fine local produce. Dinner*
*only. Closed November–*
*mid-March.*

**Park** HR III
Kenmare
Co. Kerry
Tel. (064) 41200; fax. (064) 41402
*50 rooms. Celebrated country*
*house hotel and notable*
*restaurant. Fishing, tennis, golf.*
*Closed January–March.*

**Sheen Falls Lodge** HR III
Kenmare
Co. Kerry
Tel. (064) 41600;
fax. (064) 41386
*40 rooms. Luxury resort by the*
*Sheen river, near Kenmare Bay.*
*Fishing, tennis, sauna. Closed*
*January–mid-March.*

**Aghadoe Heights Hotel** HR III
Aghadoe
Killarney
Co. Kerry
Tel. (064) 31766; fax. (064) 31345
*61 rooms. Modern. Swimming pool,*
*sauna, tennis, fishing.*

**Cahernane Hotel** HR II
Muckross Road
Killarney
Co. Kerry
Tel. (064) 31895; fax. (064) 34340
*50 rooms. Victorian house in quiet*
*lakeside setting. Tennis, golf.*

**Dingles** R I
40 New Street
Killarney
Co. Kerry
Tel. (064) 31079
*Traditional atmosphere, home*
*cooking. Evenings only.*

**Europe** HR II
Fossa
Near Killarney
Co. Kerry
Tel. (064) 31900; fax. (064) 32118
*205 rooms. Modern, on outskirts of*
*town. Closed November–March.*

**Gaby's Seafood** R III
27 High Street
Killarney
Co. Kerry
Tel. (064) 32519
*Fresh local seafood and meats too.*
*Closed February, Monday, Sunday*
*lunch.*

**Great Southern** HR III
Killarney
Co. Kerry
Tel. (064) 31262; fax. (064) 31642
*180 rooms. Traditional, friendly.*
*Sports complex with swimming pool,*
*sauna, tennis. Conference centre.*
*Closed January, February.*

**Lake** HR II
Muckross Road
Killarney
Co. Kerry
Tel. (064) 31035; fax. (064) 31902
*66 rooms. Former country mansion.*
*Closed December–February.*

**Sheila's** R I
75 High Street
Killarney
Co. Kerry
Tel. (064) 31270
*Friendly, informal bistro-style.*
*Home cooking, steaks and seafood.*
*Closed Sunday, Monday.*

**Strawberry Tree** R II
24 Plunkett Street
Killarney
Co. Kerry
Tel. (064) 32688
*Irish cooking and seafood. Closed*
*December–January.*

**Nick's**    R   ‖
Lower Bridge Street
Killorglin
Co. Kerry
Tel. (066) 61219
*Seafood, steaks, game and other
local produce. Dinner only (bar
food at lunchtime). Closed
Christmas, Monday.*

**Actons**    HR   ‖
Pier Road
Kinsale
Co. Cork
Tel. (021) 772135;
fax. (021) 772231
*57 rooms. On the quay, formed
from several quayside houses.
Favoured by groups and wedding
parties. Indoor swimming pool,
sauna.*

**Blue Haven**    HR   ‖
3 Pearse Street
Kinsale
Co. Cork
Tel (021) 772209;
fax. (021) 774268
*10 rooms. Attractively extended old
town house with good, mostly
seafood, restaurant.*

**Man Friday**    R   ‖
Scilly
Kinsale
Co. Cork
Tel. (021) 772260
*Seafood and international cuisine in
elegant surroundings.*

**Old Presbytery**    HR   |
Cork Street
Kinsale
Co. Cork
Tel. (021) 772027
*6 rooms. Friendly. Small
restaurant (‖). Closed Sundays,
Christmas.*

**Oystercatcher**    R   ‖‖
The Cross
Oysterhaven
Kinsale
Co. Cork
Tel. (021) 770822
*Fine fresh cuisine. Closed January–
mid-February.*

**Trident**    HR   ‖
Pier Head
Kinsale
Co. Cork
Tel. (021) 772301
*46 rooms. Modern, functional
concrete-and-glass block, with boat
dock. Favoured by sea-anglers.*

**The Vintage**    R   ‖‖
Main Street
Kinsale
Co. Cork
Tel. (021) 772502
*Notable seafood and international
menu. Closed January–February,
Sunday in winter.*

**Castle**    HR   ‖
Macroom
Co. Cork
Tel. (026) 41074;
fax. (026) 41505
*26 rooms. Family-run hotel in
central square. Squash and
racketball. Closed Christmas.*

**Ballymaloe House**    HR   ‖‖
Shanagarry
Near Midleton
Co. Cork
Tel. (021) 652531;
fax. (021) 652021
*30 rooms. Family-run country
house hotel on a farm. Celebrated
restaurant serving fresh,
imaginative cuisine. Swimming
pool. Associated cooking school
with own accommodation.*

**Great Southern**    HR   ‖‖
Parknasilla
Co. Kerry
Tel. (064) 45122;
fax. (064) 45323
*84 rooms. Long-established resort
hotel with fine seaside gardens and
views. Golf, indoor swimming pool,
sauna, tennis, fishing.*

**John Barleycorn**    HR   |
Riverstown
Glanmire
Co. Cork
Tel. (021) 821499;
fax. (021) 821221
*17 rooms. Adapted 18th-century
country house, close to Cork City.
Closed Christmas.*

**Quinlan's Courtyard**    R   |
Shull
Co. Cork
*Casual café. Delicatessen, cheeses,
sausages.*

**Ballyseede Castle**    HR   ‖
Killarney Road
Tralee
Co. Kerry
Tel. (066) 25799;
fax. (066) 25287
*12 rooms. Out of town towards
Killarney. Elaborate castle turned
into comfortable hotel.*

**Oyster Tavern**    R   ‖
Tralee
Co. Kerry
Tel. (066) 36102
*Fresh seafood and other local
produce. Dinner only October–May.*

**Butler Arms**    HR   ‖
Waterville
Co. Kerry
Tel. (066) 74144; fax. (066) 74520
*30 rooms. Seaside retreat on the
Ring of Kerry. Fishing, tennis, golf.
Closed November–March.*

**Aherne's Seafood**    R   ‖
163 North Main Street
Youghal
Co. Cork
Tel. (024) 92424
*Noted for good seafood. Closed
Sunday, Monday (except
July–August).*

**Devonshire Arms**    HR   ‖
Pearse Square
Youghal
Co. Cork
Tel. (024) 92827; fax. (024) 92900
*10 rooms. Traditional, friendly
hotel. Entertainment.*

# The West

**Adare Manor**    HR   ‖‖
Adare
Co. Limerick
Tel. (061) 396566;
fax. (061) 396124
*64 rooms. Luxury country house
hotel in magnificent former stately
home. Fishing, riding, indoor
swimming pool, sauna. Vast
grounds.*

**Dunraven Arms**    HR   ‖
Adare
Co. Limerick
Tel. (061) 396209;
fax. (061) 396541
*47 rooms. Old-established
traditional inn in attractive village
setting. Fox-hunting centre. Notable
restaurant. Closed Christmas.*

**Mustard Seed**    R   ‖
Main Street
Adare
Co. Limerick
Tel. (061) 86451
*Notable restaurant for fresh Irish
cooking and seafood. Evening only.
Closed Sunday, Monday,
Christmas–February.*

**Cliff House**    HR   I
The Scrigeen
Kilronan
Inishmore
Aran Islands, Co. Galway
Tel. (099) 61286
*6 rooms. Friendly guesthouse.*
*Home cooking.*

**Mainistir House**    HR   I
Kilronan
Inishmore
Aran Islands, Co. Galway
Tel. (099) 61169
*11 rooms. Informal and friendly*
*hostel and guesthouse. Home*
*cooking.*

**Prince of Wales**    HR   II
Church Street
Athlone
Co. Westmeath
Tel. (0902) 72626;
fax. (0902) 75658
*72 rooms. Central, modern*
*and pleasant with good*
*restaurant.*

**Ballynahinch Castle**    HR   III
Ballynahinch
Connemara
Co. Galway
Tel. (095) 31006;
fax. (095) 31085
*28 rooms. Stately home, now a*
*luxury hotel. Large estate. Fishing,*
*tennis. Closed February.*

**Claire's**    R   II
Ballyvaughan
Co. Clare
Tel. (065) 77029
*Small, friendly. Local seafood a*
*speciality. Closed Monday*
*(and Sunday–Thursday*
*October–Easter).*

**Gregan's Castle**    HR   II
Ballyvaughan
Co. Clare
Tel. (065) 77005;
fax. (065) 77111
*22 rooms. Friendly country house*
*hotel. Fine restaurant. Views of the*
*Burren and Galway Bay. Closed*
*November–March.*

**Hyland's**    HR   I
Ballyvaughan
Co. Clare
Tel. (065) 77015; fax. (065) 77131
*20 rooms. Old-established hotel in*
*the Burren area. Entertainment in*
*the traditional pub. Closed*
*December–January.*

**Rusheen Lodge**    HR   I
Knocknagrough
Ballyvaughan
Co. Clare
Tel. (065) 77092; fax. (065) 77152
*6 rooms. Friendly guesthouse.*
*Closed mid-December–*
*end-January.*

**Durty Nelly's**    R   I/II
Bunratty Castle
Co. Clare
Tel. (061) 364861
*Commercial complex near castle.*
*Bars, Oyster Restaurant, Loft*
*Restaurant (dinner only).*
*Traditional and international food.*
*Entertainment.*

**MacCloskey's**    R   III
Bunratty House Mews
Bunratty
Co. Clare
Tel. (61) 364082
*Elegant restaurant. Home-style*
*cooking with local produce. Closed*
*Sunday, Monday, Christmas–end-*
*January.*

**Cashel House**    HR   III
Cashel Bay
Co. Galway
Tel. (095) 31001;
fax. (095) 31077
*32 rooms. Luxury country house*
*hotel in large grounds. Fine*
*restaurant. Tennis, fishing. Closed*
*January.*

**Zetland House**    HR   II
Cashel Bay
Co. Galway
Tel. (095) 31111;
fax. (095) 31117
*19 rooms. Comfortable retreat.*
*Tennis, fishing. Closed*
*November–March.*

**Alcock and Brown**    HR   I
Main Square
Clifden
Co. Galway
Tel. (095) 21086;
fax. (095) 21842
*20 rooms. Modern, centrally*
*located.*

**Ardagh**    HR   II
Ballyconneely Road
Clifden
Co. Galway
Tel. (095) 21384;
fax. (095) 21314
*20 rooms. Family-run hotel*
*overlooking Ardbear Bay. Fishing.*
*Closed November–March.*

**D'Arcy Inn**    R   II
Main Street
Clifden
Co. Galway
Tel. (095) 21146
*Informal. International and seafood*
*menu. Closed Sunday lunch.*

**Mitchell's**    R   II
Main Street
Clifden
Co. Galway
Tel. (095) 21867
*Informal restaurant. Good seafood,*
*steaks. Closed November–February.*

**O'Grady's Seafood**    R   II
Market Street
Clifden
Co. Galway
Tel. (095) 21450
*Long-established, fine seafood.*
*Closed Christmas–mid-March.*

**Rock Glen Manor**    HR   II
Clifden
Co. Galway
Tel. (095) 21035; fax. (095) 21737
*29 rooms. Country house hotel in a*
*former shooting lodge, next to the*
*sea. Tennis. Closed November–*
*mid-March.*

**Aran View**    HR   I
Coast Road
Doolin
Co. Clare
Tel. (065) 74061; fax. (065) 74540
*16 rooms. Friendly guesthouse. Sea*
*views. Closed November–March.*

**Old Ground**    HR   II
O'Connell Street
Ennis
Co. Clare
Tel. (065) 28127; fax. (065) 28112
*58 rooms. Old-established*
*traditional hotel in town centre.*

**Admiral's Rest**    HR   I
Coast Road
Fanore
Co. Clare
Tel. (065) 76105; fax. (065) 76161
*9 rooms. Good restaurant,*
*especially seafood. Views of Burren*
*and sea. Closed November–March.*

**Connemara Coast**    HR   II
Furbo
Co. Galway
Tel. (091) 92108; fax. (091) 92065
*112 rooms. Luxury resort hotel*
*overlooking Galway Bay.Offers*
*swimming pool, tennis, sauna.*
*Conference centre.*

**Ardilaun House**     HR ||
Taylors Hill
Galway City
Co. Galway
Tel. (091) 21433;
fax. (091) 21546
*90 rooms. Extended Georgian house
in gardens. Sauna, tennis. Closed
Christmas.*

**Malt House**     R ||
Old Malt Mall
High Street
Galway City
Co. Galway
Tel. (091) 67866
*Fine local seafood and meats.
Closed Sunday, Christmas.*

**Noctan's**     R ||
Cross Street
Galway City
Co. Galway
Tel. (091) 66172
*Informal upstairs bistro-style
restaurant. Dinner only. Closed
Sunday, Monday.*

**Lakeside**     HR ||
Killaloe
Co. Clare
Tel. (061) 376122;
fax. (061) 376431
*36 rooms. On the shores of
Lough Derg. Tennis, swimming
pool, sauna, fishing. Closed
Christmas.*

**Rosleague Manor**     HR ||
Letterfrack
Connemara
Co. Galway
Tel. (95) 41101;
fax. (095) 41168
*20 rooms. Family-run country house
hotel. Tennis, sauna, fishing. Closed
November–March.*

**Spa View Hotel and**     HR |
**Orchid Restaurant**
Lisdoonvarna
Co. Clare
Tel. (065) 74026;
fax. (065) 74555
*11 rooms. Family-run hotel,
extended old farmhouse. Tennis
court. Notable restaurant. Closed
October–March.*

**Thomond**     HR |
Lisdoonvarna
Co. Clare
Tel. (065) 74444;
fax. (065) 74406
*50 rooms. Large renovated hotel
on outskirts of town. Tennis.*

**Drimcong House**     R ||
Moycullen
Co. Galway
Tel. (091) 85115
*Noted for creative cuisine, set in a
charming old farmhouse. Closed
Sunday, Monday, and January–
February.*

**Dromoland Castle**     HR |||
Newmarket-on-Fergus
Co. Clare
Tel. (061) 368144;
fax. (061) 353355
*73 rooms. Luxury country house
hotel in turreted Gothic-style
castle. Golf, fishing, tennis.*

**Cré-na-Cille**     R |
High Street
Tuam
Co. Galway
*Tel. (093) 28232
Game and seafood specialities.
Closed Saturday lunch, Sunday.*

# The North West

**Ostan Gob A'Choire**     HR |
Achill Sound, Achill Island
Co. Mayo
Tel. (098) 45245; fax. (098) 45621
*36 rooms. Traditional friendly
guesthouse on seafront. Closed
November–March.*

**The Lobster Pot**     R |
Ardara
Co. Donegal
*Informal seafood to fish and chips.*

**Woodhill House**     HR ||
Ardara
Co. Donegal
Tel. (075) 41112; fax. (075) 41516
*Good restaurant in historic country
house, with five guest rooms.*

**Belleek Castle**     HR ||
Ballina
Co. Mayo
Tel. (096) 22400; fax. (096) 22525
*16 rooms. Restored 17th-century
castle with four-poster beds and
antique trappings.*

**Danby House**     HR ||
Rossnowlagh Road
Ballyshannon
Co. Donegal
Tel. (072) 51138
*5 rooms. Innovative French-Irish
cuisine. Dinner only. Closed
Sunday.*

**Cromleach Lodge**     HR |||
Ballindoon
Castlebaldwin
Near Boyle
Co. Sligo
Tel. (071) 65155;
fax. (071) 65455
*10 rooms. Beautiful setting
among the loughs. Elegant
restaurant, imaginative
cooking.*

**Ashford Castle**     HR |||
Cong
Co. Mayo
Tel. (092) 46003;
fax. (092) 46260
*83 rooms. Palatial stately home.
Golf, fishing, tennis. Excellent
restaurant.*

**Harvey's Point Country**     HR ||
**Hotel**
Lough Eske
Donegal
Co. Donegal
Tel. (073) 22208
*20 rooms. Quiet waterside
setting, with a notable restaurant,
especially for seafood. Closed
January–February.*

**St Ernan's House**     HR ||
St Ernan's Island
Near Donegal
Co. Donegal
Tel. (073) 21065;
fax. (073) 22098
*11 rooms. Country house style
and good restaurant.
Closed November–March.*

**St John**     R ||
Fahan
Co. Donegal
Tel. (077) 60289
*Attractive restaurant serving good
fresh produce in lakeside Georgian
house. Closed Monday, public
holidays.*

**Kealy's Seafood Bar**     R |
Greencastle
Co. Donegal
Tel. (077) 81010
*On the harbour in this fishing
port. Casual dining.*

**Carolina House**     R ||
Loughnagin
Letterkenny
Co. Donegal
Tel. (074) 22480
*Fresh home cooking. Evening
only. Closed Sunday, Monday,
Christmas–New Year.*

**Malin Hotel**   HR ‖
Malin
Co. Donegal
Tel. (077) 70606
*12 rooms. Friendly hotel in the most northerly village in Ireland.*

**Fort Royal**   HR ‖
Rathmullan
Co. Donegal
Tel. (074) 58100;
fax. (074) 58103
*15 rooms. Family-owned hotel by Lough Swilly. Golf, tennis, garden setting. Closed October–Easter.*

**Rathmullan House**   HR ‖
Rathmullan
Co. Donegal
Tel. (074) 58188;
fax. (074) 58200
*23 rooms. Attractive Georgian country house. Swimming pool, steam room, quiet sandy beach. Closed January–February.*

**Coopershill House**   HR ‖
Riverstown
Co. Sligo
Tel. (071) 65108; fax. (071) 65466
*7 rooms. Country mansion in large grounds. Fishing. Closed mid-November–mid-March.*

**Ballincar House**   HR ‖
Rosses Point Road
Co. Sligo
Tel. (071) 45361; fax. (071) 44198
*25 rooms. Country house hotel, overlooking bay. Tennis, sauna. Closed Christmas.*

**Reveries**   R ‖‖
Rosses Point
Co. Sligo
Tel. (071) 77371
*Fine fresh local produce. Closed 2 weeks November, Christmas.*

**The Sand House**   HR ‖
Rossnowlagh
Co. Donegal
Tel. (072) 51777;
fax. (072) 52100
*40 rooms. Country house style next to Donegal Bay. Tennis, fishing. Closed mid-October–Easter.*

**Sligo Park**   HR ‖
Pearse Road
Sligo
Co. Sligo
Tel. (071) 60291; fax. (071) 69556
*89 rooms. Modern hotel. Sports centre with swimming pool, tennis, sauna.*

**Ardmore**   R ‖
The Quay
Westport
Co. Mayo
Tel. (098) 25994
*Friendly restaurant and bar. Fresh local produce. Closed Sunday, and at lunchtime in winter.*

**The Asgard**   R ‖
The Quay
Westport
Co. Mayo
Tel. (098) 25319
*Attractive upstairs restaurant. Irish and international cooking. Dinner only.*

**Quay Cottage**   R ‖
The Harbour
Westport
Co. Mayo
Tel. (098) 26412
*Cheerful wine bar and restaurant. Good fresh seafood and other local produce.*

**Westport Woods**   HR ‖
Louisburgh Road
Westport
Co. Mayo
Tel. (098) 25811; fax. (098) 26212
*57 rooms. Parkland setting. Tennis.*

# Northern Ireland

**Glassdrumman Lodge**   HR ‖
85 Mill Road
Annalong BT34 4QN
Co. Down
Tel. (03967) 68585;
fax. (03967) 67041
*9 rooms. Family-run guesthouse and restaurant near the sea and the Mountains of Mourne. Tennis.*

**Ben Madigan**   R ‖‖‖
Belfast Castle
Antrim Road
Belfast BT15 5GR
Tel. (0232) 776925
*In the baronial-style castle overlooking the city. French and local cuisine.*

**Duke's Hotel**   HR ‖
65 University Street
Belfast BT7 1HL
Co. Antrim
Tel. (0232) 236666;
fax. (0232) 237177
*21 rooms. Modernized Victorian building in Botanic Gardens area. Good restaurant. Sauna.*

**Forte Crest Belfast**   HR ‖
300 Kingsway
Dunmurry BT17 9ES
Belfast
Co. Antrim
Tel. (0232) 612101;
fax. (0232) 626546
*82 rooms. Modern hotel, in garden setting 15 minutes' drive from city. Squash.*

**Nick's Warehouse**   R ‖‖
35–9 Hill Street
Belfast BT1 2LB
Co. Antrim
Tel. (0232) 439690
*Bistro-style restaurant and informal wine bar. Closed Saturday, Sunday.*

**Restaurant 44**   R ‖‖
44 Bedford Street
Belfast BT2 7FF
Co. Antrim
Tel. (0232) 244844
*Attractive restaurant serving French-international menu. Closed Friday evening and Sunday.*

**Roscoff**   R ‖‖‖
7 Lesley House
Shaftesbury Square
Belfast BT2 7DB
Co. Antrim
Tel. (0232) 331532
*Fine, award-winning modern French and Mediterranean cuisine. Closed Saturday lunch, Sunday.*

**Wellington Park**   HR ‖
21 Malone Road
Belfast BT9 6RU
Tel. (0232) 381111; fax. (0232)
*50 rooms. Attractive and friendly hotel in Queen's University area.*

**Auberge de Seneirl**   HR ‖
28 Ballyclough Road
Bushmills BT57 8UZ
Co. Antrim
Tel. (0265) 741536
*5 rooms. Fine restaurant, French cuisine. Near Giant's Causeway.*

**Bushmills Inn**   HR ‖
25 Main Street
Bushmills
Co. Antrim  BT57 8QA
Tel. (0265) 732339;
fax. (0265) 732048
*11 rooms. Restored old coaching inn, comfortable and traditional. Good local food.*

**Hillcrest**  R
306 Whitepark Road
Giant's Causeway
Bushmills BT57 8SN
Co. Antrim
Tel. (02657) 31577
*International menu and local
seafood. Closed Monday to
Friday from November
to April.*

**Londonderry Arms**  HR
Harbour Road
Carnlough BT44 OEU
Co. Antrim
Tel. (0574) 885255;
fax. (0574) 885263
*21 rooms. Family-run, old-
established hotel. Fishing.
Near the sea and the Glens of
Antrim. Closed Christmas.*

**Blackheath House**  HR
112 Killeague Road
Blackhill
Coleraine BT51 4HH
Co. Londonderry
Tel. (265) 868433
*5 rooms. Quiet family-run
guesthouse. Good restaurant.
Closed Christmas–New Year.*

**Brown Trout Golf and**  HR
**Country Inn**
209 Agivey Road
Aghadowey
Near Coleraine BT51 4AD
Co. Londonderry
Tel. (0265) 868209
*15 rooms. Family-run, with 9-hole
golf course and fishing. Good
local food. Short drive to Giant's
Causeway.*

**MacDuff's**  R
112 Killeague Road
Coleraine BT51 4NN
Co. Londonderry
Tel. (0265) 868433
*In the cellar of a Georgian
house. Good home cooking.
Closed Sunday, Monday.*

**Abbey Lodge**  HR
Belfast Road
Downpatrick BT30 9AV
Co. Down
*21 rooms. Comfortable family-run
hotel with moderately priced
restaurant.*

**Adelboden Lodge**  R
38 Donaghadee Road
Groomsport
Co. Down BT20 5RU
Tel. (0247) 464288
*Traditional home cooking and
baking. Vegetarian alternatives.
Closed Sunday, Monday.*

**Culloden**  HR
Holywood BT18 OEX
Co. Down
Tel. (0232) 425233;
fax. (0232) 426777
*91 rooms. Luxury hotel in former
bishop's palace. Noted restaurant.
Tennis, squash, sauna. Closed
Christmas.*

**Magheramorne House**  HR
Magheramorne
Larne BT40 3HW
Co. Antrim
Tel. (0574) 279444;
fax. (0574) 260138
*22 rooms. Country house in
woodland setting. Swimming pool.*

**Beech Hill House**  HR
32 Ardmore Road
Londonderry BT47 3QP
Tel. (0504) 49279; fax. (0504) 45366
*15 rooms. Country house hotel in
large grounds. Good restaurant.*

**Bayview**  HR
2 Bayhead Road
Portballintrae BT57 8RZ
Co. Antrim
Tel. (02657) 31453;
fax. (02657) 32360
*16 rooms. Overlooking the sea.
Swimming pool, sauna.*

**Magherabuoy House**  HR
41 Magherabuoy Road
Portrush BT56 8NX
Co. Antrim
Tel. (0265) 823507;
fax. (0265) 824687
*38 rooms. Comfortable seaside
hotel with good restaurant
specializing in local seafood.*

**Ramore**  R
The Harbour
Portrush BT56 8DF
Co. Antrim
Tel. (0265) 824313
*Creative menu, fresh local produce.
Dinner only. Wine bar for lunch.
Closed Sunday, Monday,
Christmas–New Year.*

**Grange**  R
Main Street
Waringstown BT66 7QH
Co. Armagh
Tel. (0762) 881989
*Imaginative cooking in a fine old
house. Closed Monday, mid-July,
Christmas.*

# Index